Yvon Busson & René Gast

# ONE HUNDRED & ONE
## *Beautiful* TOWNS *in France*

# FOOD & WINE

edited by
Simonetta Greggio

*RIZZOLI*
NEW YORK

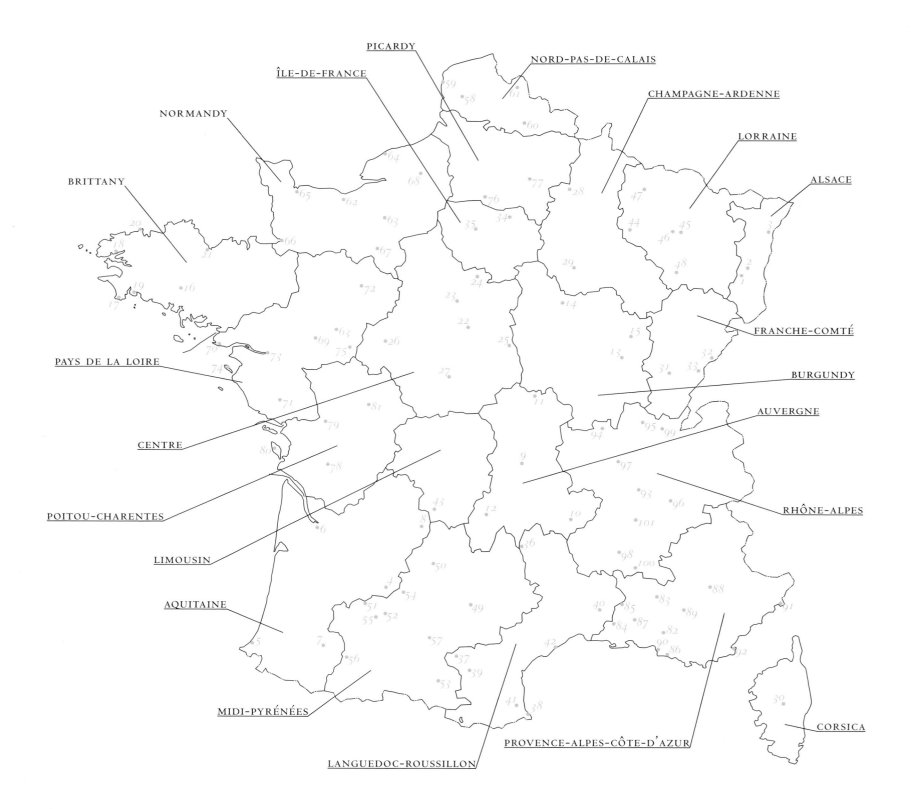

PICARDY

ÎLE-DE-FRANCE

NORD-PAS-DE-CALAIS

NORMANDY

CHAMPAGNE-ARDENNE

LORRAINE

ALSACE

BRITTANY

FRANCHE-COMTÉ

PAYS DE LA LOIRE

BURGUNDY

AUVERGNE

CENTRE

POITOU-CHARENTES

RHÔNE-ALPES

LIMOUSIN

AQUITAINE

MIDI-PYRÉNÉES

CORSICA

PROVENCE-ALPES-CÔTE-D'AZUR

LANGUEDOC-ROUSSILLON

# REGIONAL CONTENTS

# ALPHABETICAL CONTENTS

# P R E F A C E

As varied as the regions of France are, from Provence to Brittany and from Aquitaine to Franche-Comté, the art of living and the enjoyment of fine dining are two pleasures so quintessentially French that they surpass any differences presented by terrain or climate. In Provence, shops close following lunch and shopkeepers retreat to their shuttered homes, where a merciful and welcome shade offers refuge from the afternoon sun. The cafés empty of their customers and only solitary metal chairs remain out in the sun. After some pastis and a pissaladière, the pétanque players retire to the shade of their own dining rooms for a postprandial slumber, often with a news-paper over their faces. Though Brittany's climate may encourage greater activity, just as keen a pleasure is taken in a platter of seafood with some crusty bread and a pat of salted butter. Experiencing flavors to the fullest is a key element in the way the French enjoy food and wine. Olivier Roellinger, one of France's greatest chefs, has described how to savor one particular coastal specialty: "I know that the moment I open the shell, I shall find in the silky softness of its pearly interior a green, black-rimmed jewel, ready to eat, from the waters of life that come from the seabed. An oyster should not be swallowed whole. It should be chewed to release all its richness. It deserves ritual of the kind that an old English aristocrat recommended with regard to an exceptional and ven-erable spirit, 'First you look at it, then you breathe in the smell of it. Then you taste a little. Then you put down your glass to talk about it.'"

Roellinger is one among a group of leading French chefs, along with Michel Bras, the bard of herbs and spices, based in Laguiole; Alain Ducasse, heir to the greatest and the best; Pierre Gagnaire, a perfectionist to the core; and Alain Passard, who possesses the good looks of an actor and the acuteness of a writer of psychological thrillers; not to mention a wealth of other talents. Chefs in France are poets and parachutists, ramblers and sailors, historians and painters. Everyone knows the greats, but what about all those who are not media person-alities—that formidable army of connoisseurs, of excellent, passionately dedicated cooks who preserve a par-ticular taste, a rare strawberry, a breed of cattle that perhaps produces less milk but a better cheese. Knowing how to cook is a way of safeguarding the traditions of a particular region and preserving the philosophy of a place. While the south adores chilies, sardines, sea urchins, and garlic, as well as white wine and rosé to quench the thirst, the north prefers strong cheeses and red wines to invigorate and warm the blood. In the middle, the rest of France's bounty—quite a bounty—is enjoyed to the fullest.

There is no geography, or history, without appreciation of food, without sensual curiosity. To get to know a country you need to taste it, smell it, touch it, listen to it, see it. In France, it is through the body that you reach understanding—through happiness. One of the underlying ideas of the French art of living is this: Happiness is a matter of determination. It takes more courage to be happy than unhappy. Since the dawn of time people have discovered that one of the best ways to achieve this is through the understanding of pleasure—and enjoying good food and wine is an essential part of this undertaking.

# MUNSTER

MONK'S CHEESE

WALKING THROUGH THE STREETS OF THIS MODEST TOWN, it is hard to imagine that it formed part of the prestigious Decapolis, a league of the ten wealthiest Alsatian towns, from 1354 to 1679. These towns were united by a treaty of military and political cooperation that gave them autonomy in the face of the powerful Germanic Holy Roman Empire. Munster is nestled in one of the loveliest of the Vosges valleys, and its

*Charming old buildings around the market square have a distinctive European character.*

*facing page*
Rounds of creamy and mild-flavored Munster cheese, named after the town.

history is linked to that of an influential monastery—*Munster* in German—founded in AD 660 by Benedictines from Ireland. Unfortunately, the town was almost completely destroyed during World War I; the only examples of ancient architecture that survived were a Renaissance town hall, part of the abbey palace, and a fountain bearing a sculpted lion, a symbol of a victory for the Protestants who, at the time of the Wars of Religion, obtained the right to observe their faith despite the opposition of the monks and their abbot, who was lord of the valley.

These same monks spurred the economy of town and valley by developing dairy farming on the *chaumes*, land high on the Alsatian side of the Vosges that was unsuitable for cultivation. The quality of the milk produced by the abbey's herd soon gained such renown that before long all the chaumes, including those on the Lorraine side of the mountain, were devoted to dairy farming. The abundance of milk naturally led to cheese-making, the only known way to preserve milk at that time. It was around the ninth century that the monks probably "invented" Munster, called Gérome in Lorraine (based on the name of the town where it was made, Gérardmer).

A high-fat cheese made from full-cream milk, Munster has a strong smell that contrasts with the mildness of its creamy texture. It is created by *marcaires*, from the German *melker* (milker of cows), who spend May to September with their herds in the mountain pastures, and then come down to spend the winter on their farms in the valley. The Munster, made from heated milk and curdled with rennet—three gallons produces two and a quarter pounds of cheese—is matured on wooden planks for three to six weeks. It is eaten without accompaniment, seasoned with a few caraway seeds, or it is served with unpeeled boiled potatoes. For the connoisseur, it is at its most flavorful and aromatic between the end of spring and the end of autumn, when the cows' milk is rich with the fragrance of the herbs and wild flowers of the mountain pastures.

By the end of the nineteenth century it was customary for hikers to seek hospitality from *marcaires*, who would serve them a snack and sometimes offer them basic lodging for the night. This practice has continued and the number of *fermes-auberges* (as the marcaires are now called) has increased to become an important tourist resource. The quality of accommodation has improved considerably, and the meals served—with dishes that use farm products and reflect local culinary traditions—are more varied and sophisticated than in the past. Information about this network of excellent fermes-auberges can be found at the tourism office in Munster.

Alsatians may protest, but never mind: the close relationship between *flammekueche* and pizza demands comparison. The tarte flambé, a thin-crusted pizza spread with crème fraîche, Speck, and onions, is a dish still largely unknown outside Alsace. In houses that had bread ovens, the tart was baked in the initial flames of the oven while it was still heating up—hence the name *tarte aux flammes*, now commonly called tarte flambé. In the Munster Valley Munster cheese is added to the flammekueche.

# RIQUEWIHR

## THE PEARL OF THE ALSACE

facing page
Evoking the old
world is this typical
Alsatian building
with its half-
timbered facade.

*below*
Dry white wines,
as well as those
made from late-
harvested grapes
such as the famous
Vendange Tardive,
prevail in Alsace.

IT IS BEST SEEN FOR THE FIRST TIME ON AN AUTUMN AFTERNOON, when the sun gilds the vines climbing up its ramparts. The luminous charm of Riquewihr—with its cobbled streets, the half-timbered houses of its vine growers, its fountains and wells, the mystery of its courtyards with their wooden balconies—is never exhausted. Miraculously, time has stood still, and its sixteenth-century flavor pervades amid the castle of the Dukes of Wurtemberg, the Thieves' Tower, and the medieval Dolder Gate. It is present in the emblematic signs creaking on the fronts of buildings, in the richly carved surfaces of the gables and oriel windows, and in the cellar porches decorated with symbols that recall the town's wine-producing vocation: the vine growers' pruning knives, the coopers' hammers and tools, or the six-pointed stars. For Riquewihr is not just one of the most unforgettable stops on the Alsace Wine Trail (the Route des Vins d'Alsace), it is the heart and soul of it. Alsace's love affair with wine goes way back—the Romans planted the first vines. Here, near the Europe of beer drinkers extending east of the Rhine, the quality of the terroir and exceptional sunshine for such a northerly region gave birth to one of the largest wine-making regions in France, with over 50 square miles producing one hundred million bottles.

Unfortunately, the wines of Alsace were long regarded by wine lovers with derision. There were two reasons for this: the first was that some less-than-scrupulous wine producers contributed to this poor reputation by favoring quantity over quality. In recent years, considerable effort has been made by the profession's elite to restore these wines to their rightful position: among the great classics, worthy of being served at the best tables. The second reason is that the French remain disconcerted by the Alsatian tradition of designating wines not by their terroir—château, *climat*, village—but by the grape variety, of which there are seven, all protected by an Appellation d'Origine Contrôlée: Sylvaner, Riesling, Pinot Blanc, Pinot Gris, Pinot Noir, Muscat, and Gewürztraminer. Edelzwicker, a blend of several grapes, and Crémant, a sparkling wine produced using the champagne method, complete this very extensive range. The quality of the wine obviously depends on the producer. You can be sure of drinking an outstanding bottle by buying a grand cru that has these words on the label and the name of the commune where it originates, or a wine made from late-harvest grapes in a vintage year.

Approximately 19 miles to the north of Riquewihr, the Val de Villé is home to some of the best Alsation distillers. Even more than the spirits made with pear, mirabelle plum, quetsch (a type of plum), or raspberry, it is kirsch that has made the valley famous. Composed of different varieties of late-harvest cherries that have reached their maximum sugar content, including blackheart, morello, and wild cherry—once distilled 40 pounds of cherries will produce 34 fluid ounces of spirit—it is then aged, sometimes for a long time, up to ten years for the best-quality kirsches. A good kirsch should have a real cherry bouquet to which the uncracked kernels lend a slight hint of almond; this liqueur should be fruity and not burn the palate.

Extending over 62 miles, from Marlenheim in the north to Thann in the south, all along the hills and slopes that border the Vosges, this wine-producing region enjoys a favorable climate thanks to the shelter of the mountains. Surrounded by magnificent landscapes, it passes through nearly 100 villages and towns, some of which—Colmar, Ribeauvillé, Barr, Dambach-la-Ville, Kaysersberg, Obernai, to name but a few—are among the most beautiful of Alsace. In addition, there are many impressive castles, churches, and food destinations.

# STRASBOURG

PICTURE-POSTCARD BEAUTY

THIS CITY DAZZLES AT FIRST SIGHT. THOUGH IT CAN BE DIFFICULT TO SEE WHEN DAZZLED, Strasbourg is beautiful, with its pink cathedral, its old houses decorated with flowers, the embankments of the Petite France district, and the Ill River strung like a necklace aound the old town. Not that there is any need for yet another description of the cathedral, the half-timbered houses leaning coquettishly over the canal, the covered bridges that are no longer covered, the Barrage Vauban (Vauban weir), and the streets so quaintly or poetically named—the rue du Bain-aux-Plantes, rue des Pucelles, rue de l'Outre—that the fanciful visitor can plan a walking route based solely on the names of the streets and squares.

A bridge crossing the Ill River, a tributary of the Rhine that flows through the city.

*facing page*
Typical dishes of Alsace include a variety of hearty pork products and choucroute.

The miracle is that this medieval quarter is not just fixed in picture-postcard paralysis. The houses are not merely facades; there is life inside. There are children chasing one another down the streets, and old ladies toting shopping baskets. Even beyond this historic center, "the other Strasbourg"—more solemn, more spacious, more formal, in a word, more German, with its broad avenues, huge squares, and bourgeois houses puffed up with pride—has managed to remain a place that is lived in, not an open-air museum. "Visiting the new town after having wandered through old Strasbourg is like attacking an array of strong cheeses after an exquisite light supper. But a good stomach can only derive pleasure from it," declares a local writer. A culinary comparison comes naturally to the pen of an Alsatian.

It is true that Alsace, although long disputed between France and Germany, has managed to preserve a strong culinary identity. Its mild climate and its varied landscapes and different terroirs—rivers, lakes, forests, meadows, alpine pastures, vineyards, mountains—supply it with an extraordinary gamut of produce, from freshwater fish to cattle and poultry; fruits and vegetables; wines and grains. Its residents have transmuted this abundance into a cuisine of rare wealth.

"In Germany, there is plenty but it isn't good. In France, it's good but not plentiful. In Alsace, it's good and plentiful." This is how natives describe it. In fact, Alsatian cuisine unites two qualities that are rarely combined: generosity and refinement, and for chefs there it is a point of honor to satisfy both the gourmet and the healthy appetite.

A list of all the dishes that make Alsatian cuisine so remarkable could go on forever. Apart from the wines, spirits, and cheeses (see the entries for Riquewihr and Munster), among the most typical are the famous *choucroute* (sauerkraut), *foie gras d'oie en croûte, cuit avec une farce de veau and de lard hachés* (goose foie gras in pastry with a veal and lard stuffing), *baeckeoffe* (a meat stew slow-cooked with potates, onions, and carrots), the vast range of charcuterie, such as bratwurst (sausage to be cooked), leberwurst (pork liver sausage), or presskopf (head cheese, or brawn), and the pâtisserie: pain d'épices (gingerbread), bretzels (pretzels), tartes, beignets (fritters), or kougelhopf. Don't be deceived by the apparent rusticity of these foods. Great Alsatian chefs—Émile Jung, Antoine Westermann, and the Haeberlin brothers, among others—bring a strong foundation in tradition to their cooking, and raise Alsatian cuisine to the highest ranks of haute gastronomy.

These temples of good food are to Strasbourg what the bouchons are to Lyon. A few tables, beamed ceilings, paneled walls, ceramic-tiled stoves are the typical décor. Choucroute, charcuterie, pastries—these are the dishes served in generous portions. Seats are close together—legislators sit beside masons; construction workers sit beside lawyers. Winstubs are the heart and soul of Alsace, and no one can claim to know the region without having dined in at least one.

This is the Alsatian dish par excellence, like cassoulet is to the southwest or bouillabaisse is to Provence. The base of it is the *chou pommé* (a full-hearted cabbage), whose finely sliced leaves are pickled for a month with juniper berries, caraway seeds, bay leaves, and salt. This choucroute is then cooked with white whine or beer, and sometimes a dash of kirsch. Then a few boiled potatoes are added, along with an impressive assortment of pork: *saucisses de Strasbourg*, ham knuckle, smoked belly, blood pudding, cervelas (a type of sausage), *chine*, *palette* (a shoulder cut), and *saucisson á l'ail* (garlic sausage). Choucroute can also be accompanied with fresh fish such as pike-perch or salmon, and smoked fish such as haddock or herring. Finishing such a dish is a feat that very few non-Alsatians can accomplish.

*left*
A picturesque view of bridges over the Ill, along with a cathedral and half-timbered houses.

*above*
Pretzels, typically of the savory variety, are an area specialty and often accompany the local brew.

*below*
An Alsatian favorite, *pain d'epices* is a gingerbread flavored with spices and honey.

# AGEN

## FRUIT OF THE CRUSADES

NO ONE WOULD PRETEND THAT AGEN'S ARCHITECTURAL RICHES RIVAL those of the major cities of the southwest, Bordeaux or Toulouse. However, Agen can pride itself on a considerable heritage: its medieval quarter and half-timbered houses, its private mansions, the twelfth-century St. Caprais Cathedral, and the Jacobin Church—the oldest Gothic church in southern France—and, last but not least, its spectacular bridge-canal with twenty-three arches that straddle the Garonne River. It is truly a town of art and history. And it is such a lovely place to spend time, with its fine brick facades, its shady embankments, and its lively squares and broad avenues. Agen is rated as one of the best places to live in France—and it is truly a joy to linger there.

Place de la Mairie is lit up at night during a local festival.

Because of the area's mild climate, the neighboring countryside is a vast orchard, and the most representative product is the Ente plum—"mother" of the Agen prune. With its shiny black, wrinkled skin, its melting amber and golden yellow flesh, its delicately sweet taste, this delicious fruit long ago established itself as an important product. The Crusades brought the plum to France; and the monks of the Clairac Abbey made it possible to eat them year-round. In 1148 the knights of the second Crusade were repelled outside the walls of Damascus. Before returning home, some of the knights took indigenous plants, the fruit of which they called the "Damascus plum," or damson. Grafted onto Aquitaine plum trees, they produced the Ente plum, so succulent and tasty that cultivation of them spread rapidly. But they have a short season. How might they be eaten throughout the year?

This is where the monks come in. They tried drying them in the bread oven before storing them away from the light to keep mold from forming. The result? Prunes were created. Pilgrims to Santiago de Compostella, who very quickly favored this easy-to-transport, nutritious, and energizing food, contributed to its dissemination throughout Christendom. Even into the nineteenth century, whole cargo loads of prunes were transported via the waterways to Bordeaux, to be shipped to England, where they were in high demand.

Eaten as it is like a sweet, the Agen prune is in itself delicious. But its gourmet uses go well beyond this; for example, as an appetizer it can be served stuffed with cheese, wrapped in a thin slice of bacon, or stuffed with almonds. It is delicious with skewers of duck or lamb, with pot-roasted quail, pork chops, or roasted rabbit. It gives an unusual flavor to a skewer of monkfish, or, in a stuffing, to a whole salmon. For dessert, it can be used in an inexhaustible array of recipes from tarts to charlottes, sponges, ice creams, or pies. Sweet-savory flavors are not confined to Asian cuisines, and classic French cuisine has never overlooked them. There is nothing unorthodox or unusual about the use of prunes with meat and fish.

The plums are picked at the end of the summer, when the fruit has gorged on a season's worth of sunshine. Then follows the dehydration process, during which seven pounds of plums become about two pounds of prunes. The term "pruneaux d'Agen" is exclusively reserved for prunes made with the Ente plum.

The excellence of the great aristocrats of neighboring Bordeaux overshadow the minor nobility of the wines of the Agen, which is unfortunate. Some of these wines deserve recognition; for example Buzet, which is aged in oak barrels and acquires a wonderful complexity and bouquet; Côte-de-Brulhois, nicknamed "the black wine of the southwest," whose powerful, generous reds improve with age; and crisp, quaffable rosés, which are typical of these terroir wines and are always a delight to discover.

*facing page*
Agen prunes are produced from Ente plums, which have a particular taste and consistency.

# BAYONNE

S P I C E D   H A M

ON THE BORDERS OF GASCONY AND THE PAYS BASQUE, BAYONNE stands at the confluence of the Nive and Adour rivers. These two rivers mark the boundaries of three very distinct neighborhoods. Founded in the twelfth century, the St. Espirit district was the part of town where migrants settled around the collegiate church of that name; the monks there ran a hostel for pilgrims on their way to Compostella. In the sixteenth century the Portuguese Jews who were driven out of their country came and settled here; they brought the art of chocolate making to the town. On the other side of the Adour lies the upper town of Grand Bayonne and the lower town of Petit Bayonne, both surrounded by the remains of the citadel constructed by Vauban at the end of the seventeenth century. Grand Bayonne, the historic city center, has retained its half-timbered houses, its arcaded facades, and the St. Marie Cathedral, built in the Gothic style of the Champagne region. The rue Port-Neuf is a reminder that the town developed alongside canals that are now filled in, and it is one of the city's busiest shopping streets. Here, you can stock up on regional products: Espelette chilies, chocolates, and ham.

Commonly seen in Espelette, a small town near Bayonne, are chili peppers hanging outside to dry.

The term "jambon de Bayonne" (Bayonne ham) comes from the place where it was traded. The Port of Bayonne is where the cooked meats made from pigs raised in the Adour region were shipped abroad. This part of the Pyrénées-Atlantiques, rising between the sea and the mountain, has a unique climate: dry weather, attributable to the *foehn*, the wind that blows from the south, alternating with dampness coming in from the Atlantic Ocean. The resulting range in humidity causes the ham to be alternately dehydrated, then rehumidified. Jambon de Bayonne is matured slowly, acquiring its characteristic lusciousness. Every manufacturer has his own way of preparing the ham, the quality of the pork being most important to the taste of the final product. The ham is first salted with natural salt of the Pays de l'Adour, then placed in the drying chamber where it matures for a minimum of nine months. It is rubbed with Espelette chili, which gives it its distinctive orange-red color. It is best to purchase Jambon de Bayonne on the bone, which preserves its freshness much longer. It is eaten raw in thin slices, or in thicker slices fried with shallots. For more than five centuries, Bayonne has held its annual ham fair from Maundy Thursday to Easter Sunday.

Garlands of red chili peppers can be seen drying in rows in front of half-timbered houses. The chilies absorb the sun before being pulverized into powder. Introduced in the sixteenth century by Basque seamen, the chili has been cultivated in the region of Espelette since that time. From the seventeenth century, Bayonne was the leading chocolate producer in the area, and the Espelette chili was first used to add spice to some chocolate recipes. More aromatic than hot, it is regarded as a kind of pepper; it was used in simple dishes such as omelettes, fried eggs, grilled sardines, and in classic recipes for *pipérade* (a vegetable dish of green bell peppers, tomatoes, and onions), *axoa* (lamb stew), or *marmitako* (tuna and potato casserole). It also brings out the flavor of cheese made from goat's milk or ewe's milk. An annual pepper festival is held in Espelette on the last weekend of October.

In Basque, *izarra* means "star." The recipe for Izarra, a liqueur made from plants of the Pyrenees and from the East, has not changed since 1835. Green Izarra and yellow Izarra are distinguished by their taste and alcohol content. Forty-proof yellow Izarra is the product of the maceration and distillation of thirty-two plants. Forty-eight-proof green Izarra is made from forty-eight plants. Interestingly, few of the plants are common to both liqueurs. Fruit macerated in aged Armagnac also goes into the making of these liqueurs. Yellow Izarra has a bitter almond taste; green has one of peppery mint.

*facing page*
Bayonne ham, cured with natural salt, dries for many months aided by the area's unique climactic conditions.

# BORDEAUX

# THE ARISTOCRAT

THERE IS BORDEAUX AND THERE IS BORDEAUX: THE NAME IS SHARED by both a magnificent town and one of the world's greatest wines. It is impossible to speak of one without the other, so closely linked have their destinies been throughout history. And it is to the wine that the old city owes the splendor of its monuments, churches, and homes. Thanks to the Port of Bordeaux, situated though it is on the Garonne River, almost 60 miles from the sea, this same wine was able to conquer the world.

"Bordeaux is undeniably the most beautiful town in France," Stendhal declared. With the medieval layout of its older districts, parks, gardens, and eighteenth-century houses wrought like jewels, it offers a setting of undeniable splendor. The heart of the city is within a triangle whose base is formed by the Garonne embankment and whose three corners are marked by the Esplanade des Quinconces, Place Gambetta, and Porte Cailhau. The number of sites, monuments, and examples of architectural beauty are too numerous to mention by name. But even the time-pressed visitor must take a look at the most famous of them—the Esplanade des Quinconces. At 31 acres it is the largest square in Europe. Within are statues of two famous native sons of Bordeaux—Montaigne and Montesquieu; the St. André Cathedral (built from the twelfth to sixteenth centuries), with its thirteenth-century Porte Royale decorated with statuary of exceptional craftsmanship; the hôtel de ville, a magnificent example of Louis XVI architecture; the late-eighteenth-century Grand-Théâtre, a masterpiece by the architect Victor Louis and of imposing dimensions—289 x 154 feet; the basilica of St. Michel, in florid Gothic style; St. Seurin Church, built in the eleventh century on a Paleo-Christian necropolis that can still be visited; and Porte Cailhau and the Grosse Cloche (the Big Belle), vestiges of the ancient ramparts.

Even more than these buildings, a walk through the streets and squares will give you a better insight into the city's soul. How could anyone not succumb to the charm of the St. Pierre neighborhood, with its fine eighteenth- and nineteenth-century residences bordering the lovely Place du Marché-Royal, or to the busy cheerfulness of rue St. Catherine, a three-quarter-mile-long pedestrian street lined with shops and cafés? Lastly, it would be a mistake to leave without first visiting the Chartons district in the northern part of town, where English wine merchants, who for a long time dominated the trade, built superb private houses.

Wine and Bordeaux are synonymous. The quality of wine produced here is unrivaled.

*facing page*
Full-flavored red wines are the primary production of Côtes de Bourg's vineyards.

Bordeaux owes a great deal to the English. Due to the quirks of inheritance, for three centuries during the Middle Ages the Aquitaine region was a fiefdom of the English crown. Even at that time, Bordeaux wine, called claret across the Channel, was exported in massive quantities to northern Europe. After France regained control of the province, English wine merchants continued to play a major role in the Bordeaux wine industry. The town has actually retained a few characteristics of that "British way of life," distinguished by its slightly puritan stiffness, and a reserved, somewhat aloof style. That said, the justified reputation of Bordeaux wines is essentially due to the extraordinary range of grapes cultivated in the region's great vineyards and the expertise of the vine growers, who have succeeded in getting the best out of grape varieties wonderfully suited to the terroir. Of course, success has its downside, and there is both mediocre and superb wine produced. But the real wine lover, even if unable to afford one of the best extremely expensive vintages, can always track down one of those *petits châteaux*, which would be welcome at any table.

The wine-producing area of Bordeaux is the largest consolidation of vine-growing territory in the world, with nearly 450 square miles of vineyards of which 85 percent come under the AOC designation. Its 4,000 *châteaux* produce about eight hundred million bottles per year, almost equally divided between red and white. Blended red wines are made with Cabernet, Sauvignon, and Merlot grapes; whites are made with Sauvignon and Sémillion. Bordeaux comprises five wine regions: Médoc, on the left bank of the Gironde River, which produces mostly reds; Blaye and Bourg, on the right bank, which produce both reds and whites; Libourne-Saint-Émilion, Fronsac, and Pomerol, which lie on the right bank of the Dordogne River; Graves and Sauternes, on the left bank of the Garonne River; and, lastly, the vines of Entre-deux-Mers, which occupy the space between the Dordogne and the Garonne.

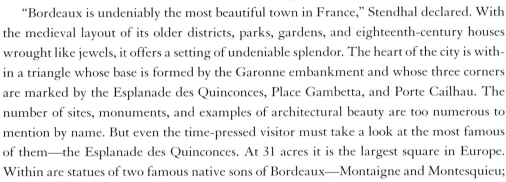

Mediocre cuisine could never satisfy the discriminating palates of Aquitaine. Natives of Bordeaux eat *à la bordelaise*: *lamproie à la bordelaise* (lamprey with leeks and red wine), *entrecôte à la bordelaise* (steak with shallots, marrow, and red wine), and *cèpes à la bordelaise* (porcini mushrooms fried in oil with garlic and red wine). In addition to these sumptuous dishes are *grenier médocain* (pork-blanket tripe cooked in a court bouillon), the Aquitaine white asparagus, Gironde caviar, Arcachon oysters, and, for dessert, the Saint-Émilion macaroon and the *cannelé*, a little baked pudding made with eggs and sugared milk flavored with rum and vanilla.

*right*
Cèpes de Bordeaux (Bordeaux porcini mushrooms) are often sautéed and served as a side dish.

*below*
In the Gironde estuary sturgeon were fished for their prized caviar, but this practice was banned in 1982.

*far right*
Pont de Pierre is a beautiful arched bridge over the Garonne River.

# P A U
## SAVORY STUFFED CHICKEN

CAPITAL OF BÉARN, PAU IS CALLED THE TOWN OF A THOUSAND PALM TREES and faces the Pyrenees. In the nineteenth century, drawn by the climate and its healthful benefits, the British gave Pau the appearance of a garden town (this is still so today). The British found the place to their liking, settled down, created the first golf course in France in 1856, and even founded a rugby club, the first on the continent, in 1902. The town quickly became known for its sports.

Thanks to construction carried out by the English, extravagant villas surrounded by parks lush with exotic species of trees helped to make Pau a green city ahead of its time. In fact, one of the loveliest walks in Pau links two parks: the Boulevard des Pyrénées runs between Parc Beaumont and Château de Pau, and offers a panoramic view of the nearby mountains. Rising above the ancient Navarre parliament building and Place de la Monnaie, lined with sixteenth- and eighteenth-century houses, is the castle. Also overlooking the Gave de Pau is the Hédas district, which has retained both its historic character and working-class population.

Henry IV's castle, with its noble square towers, is easy to find. The original foundation was extensively restructured by Gaston Fébus in the fourteenth century. It contains a few precious objects that belonged to King Henry, along with a tortoiseshell cradle (a copy of the one he lay in as an infant). At the foot of the castle is a reconstruction of the gardens of Jeanne D'Albret, mother of good King Henry. In the middle of an austere grid layout, vegetables and flowers flourish side by side.

"No peasant in my kingdom should be so poor that he cannot have a chicken in his pot every Sunday," Henry IV supposedly said, but anxious though he was for the well-being of his people, this would turn out to be the first of a long series of political promises. While *poule au pot* has since been cooked in numerous ways, when it is served in the style of Henry IV of Béarn, it is not in any way a simple dish to make. According to traditional preparation, it takes a good two days' work and several stages of cooking. Chicken is stuffed with ham and chopped giblets, to which chicken livers, breadcrumbs, and seasoning are added. It is served with a medley of vegetables: turnips, carrots, cabbage, and leeks. To accompany it, a light fruity wine—a red Anjou or Brouilly—is recommended.

In 1925 Adrien Artigarrède opened a patisserie at Oloron Ste.-Marie. There he created an almond-based cake adapted from a recipe dating from the nineteenth century. Since the best almonds came from the Crimea at that time, and since the sugar icing on his pastry suggested the snow-covered plains of Russia, this typical pastry of Oloron is called a Russe (Russian). Its reputation has long since expanded beyond the local area. His grandson is carrying on the tradition and it will surely continue to be passed down through the generations.

Henry IV's father bought some vines in 1550. When his son was born, he made the child sniff his wine, then gave him a few drops to drink and rubbed his lips with a clove of garlic. The tradition of the béarnaise baptism was born, and Jurançon wine thereby acquired symbolic status. This four-square-mile vine-growing area is planted on the slopes facing the Pyrenees mountains. Local grape varieties, such as Gros Manseng, are grown; they are the main component of these wines, which are blended with Petit Manseng and Lazet. Jurançon (a sweet wine) and Jurançon sec (dry) are the two AOC-designated wines of this area and were among the first French wines to be awarded this distinction in 1936.

# S A R L A T
## A  M A T T E R  O F  T A S T E

EARLY MAN SETTLED HERE THOUSANDS OF YEARS AGO, SECURING PÉRIGORD'S reputation as a congenial place. It is no accident that our ancestors were born on the banks of the river running through these gentle valleys located exactly halfway between the North Pole and the equator. The Vézre Valley, notably where the Lascaux Cave is located, has even been dubbed the "Cradle of Humanity" and listed by UNESCO as a world heritage site. Henry Miller called this part of the Périgord the "Frenchman's paradise."

Sarlat-la-Canéda, the area's full name, is the capital of Périgord Noir; it is known for its first-class cuisine. But the town also boasts an exceptional architectural heritage. An abbey seigneury, it reached its height in the thirteenth century when this flourishing town numbered 5,000 inhabitants. Destroyed during the Hundred Years' War, it began to thrive again in the fifteenth century thanks to privileges conferred by the king. In the nineteenth century, the town was divided in two by a road, but Sarlat has not suffered too greatly from this sacrilege and among its many treasures is the St. Sacerdos Cathedral, built between the twelfth and eighteenth centuries; the twelfth-century St. Bernard tower (also known as the Lanterne des Morts); the seventeenth-century chapel of the White Penitents; as well as many impressive private residences: the Hôtel Plamon, de Gisson, de Grezel, de Vassal, de Vienne, and also the house where Montaigne's great friend Étienne de la Boétie was born, located near Place du Peyrou and inspired by the Italian Renaissance.

Every Saturday is market day on the Place de la Liberté, which is lined with arcaded houses. In winter there is also a truffle and foie gras market; both goose and duck foie gras are sold. Goose foie gras is delicate and subtle, while duck foie gras has a more pronounced taste. Free-range goslings and ducklings are raised until fully grown, which takes about twelve weeks. Only the males are fattened: three weeks for geese, two weeks for ducks. Foie gras is sold in various forms. Whole foie gras consists of one or more lobes with the membrane removed; it is seasoned and then sterilized. If it is "half-cooked," it should be kept in the refrigerator and eaten soon after buying it. The *bloc* of foie gras is a reconstitution of fragments of lobes blended and emulsified. Foie gras should be served chilled and is best accompanied by a glass of Sauternes or a sweet Bergerac.

Périgord Noir's vineyards once extended over nearly 7,400 acres (11.5 square miles), but they were devastated by phylloxera at the end of the nineteenth century. Today, making a brave comeback with some 49.5 acres, the Domme vine-growing area is one of the smallest terroirs in France. It occupies the slopes of the Vallée du Céou and has brought together some fifteen enthusiastic producers who, for quality-control purposes, have decided to limit their production and to pick the grapes by hand. Noble grape varieties—Merlot for its generous rounded flavor, and Cabernet Franc, with its austerity and finesse—are used to make a rosé wine (the grapes are macerated), and various reds, including a special cuvée matured in oak barrels and imbibed at room temperature, approximately 61- to 64-degrees Fahrenheit.

*facing page*
Foie gras and cep mushrooms are local products prized by gourmands.

*below*
Sarlat geese, commemorated in town by a small monument, are raised in surrounding areas.

Cro-Magnon man ate walnuts more than 17,000 years ago, and in the Middle Ages the walnut was regularly used by the peasants of Périgord as a form of payment. In the eighteenth century walnut oil had become a popular product, transported by barge down the Dordogne River to the markets of Libourne. Four types of walnut are found in the region: marbot, very early to fruit and eaten fresh; corne, a hardy variety; grandjean, strongly flavored with a hint of bitterness; and, finally, franquette, imported from Isre some fifty years ago. Near Sarlat, the water mill of St. Nathalne dates from the sixteenth century. Here, virgin oil—walnut, hazelnut, and almond—is produced by artisanal methods. It is even possible to press one's own walnuts.

# CLERMONT FERRAND

## A VARIETY OF CHEESES

"THE AUVERGNE IS KNOWN FOR ITS MINISTERS, CHEESES, AND VOLCANOES," the writer Alexandre Vialatte used to say. Had he lived longer, he could have added presidents of the Republic. The chain of the Puys, a line of volcanic craters polished with age, surrounds the great Auvergne metropolis of Clermont-Ferrand. The beautifully situated city can be seen from Puy de Dôme's summit, which is nearly 5,000 feet high. Standing in the heart of the town's historic center, the Notre Dame de l'Assomption Cathedral, its two black-spired bell towers reaching toward the heavens, is an impressive structure. The cathedral was built in the black volcanic stone of Volvic and its stained-glass windows, depicting the life and occupations of St. Mary Magdalene, are remarkable for their precision and richness of color. From the summit of the Puy de Dôme, the view extends as far as Mont Blanc. This area encompasses around 100 inactive volcanoes, some filled with dark lakes. Meadows climb slopes smoothed by erosion, on which herds of russet cattle graze.

Saint-Nectaire is one of the five Auvergne cheeses with an *appellation* designation, but it is also the name of a village that has some other surprises in store. The lower town is dedicated to spas, thanks to some twenty springs, while the upper town has one of the most beautiful Romanesque churches in the Auvergne. A semi-hard cheese with a bloom on the rind, Saint-Nectaire is uncooked, pressed, and salted. A round cheese, it is approximately eight inches in diameter, two inches thick, and weighs nearly four pounds. The first artisanal cheese in France to attain AOC designation (in 1955), Saint-Nectaire is made within the AOC area from the milk of a single herd belonging to that same area.

Another cheese produced nearby, Cantal, takes its name from another chain of volcanoes with more jagged silhouettes located to the south. Pliny the Elder mentioned it in his *Natural History* as long ago as the first century AD, while Diderot and D'Alembert refer to it in the eighteenth century in their *Encyclopedia*. To satisfy the most demanding palates, Cantal comes in three different types: *jeune* (young), *entre-deux* (medium), and *vieux* (seasoned). This cow's-milk cheese is uncooked and pressed, and comes in a wheel weighing 80 to 90 pounds. After only one month's ripening, Cantal jeune has a fresh, sweet taste under its thin gray rind. After two months, the cheese has a golden rind and a fruity flavor. When it is aged between two to six months, its taste develops further; this is called *entre deux*. After more than six months' aging, it displays a bit more character and is called *vieux*.

Notre Dame de l'Assomption Cathedral, in the center of town on the Place de la Victoire.

*facing page*
St. Nectaire cow's-milk cheese is aged in natural caves. The aging process imparts an earthy, mushroomy flavor.

Auvergne agriculturists want to promote wheat production and have developed an original initiative for what they call Combrailles bread. This bread is made from wheat that grows on the Auvergne uplands at an altitude of about 2,460 feet. Combrailles wheat is exclusively of the Camp Rémi variety. It is untreated, and the same is true for the flour that is made from it. A baker in Volvic, Christian Nury, uses it to make one of his creations, Brayaud bread; it is made in many shapes and flavors.

Auvergne is a region that produces a lot of fruit, but its winters are often long and harsh. To preserve the sun's bounty during the cold season the people of Auvergne showed ingenuity from very early on. In the fifteenth century they made "dry jams" that today we call fruit jelly. The establishment of a sugar refinery in the port of Clermont-Ferrand in the middle of the nineteenth century aided the development of this artisanal industry. Enjoying the spa experience, at that time a popular activity, garnered attention for the sweets served in tearooms. Fruit jelly is made from fruit pulp, while fruit that will be candied is picked when just ripe and then dipped in a progression of increasingly concentrated sugar syrups. When the fruit's moisture has been totally replaced by sugar, the fruit is then covered with a thin coating of confectioners' sugar. It will keep for months without losing its flavor or color.

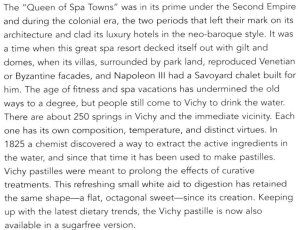

The "Queen of Spa Towns" was in its prime under the Second Empire and during the colonial era, the two periods that left their mark on its architecture and clad its luxury hotels in the neo-baroque style. It was a time when this great spa resort decked itself out with gilt and domes, when its villas, surrounded by park land, reproduced Venetian or Byzantine facades, and Napoleon III had a Savoyard chalet built for him. The age of fitness and spa vacations has undermined the old ways to a degree, but people still come to Vichy to drink the water. There are about 250 springs in Vichy and the immediate vicinity. Each one has its own composition, temperature, and distinct virtues. In 1825 a chemist discovered a way to extract the active ingredients in the water, and since that time it has been used to make pastilles. Vichy pastilles were meant to prolong the effects of curative treatments. This refreshing small white aid to digestion has retained the same shape—a flat, octagonal sweet—since its creation. Keeping up with the latest dietary trends, the Vichy pastille is now also available in a sugarfree version.

*far left*
Vichy became a
fashionable spa
town during
the nineteenth
century thanks to
its "miraculous"
waters, which were
discovered by the
nobility vacationing
there.

*above left*
Today Vichy water is
considered to be of
very high quality and
is bottled for sale.

*above*
Among Clermont-
Ferrand's many
notable products are
candied fruits.

# LE PUY
## EN VELAY
### BLACK STONE AND GREEN LENTILS

A VERDANT AREA ON THE EDGE OF THE AUVERGNE, VELAY lies in the midst of a basaltic plateau and extinct volcanoes. Between the Rhône and the Allier rivers, the fertile land of the valleys gives way to meadows— vast grassy areas for cattle grazing on which cold winds blow in the winter. A modest regional capital, Le Puy-en-Velay is a town distinguished by its physical location—and by religion. Every black-stone rock jutting out of the earth is adorned with a religious monument at the summit. Mount Corneille bears a massive statue of Notre Dame de France, cast in 1860 out of cannons brought back from the battle of Sebastopol. On top of the slender peak of Aiguilhe is a chapel dating from the twelfth century and dedicated to St. Michel; the cathedral, Notre-Dame-du-Puy, designated a UNESCO World Heritage site, stands on a broad terrace.

From the eleventh through the fourteenth centuries Notre-Dame-du-Puy, reached by climbing 134 steps, was one of the most important places of pilgrimage dedicated to the Virgin Mary. People came from far and wide to venerate a mysterious Black Virgin, which was consumed in a fire at the end of the eighteenth century but whose reproduction still draws crowds. People also embarked on long journeys from there, since the town was the starting point of one of the main routes to Compostella. To brighten up its landscape of dark stone, Le Puy has covered its roofs with red tiles and decorated the facades of buildings in the center of town with lively paintings. There is also artistic appreciation and talent in the Velay capital. Since the sixteenth century, some of the finest French bobbin lace has been made here.

In addition to cattle, the high plateaus of Velay are devoted to the cultivation of an unusual crop. Originally grown in the Mediterranean, the green lentil became established in the Puy region over 2,000 years ago. Sowing takes place from March to April, and the harvest is from August 1 to September 15. Cultivated without the use of fertilizers or irrigation, this pulse is rich in minerals, amino acids, trace elements, and proteins, but low in lipids, which is why it is often described as "vegetable beefsteak." The region's climate—the plant first endures the cold, then benefits from the summer sun that promotes ripening—imparts a distinctive flavor to it. Puy lentils have unique characteristics: lovely green thin skins and non-floury kernels, which allow quick cooking that retains the delicacy of the lentils' flavor. In 1996 the green Puy lentil was the first legume to be included on the very restricted list of AOC designated products.

A panoramic view of the town and its inactive volcanoes, with Notre-Dame du Puy Cathedral.

*facing page*
Small with an intense aroma, the Puy green lentil is speckled with a blue pigment.

One of Auvergne's iconic products since 1859, when an apothecary and skilled herbalist concocted a mixture of more than thirty plants in his laboratory, is Verveine du Velay liqueur. It includes a distillation of vervain picked on the sides of the volcanoes. This is how Joseph Rumillet Charretier developed the formula for Verveine du Velay. Some time later Victor Pagès took over the distillery that thereafter bore his name. From generation to generation the secret of how the liqueur is made is handed down. Both green and yellow Verveine du Velay are aged in oak barrels—and both are drunk on ice or used in cocktails. They are also used in the preparation of some dishes.

This pressed, uncooked cow's-milk cheese is formed into a cylindrical shape four inches in diameter and about two inches in height. Its uniqueness comes from the preparation of the milk. After ripening, the previous day's milk is semi-skimmed, then mixed with fresh milk before rennet is added. From molding to salting, Velay is worked by hand in the same way it has been for centuries. It is drained for two to five days before being laid on wooden trays made of poplar that encourage the development of *artisous*, the cheese mites that sculpt its rind. Maturing in the cellar lasts three weeks, but connoisseurs will readily enjoy a cheese aged for two months.

# MOULINS
## AUVERGNE
## DISCREET WEALTH

WINDMILLS USED TO LINE THE BANKS OF THE ALLIER RIVER, and perhaps that's the origin of the town's name; no one knows for sure. In the heart of a gentle and fertile landscape, Moulins grew slowly, becoming the capital of the Bourbonnais, then the largest duchy in France in the fifteenth century. Of this glittering ducal period, when the blaze of the town's glories reached even the French court, there remain a few vestiges and a lingering taste for fine things.

The most beautiful evidence of its previous splendor is owed to an unidentified person known as the Master of Moulins. In the town's Notre-Dame Cathedral this artist created a triptych of the Coronation of the Virgin, depicting the Virgin and child seated on her throne, with the Duke of Bourbon and his wife, Anne of Beaujeu, on either side. Painted in 1500, and an important work of medieval art, it has not been restored but, remarkably, its colors remain vibrant. The Malcoiffée (inappropriately capped), which owes its name to its mansard roof, is the oldest monument in town, the remains of a keep of the former dukes' castle. A symbol of municipal freedoms, the Jacquemart belfry, a 750-foot tower, has burned down several times but has always been rebuilt exactly as it was; its bell chimes every hour.

*Poulet à la moutarde de Charroux* (spring chicken with Charroux mustard), *tatin de boudin noir aux pommes* (black pudding and apple tart), *pâté bourbonnais* (Bourbonnais pie)—the Moulins region has an original cuisine with strong flavors that reflect the terroir. Pâté bourbonnais, often served with a green salad, is a traditional dish made with potatoes, bacon, and fresh cream and baked in a pie crust. It was created in the Allier countryside in 1789, the year of the Revolution but also of a serious food shortage in the region. Peasants at that time were very observant Christians, so they didn't eat meat on Fridays. Bourbonnais lakes had plentiful supplies of fish, but the poor were not entitled to eat it. With the few ingredients they could gather, peasants made a potato pie, covering it with a short pastry to be baked in the oven; they added fresh cream once it was cooked. A peculiar characteristic of this dish is that, before cooking, a hole is made in the pastry top. When the pie is taken out of the oven, cream can then be poured down the hole; the pie pan is tilted back and forth so that the cream can be absorbed by the potatoes.

Palet d'or, a subtle mix of bittersweet chocolate coating a ganache of chocolate and fresh cream flavored with coffee, and then sprinkled with gold, was created in Moulins in 1886 by Bernard Sérardy. A great classic of the master chocolate-maker's repertoire, it became a treat unique to Moulins, replacing sugared almonds at weddings. In the 1920s it was copied by a somewhat unscrupulous chocolate maker, which led to a legal battle and a protest by locals. The dispute ended with a victory for the authentic palets d'or of Moulins, which now have the imprimatur *Bernard Sérardy Createur.*

Vines that supposedly predate those planted by the Romans can be found in Saint-Pourçain-sur-Sioule. Saint Louis, King of France, used to serve this wine at his table, and the popes of Avignon had it shipped to them despite the prohibitive costs of transporting it at that time. Today nineteen districts around Saint-Pourçain covering approximately two and a half square miles produce white, rosé, and especially red wines that have a VDQS (wine of superior quality) *appellation d'origine*. The whites are dry and fruity with citrus notes. They go just as well with white meat as they do with a Saint-Nectaire cheese or a Cantal. The fruity, slightly spicy reds are made with Gamay or Pinot Noir and are the perfect accompaniment to charcuterie. Light and fruity rosés are drunk chilled during the summer. They can also be served as an aperitif.

# SALERS

A HEARTY BREED

"CARVED OUT OF THE LAVA IN THE HEART OF THE HIGH COUNTRY," Salers's hour of glory came in the mid-sixteenth century. Set amid pastureland at an altitude of about 3,300 feet, the town has preserved a rare assemblage of ramparts and remarkable private houses reflecting its military and judicial past. In 1550, on the orders of the king, it became the seat of the Bailliage des Hautes Montagnes d'Auvergne. This was a tribunal presided over by a lieutenant-general and composed of a dozen officers. Wealthy residences that constitute a body of architecture at once sober and elegant were then built within the ramparts. These turreted mansions were constructed of dark volcanic rock and covered with heavy roofing stones. Among the most handsome are the Maison du Bailliage, the Hôtel de la Ronade flanked by a four-story tower, and the Maison des Templiers, today a museum. During the Revolution, Salers lost its privileges and soon returned to being a town of ordinary status. It played only a local commercial role with its livestock fairs and cheese market.

One of the town's prettiest squares bears the name, and has a statue, of Ernest Tyssandier d'Escous (1813–1889). A landowner and biologist, he was interested in the local cattle stock. By selective engineering, he sought to improve the qualities and attenuate the weaknesses of an age-old breed. Advocating better methods of feeding and strict sanitary regulations, he encouraged breeders to present their finest specimens at agricultural competitions. Through force of perseverance, in 1852 Tyssandier obtained from the Ministry of Agriculture official recognition for Salers cattle. With its mahogany coat and lyre-shaped horns, the Salers's robust character is forged on the upland plateaus of the Massif Central. Thanks to its hardiness and adaptability, Salers breeders are found in the United States, Canada, South America, and Australia. Salers meat is dense and evenly marbled—and it has a considerable capacity for water retention, so it remains very moist when cooked. It is finely textured, with a distinctive deep red, slightly dark coloring. Salers meat gives full expression to all its organoleptic qualities after a minimum of twelve days' aging. Then at its prime, it has a silky, melt-in-the-mouth tenderness.

Large wheels of hard, uncooked Cantal cheese, the oldest French cheese, along with Salers, a similar type of product.

*facing page*
Lovely Place Tyssandier d'Escous lined with typical Renaissance houses.

The recipe for Salers dates from 1885 and has never been altered. Salers is the oldest brand of gentian liqueur from the Massif Central, and the company prides itself on continuing to distill the same product. Yellow gentian grows naturally on the volcanic terrain of the Auvergne. The roots, which are deeply anchored in the soil and weigh up to 13 pounds, are picked between June and September. They are sorted, washed, and crushed, and then macerated in alcohol for months. Distillation follows, with additional infusions of aromatic plants to perfect the flavor; the final bottled product is 16 to 25 proof.

An exclusively artisanal cheese, Salers is made with whole untreated cow's milk. Its manufacture is authorized only from May 1 to October 31, when the cattle are put to pasture. The wild plants and grasses of the high-altitude Auvergne plateaus give the cheese its distinctive character and flavor. Immediately after milking, rennet is added to the milk; it is then turned in a wooden vat. Drained, worked, salted, and placed in molds, the curd undergoes a second pressing for 48 hours. The cheese is matured in a deep, cool, damp cellar for three months to one year. Salers is a firm-textured, 45-percent fat cheese that has a thick, dry crust with a bloom on it. It is cylindrical with a diameter of 15 to 19 inches, and it can weigh nearly 100 pounds.

# BEAUNE
WINES OF DISTINCTION

THERE IS NO END TO THE LIST OF LEGENDARY NAMES: MEURSAULT, POMMARD, Volnay, Aloxe-Corton, Romanée-Conti, Chambolle-Musigny, Nuits-Saint-Georges, Gevrey-Chambertin, Montrachet, Mercurey, and Corton-Charlemagne. These are exceptional wines, produced in vineyards sometimes as tiny as Japanese gardens by winegrowers—artists of viticulture—whose talent rests on a 2,000-year history. These wines express a mysterious alchemy between grape variety, soil, climate, and human expertise, and their infinite nuances—from the sweet to the full-bodied, mineral, and floral; powerful to silky—along with their strength, grace, and aromatic complexity, are a welcome challenge to the uniformity of taste increasingly imposed by the market.

It is not a matter of establishing a hierarchy and claiming that Burgundies are better than Bordeaux or Côte du Rhônes. But the number of small vineyards—some producing wines that any educated amateur would be capable of distinguishing blindfolded—are on plots separated from each other by only a few dozen feet, or even just a wall, and the diverse expertise of every wine producer exalts as nowhere else the virtues of the terroir, creating a unique and rich oenological universe. Every village is, in effect, a small wine principality in the Burgundian kingdom, and every *clos*, or walled vineyard, has its own story to tell.

However, one town more than any other sums up the magic of the old province and its wines. Beaune has allowed Dijon to claim the title of capital of Burgundy and kept for itself the even more prestigious title: capital of Burgundy wine. But everything is a reminder that Beaune was an immensely important center of art and culture in the Middle Ages: its old houses, the Hôtel des Ducs—where the Musée des Vins (Wine Museum) is now located—its twelfth-century collegiate church, Notre-Dame, which is decorated with an exceptional collection of Aubusson tapestries, its ramparts that have found a new use in accommodating millions of bottles of wine stored within its thick walls, and, lastly, the town's most important monument, the Hôtel-Dieu.

In 1440, the duke of Burgundy's chancellor, Nicolas Rolin, decided to found a hospital for the poor. When construction was completed in 1457, a masterpiece of medieval architecture was born. With deep roofs of glazed tiles and its immense 236-by-66-foot *Salle de Pôvres* (Paupers' Room) with painted beams, this wonderful building is "closer to a royal castle than a paupers' dwelling," according to one contemporary writer.

This large vineyard produces Pommard, a robust and tannic red.

*facing page*
A wine shop in the heart of Burgundy.

If there is one region where wine is part of its past and its present, it is certainly Burgundy. The Route des Vins (wine tour) offers a way of getting to know its vineyards, but also its landscape, heritage, and way of life. There are five different wine tours: Route des Grands Crus, Routes des Grands Vins, Route des Vins du Maconnais-Beaujolais, Route des Vignobles de l'Yonne, and Route des Côteaux de Pouilly-Sancerre, with bilingual (French-English) guides issued by the Bureau Interprofessionel des Vins de Bourgogne (see Addresses, page 252) and distributed at tourist offices.

Ever since it was founded, the Beaune Hospice needed benefactors in order to continue treating the sick and the poor. Today, as a result of nearly six centuries' worth of gifts of money, land, houses, and, especially, vines, it is in possession of more than 140 acres of grands cru and premiers cru vineyards. Every year during the first two weeks of June, in a tradition that started hundreds of years ago—the most famous charity auction in the world takes place. All the wines purchased have been aged in barrels before being bottled, and every one will then be labeled with its "appellation, the name of the cuvée, the year, and the name and address of the buyer." This sale also serves as a gauge for the Burgundy wine trade.

# CHABLIS

## GOLDEN GATE TO BURGUNDY

THIS IS A LAND OF STEEP HILLSIDES TIGHTLY STITCHED TOGETHER BY A NETWORK OF VINES, of white-stone villages nestled in valleys, of meandering rivers—the Serein and the Armançon, and of forest and pasture. In the heart of this picture-postcard landscape, almost a cliché of the rural France of myth and legend, Chablis presides over one of the jewels of the country's wine-producing regions. Yet this is northern Burgundy, where the summers can be blazing hot and the winters long and harsh. But is it not said (wine being the blood of vines) that the best wine comes from those that have suffered most?

Chablis is known for its white wines made from the Chardonnay grape, classified as Petit Chablis, Chablis, Chablis Premier Cru, and Chablis Grand Cru.

In Chablis every successful harvest is a kind of miracle. To appreciate the truth of this, you have only to see the hundreds of braziers situated between the rows of vines, which the viticulturists, who keep their eyes on the thermometer day and night, light up at the first sign of potential frost. The results measure up to these monumental efforts: refined, crisp, dry yet fruity with a lovely gold-green color, Chablis is considered the best white wine in the world. Though often copied, its mineral tang and delicate bouquet have never been matched. At the top of the hierarchy are the seven grands crus—Blanchots, Bougros, Les Clos, Grenouilles, Les Preuses, Valmur, Vaudésir—produced from vines rising above the right bank of the Serein on the steepest and stoniest slopes. Then come the premiers crus—Beauroy, Fourchaume, Montmains, and Vaillons, for example—which in vintage years may rival the grands crus. Lastly, there are Chablis and Petit Chablis, made from vines planted on slopes that are less well-exposed or on the plateaus, but often still remarkable.

Famous since the Middle Ages, when these wines were shipped throughout France, the vines have survived phylloxera, and they almost disappeared at the end of the nineteenth century, as did all those from this part of Burgundy. But through the fierce determination of the vine growers these vineyards have made

While Chablis may cast the other wines of this region into the shadows, it should not be forgotten that until the phylloxera catastrophe at the end of the nineteenth century, northern Burgundy had one of the most extensive vine-growing areas in France. Although at the northern limit of the prime red-wine producing area, there are some fine reds to be found around Auxerre and Tonnerre, some of which bear comparison with the red Burgundies from farther south. An interesting consideration: for the same quality their prices are definitely more affordable. Especially worth discovering are the wines of Irancy, Épineuil, Coulanges, St. Bris, as well as Côte St. Jacques, produced around Joigny. Also notable is the Crémant de Bourgogne, a sparkling wine made with the méthode champenoise. It is lovely as an aperitif or as a dessert wine.

a comeback; reducing the amount of land under cultivation no doubt improved the quality. Chablis has regained its prosperity of old, when boatloads of its wines were transported to Paris by barge on the Yonne River and the Nivernais Canal. You will certainly not find the same architectural riches that neighboring Auxerre and Tonnerre offer. But this small town has its own charm, and its fine houses built in the Burgundy style, and its collegial thirteenth-century St. Martin Church, a small-scale replica of Sens Cathedral, deserve more than a passing glance.

Yet another andouillette? Though a few have been described in this book, this one is not like any other. Traditionally made, solely from pork intestines and also cased in pork intestine, it is not, as one might suppose, cooked in the local wine as part of the initial preparation. For the rest, every chef and home cook has his or her own secret recipe. For serving, it may be cooked in Chablis and, of course, consumed with a glass—or several—of this inimitable nectar.

*facing page*
Chalky, clay-rich soil gives the wines produced by these vineyards a fresh mineral bouquet.

# DIJON

## MUSTARD CAPITAL

"AH, WHAT A BEAUTIFUL CITY!" KING FRANÇOIS I IS SUPPOSED TO HAVE EXCLAIMED when he saw Dijon for the first time. It is true that the architectural splendors of what is today a slightly sleepy provincial town are reminders of the time, at the end of the Middle Ages, when it was the capital of the rich and powerful dukes of Burgundy. Within the city's twelfth-century walls visitors can take a lovely stroll through the past of the grand dukes of the west: There are innumerable Gothic, Renaissance, and classical mansions—among them the twelfth-century Maison du Change, the late-fifteenth-century Hôtel Chambellan, and the early-seventeenth-century Maison des Cariatides; the St. Benigne Cathedral, and the churches of St. Michel, St. Philibert, and St. Jean; the ducal palace and the palace of justice, former seat of the Burgundian parliament; and the exceptional holdings of the Musée des Beaux-Arts. All of these notable landmarks contribute to Dijon's place as one of France's most sumptuous places to view art. But it is one of the least well known. While it should be famous for these treasures alone, it is mustard with which its name is inextricably linked.

"The gods of Olympus were not great food lovers," Alexandre Dumas remarks in his *Dictionary of Cuisine*. "To be satisfied with nectar and ambrosia—what lack of imagination! The sweet, smooth, sugary, and unctuous for all eternity—pah! It is true that greed is a sin the gods have always condemned. Why this divine fury against a pleasure that harms no one? Perhaps because genuine cuisine requires condiments, that is to say, all those things that excite the palate and inflame the senses." Here is the explanation: the sin of greed could not arise from the sweet and the smooth, it required the hot and the fiery—indeed, the devilish—to exist.

While the spice trade was the driving force behind the Europeans' exploration of the world, there was no need to travel far to find mustard. This modest plant grows everywhere, so much so that even in the Middle Ages it was on every table, and every town had its own organization of vinegar and mustard makers. But gradually Dijon imposed itself as the home of "real" mustard. Why? Very simply because the plant is easily cultivated in the clearings of its neighboring forests, and its vineyards provide verjus and vinegar

*facing page*
Crocks and jars of Dijon mustard, famous for its particularly strong taste, with the customary wooden serving spoon.

*below*
A view of Porte Guillaume at night.

in abundance. Few mustards have managed to resist the crushing domination of Dijon's product. The facts speak for themselves: of the over two pounds of mustard per year consumed by every adult in France, most of that (1.75 pounds) bears a Dijon label.

The black currant grows well in Burgundy's soil. Black-currant liqueur, reputed in the past to be a life-prolonging elixir, has for at least three centuries been emblematic of Dijon's gourmet delights. It was traditional among peasants and workers to offset the acidity of poor-quality wine with black-currant syrup. Félix Kir, a colorful character and the mayor and parliamentary representative of Dijon during the Fourth Republic, popularized the aperitif that today bears his name. Kir is made with one-third crème de cassis and two-thirds white Burgundy. Champagne may be used instead of white wine in the same proportions. Cassis with red wine is called a "communard" (the "communards" being the Paris revolutionaries of 1871); with marc, a "marcassin"; and with ratafia, a "ratacas."

There is no end to the delights of Burgundy's cuisine. Typical examples are *boeuf bourguignon* (shin of beef braised in red wine with seasonal vegetables), *oeufs en meurette* (eggs cooked in a ramekin with a red wine sauce), *jambon persillé* (ham with parsley), *gougère au fromage* or *au jambon* (Burgundian pastry with cheese or ham), *cassissine* (a black-currant sweet with a liquid center), or *pain d'épices* (gingerbread)—and all are part of the French culinary heritage. And then there are *les escargots* (snails) served in their shells with parsley butter.

*far left*
Place de la Libération was designed by Jules Hardouin-Mansart in the seventeenth century to increase the value of the Palais des Ducs. Today the square is bordered by cafés where reposing and admiring the Ducal Palace is best accompanied by a petit café.

*left*
Crème de Cassis (blackcurrant liqueur) and sparkling white wine combined make a Kir Royal, a splendid aperitif.

Escargots de Bourgogne is a local specialty prepared with butter and garlic and it's preparation is tedious yet rewarding. The snails are removed from their shells and soaked for two days, after which they are cooked for three hours in a mixture of water, white wine, carrots, garlic, and fine herbs.

# GUÉMENÉ
## SUR-SCORFF
### SMOKED ANDOUILLE

IN THE MIDDLE OF WOODS-ENCLOSED PASTURELAND BESIDE A QUIET RIVER, the little town of Guéméné is the capital of the Pays Pourlet, which today comprises a handful of villages. During its turbulent history, this territorial enclave passed from hand to hand, sometimes under English control, sometimes Breton; relics of its early past disappeared during the French Revolution. Little remains of the feudal castle, and the old covered markets have been destroyed. Guéméné has managed to preserve a few old granite buildings and a fine half-timbered medieval house. History has dealt harshly with the place, but gourmets have made it one of Brittany's temples of gastronomy.

Even in the eighteenth century, the Breton andouille enjoyed considerable renown. But it was not until after World War I that fate took its revenge and the Guéméné andouille prevailed over its local rivals, becoming the worthy heir of the rich and ancient tradition of Breton charcuterie. What distinguishes the Guéméné andouille is that it is made with pork *chaudins* (large intestines) encased in one another. About twenty chaudins are required to make one andouille. They are first cut to the same length, then sorted by size, from the narrowest to the widest. The narrowest form the core, over which the other chaudins are drawn one at a time. The whole thing is then cased in a pouch of beef intestine. Each chaudin is scraped and stripped of fat, then peppered. Assembling the Guéméné andouille in this unique way requires about twenty minutes' work (when sliced the Guéméné andouille has distinctive concentric circles).

Once it has been prepared, the andouille is smoked with oak or beechwood for one week to six months before being left to dry. The drying period may last from one to nine months. After being pricked at the base to drain off excess fat, the andouille is cooked slowly in a hay-scented broth. It is first immersed in cold water, brought to the boil, and then left to simmer for three to four hours to obtain its unique flavor. Nowadays it is mostly eaten cold and sliced with buttered bread. It may also be eaten hot in a buckwheat pancake or with mashed potatoes.

*facing page*
An annual festival, the Confrérie des Goustiers de l'Andouille, is held in honor of the area's renowned sausage.

*below*
Handmade from pork intestines is this andouille sausage, which is smoked over a fire for three weeks.

The cider press came to Brittany in the thirteenth century—and soon after came cider production. While it is not a particularly old product, Royal Guillevic is nevertheless venerable and original. Made in Auray, Vannes, and Lorient, this cider is distinctive because of its ingredients. Unlike other ciders produced from a blend of apples, Royal Guillevic is made from only one variety: the guillevic. It is characterized by its pale yellow color, delicate fragrance, and fresh fruit aromas. Connoisseurs appreciate its long-lasting bubbles and its mellowness with a delicately acidic spike. To fully enjoy its flavor, it should be cooled in an ice bucket before being served in a champagne flute. This was the first cider from Brittany to obtain the label rouge, guaranteeing its quality.

Breton's specialty is the kouign amann, a multilayered galette, and the kouign patate (potato pancake). This tasty combination of two staple products grown in Breton, the potato and buckwheat, is beginning to enjoy success in restaurants in the Pontivy region, as well as local grocery stores. It is a mixture of mashed potato and flour, with the potato predominating. The kouign patate is smaller than the ordinary galette but thicker. It is eaten hot, with an egg, cooked ham, or grated cheese—and browned in salted butter.

CONFRERIE
des
GOUSTIERS
de
L'ANDOUILLE
de
GUEMENE
sur SCORFF

# LE GUILVINEC

FRUITS OF THE SEA

IT WOULD BE A MISTAKE TO REDUCE THE LAND OF THE BIGOUDEN (the name of an ancient Breton tribe and also of the traditional Breton headdress) to the south of Quimper, to a folkloric stovepipe coif that no more than a handful of old women still wear—and only on festival days. This flat, green countryside, where the bell towers serve as landmarks for boats, lies open to the sea. Strung out along barely twelve miles of Brittany's southwest coast, the ports of Le Guilvinec, Loctudy, St. Guénolé, and Lesconil alone constitute France's most important fishing area, accounting for 17.5 percent of the national fishing industry. Practically every kind of working vessel can be found alongside the quays of Le Guilvinec, which everybody calls «le Guil,» a word synonymous in these parts with strength. It is France's third largest fishing port (in tonnage and value), after Lorient and Boulogne, and the leading artisanal fishing port. It was created out of nothing in 1850, when fish canneries first opened.

Curiously, Le Guilvinec is renowned for its Dublin Bay prawns (also called Norway lobster and scampi), which many consider the best on this coast. Canning this crustacean, with its long, thin claws, has never been done successfully. Every day, from 4:30 P.M. onward, the fishing boats return to port in a procession escorted by flocks of screaming seagulls. You would swear the boats were racing each other, but they arrive every time in exactly the same order. The fishermen unload the catch, load up the empty crates for the next day's fishing expedition, and then dock the boats in the harbor; all this happens in only a few minutes.

Dublin Bay prawns are curious creatures that live in burrows in the seabed; they emerge at dawn and at sunset to search for food. It is at these times of day that the trawlers can dredge for them off nearby Glénan Island archipelago. This allows them to sell their Dublin Bay prawns live, the same day, satisfying half the total French market. As soon as they are unloaded, the prawns are sold at the evening auction, a process whose mysterious and theatrical rituals of old have been lost to technology. For early risers, the morning auction is reserved for deep-sea fishing boats that catch angler, hake, or ray. Prawns cannot be tinned just as they are, but they can be found as tinned cream of scampi (prawns), soup, or mousse, sometimes flavored with a drop of Armagnac. It goes without saying that they are best fresh-caught and grilled, baked, or simply cooked in a court-bouillon.

A tranquil scene of fishing boats anchored in Le Guilvinec's usually bustling port.

*facing page*
Tinned prawns and sardines, a product of this town's canneries.

"Rebellious and refined," the very proud parents say of their child. The child in question is *cidre de Cornouaille* (Cournaille cider)—from an area of southern Brittany, to be more precise. The efforts of a dozen producers—in terms of quality of production, selection of trees, and density of planting—were rewarded in 1996 with an AOC designation. Kermerrien and douce-coetligné are the two main varieties of apple used for this orange-hued, refreshingly effervescent cider.

Often called buckwheat, Saracen corn is a grain that comes from the East. Since its introduction to France in the sixteenth century, its gray flour has long served as a staple food for Bretons, who would eat it as gruel or porridge. Today the *galette* (a Breton crêpe), not to be confused with the crêpe, made from wheat flour, is one of the key elements of Breton gastronomy. In vogue and on the menu of every creperie since the sixties, the galette is eaten in many ways—plain, or with ham, cheese, or mushrooms, to which an egg may be added. There's also the traditional *galette-saucisse* (galette-wrapped sausage) that is eaten like a hot dog. Galettes may be accompanied with cider, but traditionalists prefer a glass of *lait ribot* (buttermilk), called *babeurre* outside Brittany.

48

LE GUILVIN
ALAIN FURIC
LANGOUSTINES
AU
NATUREL
LA POINTE DE PENMARC'H

"Anyone can make it, but not everyone can make it well," is a proverbial saying in Douarnenez, a port situated at the very tip of Brittany. At first glance, the recipe for kouign amann (the name means "butter cake" in Breton) looks simple enough: it is made with flour, butter, and sugar. But the key to success lies in the proportions used, expertise, the cooking time, and the temperature. As a rule, kouign amann is made with about two pounds of bread dough (consisting of flour, water, salt, yeast) to one pound of sugar and one pound of butter. No one really knows the origins of it. It may derive from an attempt to rescue a bread dough gone wrong with the addition of some butter and sugar. It may have originated around 1865, at a time when there was a shortage of flour but butter was plentiful. It could also have been inspired by the sweetened bread that Scandinavian sailors had onboard their vessels. With no way of knowing for sure, the cake's creator is thought to be Yves René Scordia, a baker in Douarnenez in the 1860s. His recipe for kouign amann was soon copied by his colleagues and the arrival of tourists in Brittany permanently secured the renown of this caramelized butter cake.

*above*
Today more monkfish, hake, and skate are fished in Le Guilvinec than prawns.

*right*
*Kouign amann*, a typical dense, very rich Breton cake, consists of equal parts sugar and butter (a half pound each), and slightly more flour (three-quarters of a pound).

*far right*
Cheese, ham, and eggs are typical accompaniments of Breton buckwheat pancakes called *galettes*.

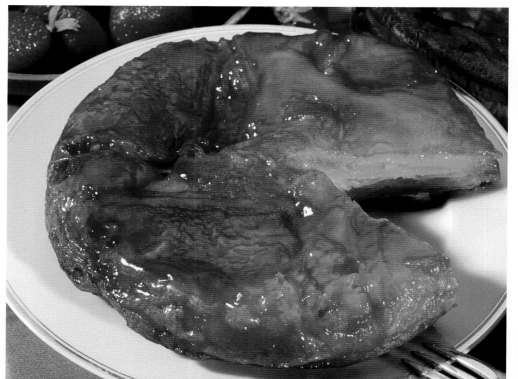

# PLOUGASTEL DAOULAS

## STRAWBERRIES FROM THE WEST

NEAR BREST AND JUST A SHORT HOP ACROSS THE ELORN RIVER, which spreads out like an inland sea, is the Plougastel peninsula. This little town has several claims to fame. It is the largest town in Finistère county. Also, it has one of the finest calvaries in Brittany, dating from the beginning of the seventeenth century and consisting of 181 figures finely sculpted in Kersanton stone. Finally, Plougastel has been the leader in France's stawberry cultivation.

Brittany owes its Plougastel strawberries to a Savoyard who had no obvious reason for going to sea. It was in the service of the king that one fine day in 1712 the appropriately named Amédée-François Frézier (the French word for strawberry is the similar-sounding *fraise*) set sail from St. Malo on a mission to spy on the Spanish ports on the west coast of South America. The results of his secret mission are unknown, but at a time when only the tiny wild strawberry was available in France, he was very impressed by a strawberry that was to become known as the Chilean white. He noted: "Its fruit are ordinarily as large as a walnut, and sometimes as big as a chicken's egg. They are of a whitish red, and a little less delicate in flavor than our wild strawberries. I gave a few plants to Monsieur de Jussieu for the royal garden, where they will be tended to make them bear fruit."

At the end of the eighteenth century, Frézier came to Brest to oversee the fortification of the naval base. He brought strawberry plants with him to present to the town's botanical garden. A Kéraliou-en-Plougastel village resident took one to plant at home, and it was here that the town's strawberry cultivation began. The strawberry found a mild and oceanic climate here, favorable soil conditions, with a good southern exposure protected from the winds that frequently sweep the Brittany headland. Cultivation continued to expand throughout the nineteenth century, reaching a peak in 1937. With over four square miles then under cultivation, Plougastel produced around 6,600 tons of strawberries—a quarter of France's total production—and was exporting them to Paris and England. The war put an end to this enormous success. Since 1996 much attention has been lavished on the Plougastel strawberry. The peninsula was first covered with greenhouses to provide strawberries from mid-March to the end of October, then the Plougastel farmers learned how to grow strawberries off the ground making it possible to obtain fruit a month earlier. Today Plougastel has an annual production of around 1,100 tons of strawberries.

*facing page*
Cultivating strawberries is one of the most important activities in the region.

*below*
With its 180 statues, the Grand Calvaire is one of the area's most famous sacred monuments.

The Bretons are major consumers of butter—salted butter, to be exact. If Breton butter is salty, it is not because the cows graze by the sea. There is a more practical reason. Before refrigeration, the addition of a small percentage of salt increased its shelf life. Because Brittany was exempted from paying the *gabelle* (salt tax), this treatment was not costly; elsewhere in France salt was rare and therefore very expensive. The tradition has survived, and the taste has remained the same. In the past, an ornately sculpted block of butter would be offered as a wedding present. On Trinity Sunday, in the Black Mountain town of Spézet, there is still a *pardon au beurre* (literally a butter pardon, a religious festival involving an offering of butter).

A quasi-mythical potion, mead was the beverage of the gods, of knights, and of brave warriors. In Brittany, where fantastic tales are also popular, it is called *chouchen* and supposedly quenched the thirst of elves. This sweet alcoholic drink is a fermentation of water and honey to which cider, apple juice, or must may be added. It is the subject of numerous legends: drunk to excess, it results in a loss of balance and falling backward. It is also said that hard-pressed peasants would put into the barrel trays from the beehive, containing traces of honey but also bees, and therefore poison, leading some people to conclude that drinking chouchen could cause madness. Chouchen is an aperitif or digestif, and is always served very cold.

# PONT-AVEN

GAUGUIN'S OYSTERS

"OLD COUNTRY OF MILLERS, PARADISE OF ARTISTS," IS HOW PONT-AVEN is often described. At the end of the nineteenth century, grain processing was the primary activity of this village, which is situated on a cascading river not far from the sea. "Fourteen windmills, fifteen houses," is how this small community, whose name was later to become world famous, could also be summed up.

A fisherman harvesting the highly prized flat Bélon oysters.

*facing page*
Picture-postcard perfect Promenade des Moulins is one of the attractions of Pont-Aven, in the past a place with many water mills.

Some locals decided to use the flour to make specialized products other than bread. In 1890 when Isidore Penven took over the family bakery business from his father, he created a new kind of cookie made from wheat flour, eggs, fresh butter, and sugar. From his oven emerged thin, crisp, buttery cookies, and some thicker ones too. These famous Penven Galettes are still produced today. The distant descendants of Isidore Penven are today running two biscuit companies, Traou-Mad, which means "good thing" in Breton, and Les Delices de Pont-Aven, both upholders of traditional excellence.

Gauguin must have tasted these cookies when he came and stayed in the town for the first time in 1886. Like Corot and a few American painters some twenty years earlier, he felt attracted by the light, the reasonable price of room and board, and by the fact that there, in the farthest reaches of little-known Brittany, locals spoke French.

Near the old bridge a plaque marks the place where Marie-Jeanne Gloanec ran her hotel, which was a refuge for painters such as Emile Bernard, Paul Sérusier, Mauffra, Meyer de Haan, and others. Over time, the windmills have been turned into inns or art galleries. The Bois d'Amour, immortalized by the Pont-Aven School, is open to people strolling, whether they are romantically linked or not, and at Trémalo Chapel, the Yellow Christ that fascinated Gauguin still hangs from a beam.

The Pont-Aven School had hardly come into being before its advocates fled the "crowds" that headed to the coast by train. They moved to Pouldu. In 1889 Gauguin and his friends turned up at the Auberge de la Plage, run by a woman known as Marie Poupée. These penniless artists paid their hostess with their artworks or by painting directly onto the walls. The Maison Marie-Henry has been carefully reconstructed two steps from its original site. "When my clogs ring out on this granite floor, I hear the dull, subdued, strong sound that I seek in painting," said Gauguin. Yet it was not long before he left for Tahiti in search of another source of inspiration and happiness.

Gauguin came to Bélon to eat the flat oysters of worldwide renown found in Brittany. Heir to four generations of oyster farmers, François de Sominihac affirms that at certain times of day the trees that line the Aven are indeed violet-colored, just as the Pont-Aven artists depicted them. He is the only one to farm these oysters, allowing them a long time to develop in the unspoiled, wooded Bélon River Valley. His ancestor, a pioneer in the field, created the first commercial oyster beds in 1864. The natural setting remains unchanged from those early days. Bélon oysters are renowned for their hazelnut flavor. This unique taste is imparted by the high-quality river water, which is fed by iron-rich springs that mingle with the seawater to create an ideal level of salinity.

There are as many as thirty fish canneries in this fishing port, one of the biggest in France; tuna is the primary haul. Sardines disappeared from the Breton coast in 1905; until that time Concarneau was one of the most important sardine ports in France. There is no mention of these tiny blue fish today, except when the Fête de Filets Bleus (Festival of the Blue Nets) takes place each year in August. Begun in 1905, the festival was originally a benefit to aid fishermen. It has become one of Brittany's most popular folk festivals. Every year Concarneau issues a commemorative tin of sardines featuring an illustration by a local artist.

# ROSCOFF

AN ADVENTUROUS ONION

ABOVE THE GRAY GRANITE QUAYS AND THE OLD TURRETED HOUSES that surround the square on which it stands, the bell tower of Notre-Dame de Croas Batz Church looks as if it were built to withstand tempests. Jutting out are two stone cannons directed toward England, the age-old enemy. Over the course of history, English ships often threatened the town. But look carefully, and between the two cannons one can find a man carrying strings of onions on his back. Despite their enmity, the people of Roscoff did not hesitate to sell their vegetables to their enemy-neighbors.

As early as 1350 there is record of a ship named the *Ste.-Marie du Conquet* that crossed the Channel loaded with animal skins and onions—but 1828 marks the official beginning of trade. That year, Henri Ollivier decided to set sail to Plymouth, England, to unload the vegetables he could not sell at home. A few weeks later he returned with his hold empty and his pockets full. Thus the British were introduced to the pink onion, nicknamed the "lard de Roscoff" (Roscoff bacon). In 1860 there were 200 "Onion Johnnies" in Great Britain. They were so named by the British, who were amazed to find so many Bretons called Jean. In 1930 there were more than 1,500 Onion Johnnies, all from the Roscoff region, in England. They would leave in August and return the following January, living cheaply in cellars and barns, saving the driest spot for the vegetables. They went door to door, with the strings of onions slung over their shoulders, or later on bicycles that they wheeled through town and countryside.

Shipowners of the past lived in grand houses; this one features a carved granite facade.

Although the age of the Onion Johnnies is long gone, this onion is still popular. Grown from seed brought back from Portugal by a monk in the mid-seventeenth century, the onion was first cultivated in private gardens. Cultivation expanded to feed the crews of merchant vessels that sailed for long periods of time without docking at ports. Easy to keep and rich in vitamin C, the onion was effective in warding off scurvy. The Roscoff pink onion is grown as it has always been, without watering, and it is harvested by hand. Both a vegetable and a condiment, it is hardy, with a pink or coppery color. Its skin is regular and its stalk is strong enough to be made into *troches*, braided bunches that facilitate storage and preservation. Eaten raw, the Roscoff pink onion is crunchy and juicy. Cooked, it is meltingly soft and sweet, retaining its fruity taste.

A traditional Breton fare which is a specialty of Léon, in the north of Brittany, is Le Kig ha farz, which means "meat and dumpling" and is related to the *pot-au-feu*, slow-cooked meat and vegetables. Every village has a unique recipe. It is prepared with beef (shin, neck, and brisket) and pork (bacon, belly, and knuckle) braised over a gentle heat for three hours in one-and-a-half to two gallons of stock and cooked with carrots, onions, turnips, and leeks (never cabbage or potatoes). The *farz en sac*, a thick paste of buckwheat flour placed in a muslin bag, is immersed in the stock halfway through cooking. Kig ha farz is a complete meal in and of itself. First the stock is served with the vegetables; then comes the meat with the farz that is crumbled or sliced.

Just off the coast of Roscoff is Batz Island, where the climate and light sandy soil are ideal for the cultivation of early vegetables. The farmers have always fertilized their fields with seaweed, to produce a much-sought-after early potato. Planted around January 15, the crop is harvested around April 15. Coming three weeks in advance of others, these are the first new potatoes to reach the market. They have a somewhat nutty taste and should be consumed within ten days of harvesting.

facing page
"Onion Johnnies" rode their bicycles around Britain selling their overstocks of onions, which they tied together in strings.

# SAINT-BRIEUC

## WHERE THE SCALLOP IS KING

A FAVORITE IN BRETON, LARGE SCALLOPS (IN LATIN CALLED *PECTEN MAXIMUS*) have an extremely delicate taste and should not be confused with the much smaller scallop, known in French as *pétoncle* and which has the scientific name *aequipecten opercularis*.

A symbol of pilgrims going to Compostella since the Middle Ages, the pilgrim scallop has become the primary resource of the Saint-Brieuc Bay in the north of Brittany. Scallop fishing—it is actually a process of dredging the seabed—began in the 1960s with about forty vessels. Soon there will be 500! There have been years when fishermen brought in 11,000 tons of shellfish; today, stocks are in danger of running out. To avoid ruin, Saint-Brieuc Bay, France's leading producer of shellfish, must be fished more carefully. The fishermen themselves impose very strict regulations on licenses, fishing seasons, and quotas. Fishing now occurs between November and April, and the duration of fishing trips is chronometrically controlled—sometimes aerial surveillance via airplanes and helicopters is also undertaken to deter poaching. After this race against the clock, the scallops are bought to be auctioned at one of the bay's three markets: Erquy, St. Quay-Portrieux, or Loguivy, where they are subject to health controls before being sold. Today,

High-quality scallops from Saint Brieuc Bay.

just under three hundred boats are licensed, with an annual production of 3,300 tons.

In April, the three main ports on Saint-Brieuc Bay, which are also major sea resort destinations, take turns hosting the Coquilles St. Jacques Festival. This event provides an opportunity to learn about fishing, scallops, and the region. For two days the quaysides are lively with the sound of music, folk dancing, and fishermen's songs. Boat trips introduce visitors to the fishing grounds and to fishing techniques.

There are countless ways to prepare coquilles St. Jacques. It can be eaten raw, carpaccio style, with a slice of lemon and a drizzle of olive oil, or tossed in skillet with butter over very high heat, and served with young vegetables. Should it be cooked with or without the coral? Current culinary trends advocate discarding this little red or orange tongue, which is not particularly flavorful. On the other hand, to put both color and taste on your plate, you can use it as the base for a sauce for the scallops.

In the nineteenth century, ports along the Saint-Brieuc coastline ranked as France's most important for deep-sea fishing. From as early as the fifteenth century fishermen would set sail on six-month expeditions to the Banks of Newfoundland; later they would venture into the frigid waters off Iceland. In 1845 the port town of Binic was bustling, accounting for 1,700 fishermen crewing thirty-seven ships. A sign of wealth on land was the equal number of bars. After World War I the fishing industry went into decline. All that is left in Binic today to keep the memory of those times alive is the Musée des Traditions Populaires and a major salt-cod festival, held every year in May.

A sailor brought back the seeds of coco de Paimpol, a delicious white bean from Argentina, in 1928. It was first grown by the wives of fishermen before attracting the attention of farmers. Curiously, it was in southwestern France that it first found a market: the coco de Paimpol is well-suited to cassoulet. The beans are harvested by hand, pod by pod, between July and October. Because of the unique characteristics of its terroir and its highly regarded excellence, the coco de Paimpol has enjoyed the prestigious AOC designation since 1998. Traditionally the beans are prepared with tomato and bacon.

*facing page*
A popular, busy market filled with a bounty of fresh produce gets even more crowded during the St. Michel fair in September and at Christmas.

# LAMOTTE BEUVRON

## GOURMET SOLOGNE

LAMOTTE-BEUVRON IS A TOWN IN THE FRENCH REGION OF SOLOGNE that best symbolizes one season: autumn. To the south of Orléans and the loop in the Loire are landscapes mostly defined by water and trees. When the leaves turn red, a sound that is the inevitable response to the abundant wildlife reverberates. In this area that once belonged to the kings of France, hunting and fishing are two lifelines. Deer and roe deer are numerous, and may emerge from the forest at any moment, leap out onto the road, and then flee in panic. Now and again, behind the screen of oaks, the gray mirror of some inaccessible pond may be glimpsed, far below, ringed with trees and rushes. Away from the roads, which tend to run in straight lines, countless footpaths, often straight too, lead into the depths of the countryside. Mushrooms, especially chanterelles and craterelles (also known as "trumpets of death"), are abundant here. At the end of a forest lane, the passerby not so much sees as discerns a dwelling—hunting lodge, grange, or castle—seeing at most a length of wall, a turret, or the outline of a dovecote. Certainly the vogue for fences and barbed wire continues to attract followers, albeit to the detriment of the wildlife that everyone wants, but the region of Sologne still manages to remain accessible to hikers.

A curious canal passes through Sologne, beyond the gates of Lamotte-Beuvron. Abandoned in the middle of the countryside, it gives the impression of starting nowhere and leading nowhere. It was dug by prisoners under Napoleon III who had acquired estates in the vicinity. Originally, the canal was intended to help reclaim land for the creation of model farms. It has almost never been used, and its 22 miles of towpaths are now the preserve of hikers and fishermen. The land and waters of the Sologne region have inspired many legends, some of which are sadly close to the truth. Chaon is home to an unusual place: the Maison de la Braconnage, a museum of poaching. All of the hunting practices forbidden by law but pursued here for centuries are illustrated in detail, with explanations of how the poachers managed to elude detection.

*facing page*
Packages of delicious sablés, a locally made crumbly shortbread cookie.

*below*
France's famous apple dessert was created at the Hotel Tatin in the late nineteenth century.

Many famous dishes are the result of mistakes in the kitchen. An example of one such mistake occurred in 1953, when young Jacques Fleurier accidentally invented the sablé. Seeing that the recipe had taken a turn for the worse but not wanting to waste the ingredients, his mother decided to bake the dough anyway, even though its consistency wasn't promising. The accidental creation was a hit with all those who tasted it. Success continues, thanks to artisanal production of the Maison Fleurier, which makes distinctive shortbread sablés. For many, the taste of a sablé recalls another time.

Tarte Tatin has been enjoyed in Lamotte-Beuvron, and the greater region of Sologne, for over 100 years. In the late 1800s, two sisters took over the management of the Hotel Tatin after their father died. Lovely young Caroline dealt with the guests; her hardworking older sister, Stéphanie, an excellent cook, presided over the kitchen. Stéphanie had a particular specialty: a tart with a crisp pastry dough and meltingly soft caramelized apples. According to legend, Stéphanie was a little scatterbrained. One day, during the height of the hunting season, she was particularly pressed in the kitchen and put her dessert in the oven upside down: the apples were on top and the pastry was underneath. There was no time to prepare another one for her guests, so she served the tart as it was. Everyone enjoyed it, and no one believed that her creation was a mistake. The following week, hunters flocked to the Hotel Tatin to try the new dessert. Stéphanie acquired everlasting fame for inadvertently creating what Curnonsky made famous in Paris and called "tarte des Demoiselles Tatin" (Miss Tatin's tart), a name that now appears in all good cookbooks.

# LES SABLÉS DE N

## BOULANGERIE PA

PAINS SPECIAUX

Votre boulanger.
Un artisan authentique

FLEURIER
☎ 48.51.81.19

PÂTISSERIE

SABLES de NANÇAY

*far left*
The pastry shop where, thanks to a mistake, the famous sablés cookies were invented in 1953.

*above*
Tarte Tatin is justifiably famous, with its crisp pastry and warm apples that melt in the mouth.

*left*
Jasnières is a dry, fruity white wine produced in the Loire region.

Until the beginning of the nineteenth century only the wealthy could afford asparagus, a delicate and extremely expensive vegetable cultivated in the Parisian region in the hills around Argenteuil. During the seige of Paris in 1870, Charles Depezay fled the city in a hot-air balloon, and for some unknown reason, he brought along bundles of asparagus shoots. The balloon landed in Sologne, which became the leading asparagus-producing region in France. Sologne grows a popular white asparagus. The vegetable is grown underground, without light. When the asparagus spear is fully grown, it is dug out with the aid of a specially designed asparagus knife. Sologne asparagus are available from mid-March to mid-June.

# ORLÉANS

## THE SECRETS OF VINEGAR

ORLÉANS IS MUCH MORE COMMONLY ASSOCIATED WITH A MYSTERIOUS PERSON than with a widely consumed condiment. Joan of Arc, seated on her horse, occupies a place of honor in the center of town, but were it not for the Martin Pouret company, genuine Orléans vinegar would not exist.

Vinegar has been used since earliest times, but its origins are unknown. No doubt it had its start with a little mead, barley beer, or wine left in the sun. There is evidence that it was known to the Egyptians, who may have used it for embalming mummies, and to the Greeks and Romans. It developed on the banks of the Loire River by accident at the end of the fourteenth century. The region's wines were already popular in Paris, and the riverbanks resounded with the sound of barges unloading wine casks on their way to the capital. Some casks were damaged during the journey, and the wine inside that was exposed to the air was abandoned on the quayside. This is how Orléans came to pursue an unusual business activity: making vinegar. At one point there were up to 200 vinegar makers operating in the town. Today there is only one artisan left to carry on the tradition.

Vinegar-producer Martin Pouret is the only company in France making vinegar in the old-fashioned way, by the so-called Orléans method. This method has not changed since 1797. The *vaisseau*, a 63-gallon oak barrel equipped with an eye-hole an inch or so in diameter and a gauge glass, is the key to making this vinegar. Lined up in two rows, one on top of the other, are 3,000 *vaisseaux*, which form dark, narrow corridors where the smell makes the air unbreathable. In these rooms with their sticky floors, a few small windows diffuse a dim light against which drosophila, the vinegar or fruit fly, can be seen flying around. Each vaisseau is half-filled, so there is plenty of surface area on which bacteria can work to transform the wine into vinegar; it is a long process that occurs summer and winter at a constant temperature, between 82 and 86 degrees Fahrenheit. By the end of three weeks, the bacterium *mycoderma aceti*, the object of lengthy studies by Pasteur, has completed its work. Around 13 gallons of vinegar are then drawn from the vaisseau, which is then refilled to exactly the same level with another 13 gallons of wine, so the process can be repeated. The vinegar is then placed in oak casks where it stays between six months and three years before being bottled.

How is it different from other vinegars? You only have to taste it. Mass-produced vinegar, tens of thousands of gallons of which are made in twenty-four hours, may be called by the same name but is nothing like the artisanally made variety. Martin Pouret's authentic *vinaigre d'Orléans* can be obtained from specialty food stores or directly from the producer.

*facing page*
An arched bridge over the Loire with the St. Croix Cathedral in the background.

*below*
Vinegar production in Orléans dates back to the Middle Ages.

Apart from its well-known culinary attributes, vinegar also has a place in the medicine cabinet. An antiseptic, a treatment against infection, and an antidote to poison, it was also used in the past for tiredness and as a gargle to soothe throat ailments. It cured ladies of the vapors and relieved headaches. Diluted (one spoonful to a quart of water), vinegar can also be used as a skin cleanser. A few drops rubbed into the skin act as a mosquito repellent. Finally, crystal and silver will recover all their brilliance after being immersed in a solution of vinegar and hot water.

In vinegar making, it is the scum that forms on the surface of the wine that creates the vinegar and not what is mistakenly called the "mother of vinegar," the gelatinous deposit that many carefully preserve at the bottom of their vinegar cruet. This is the enemy of vinegar, and, in fact, the graveyard of the bacterium acetobacter, carried by dust in the atmosphere and that turns the alcohol into acetic acid. In the past the mother was used to stabilize wines that had started to oxidize so that they could continue to be drunk. Another misconception: the degree level indicated on a vinegar label is not a measure of the proportion of alcohol contained in the product. Vinegar contains no alcohol, but acetic acid.

# PITHIVIERS

TWELFTH NIGHT DESSERT

THIS TOWN IS SITUATED IN THE MIDDLE OF A FLAT LANDSCAPE, on the border of Beauce and Gâtinais. It is the realm of beetroot and cereals, which has not prevented the town, the economic center of an essentially rural region, from building up a solid gastronomic reputation. Bearing in mind the name of the river that runs nearby, the Oeuf (Egg), this might even be considered perfectly natural. Indeed, a few eggs suffice to create an authentic pithiviers (a local almond confection). Whether the *fondant* version (a cake with icing) or the *feuilleté* (a pie made with puff pastry), the essential element of its preparation rests in placing a layer of almond paste in the middle of it. This traditional Twelfth Night dessert is also called *galette des rois* (Three Kings' Cake). It is almonds that have established the ducal credentials of Montargis, a neighboring town. According to legend, Duke of Choiseul Maréchal de Plessis-Praslin, was so fond of the caramelized almonds his cook made for him that they came to be called *pralines*. The tradition is carried on today in the same house where they were invented, and by the same method of production.

A land of honey, Pithiviers was also given the recipe for gingerbread by a hermit saint from the East. For many years, schoolchildren had afternoon snacks of slices of gingerbread made by the Gringoire company, whose factory was located in the town. This region is also where a much more complicated recipe originated: lark pâté. Allegedly, King Charles IX one day escaped his overbearing mother, Catherine de' Medici, in order to meet his mistress. He got lost in a forest to the south of Pithiviers, where he encountered Protestants who were hiding from persecution. They offered him a pâté baked in pastry. Charles brought some of this lark pâté for his mother, along with the complicated recipe, which subsequently led to the birth of a new profession: *pâtissier alouettier* (pastry cooks specializing in lark dishes).

Lastly, try a slice of Bondaroy, a soft cow's milk cheese made in the Gâtinais area. It is consumed between June and November. This straw yellow cheese with gray rind has a supple texture; a distinctive feature is that it is ripened in straw for five weeks. Finally, not far from the banks of the Loire, an area mostly dedicated to winemaking, beer can be enjoyed as well. The Pithiviers malthouse produces malted barley and wheat used in the manufacture of a pale ale from Orléans called Johannique, in memory of Joan of Arc, though no one knows what she herself might have drunk.

Fields with the St. Saloman et St. Gregoire Church in the background.

*facing page*
A *feuilleté* is a pie made with puff pastry and an almond-cream filling.

Honey is the oldest dessert in the world—and without any doubt the most natural. Gâtinais honey has existed since the Middle Ages and in the nineteenth century the area's proximity to Paris bolstered its success. At the time, the region was known for farming and hunting. People traveled on horseback, and the animals needed to be fed. This meant having to plant sainfoin, clover, and alfalfa, on which the bees also feasted. Today light-colored, delicately sweet Gâtinais honey is the most widely consumed variety in France. It has aromas of acacia, but more often of sunflower and rape.

Used to flavor sweet or savory dishes, saffron is appreciated for its intense peppery taste; it also imparts a lovely orange-yellow color. Saffron, *Crocus sativus*, was probably brought back to Gâtinais by a knight returning from the Crusades. The plant must have thrived here at the time of the Revolution, when annual production of this precious condiment was around 34 tons. A century later it had dropped to only 11 tons, before disappearing completely by the beginning of the twentieth century. In 1987 an association, Les Safraniers du Gâtinais (Gâtinais Saffron Producers), revived saffron production by planting 50,000 bulbs brought from Kashmir; the producers aimed to grow high-quality saffron. Harvested in September and October, saffron derives from the orange-colored stigma of the flower; once it has been extracted and dried, the powder is made. Two pounds of saffron powder are produced from the stigmas of 160,000 flowers.

# SANCERRE

THE VINTNER'S ART

Morogues, a village not far from Bourges, is squeezed between two hills. Its ungainly red-sand-stone church tower barely emerges from a sea of vines. This area has the AOC designation Menetou-Salon, from the name of a neighboring village. Two villages, two different geographies, two different climates: This could only lead to a friendly rivalry between their two labels. "Morogues is a hillside vine-growing area," points out Julien Zernott, oenologist with winemaker Henry Pellé. "The soil here is less warm. There's a week's difference between here and Menetou. The vines ripen later, but hold out longer." The Morogues whites, made from the Sauvignon grape, have a distinct mineral quality, while in Menetou the emphasis is on the fruit of the wine. Anyone for whom this matter of taste might create an awkward predicament can always sample the wines of Parassy, a village overlooking the plain and situated exactly halfway between Menetou-Salon and Morogues. "Wine is also dependent on environment," says Zernott. "Every cellar has its own personality and it should be detectable in the glass. Not to mention the intervention of man every year."

All wines are original products, because the circumstances under which they are produced are always unique. From Alphonse Mellot in Sancerre, whose family has produced nineteen generations of vine growers, you will hear the same idea. "It's my wine," he says. "I'm the one who decides." The vine-grower's approach, his experience, are factors as important as viticulture, oenology, climate, or terroir. "But above all, we must never forget that an *appellation contrôlée* is linked to a terroir," says the owner of the estate. "So it's the terroir that must find expression. The grape should bring out the terroir and not the other way around." Best expressing the quality of the soil is the vine-grower's art.

Despite the labyrinth of vaulted cellars that for hundreds of years have run beneath the hilltop on which the old town is built, Sancerre wine is completely grounded in the present. Computer technology has become its ally. Installed in strategic places, electronic sensors constantly monitor the most important factors in the development of the vine: humidity of the atmosphere, temperature (day and night), relative humidity, and humidity on the leaves. "This allows us to take informed and preventive measures to gain maturation time—a lunar month, half a lunar month. This is important because the fruit matures as the moon waxes. As the moon moves away from the earth, it draws the sap. As for bottling, that should take place as the moon wanes." Before Sancerre's harvest is taken down to the cellar, the vine grower must look to the stars.

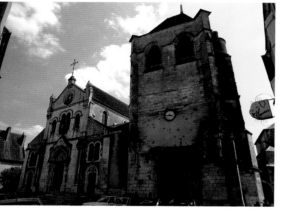

Notre Dame Church in Sancerre.

*facing page*
Crottin de Chavignol is a small goat cheese named for the small town near Sancerre where it is made. These are at various stages of maturity.

A favorite snack of agricultural workers and vine growers in the Sancerre region is Crottin de Chavignol cheese, with a texture ranging from creamy to very dry. Small, round, and ivory-colored, with a bloom on its rind, it is made from unpasteurized goat's milk in Sancerre and neighboring areas. It is matured in a cellar for about ten days. For a more subtle taste, it can be grilled or steeped in white wine. This cheese has had an appellation contrôlée designation since 1976, but has always been made with great care. In 1928 one writer reported that the cheeses were first ripened in the attic before being matured in a very cool cellar.

In August, when night falls on Bué, strange silhouettes emerge from the vines: wizards accompanied by figures dressed in white capes and wearing death masks called *les birettes*. Birettes were created by a priest in 1945, in order to promote the vineyard. Scouring the folk memory of a part of the country that claimed a few witches burned at the stake on the Place de Grève in Paris, Abbé Barreau decided to pay tribute to the terrors of the past in a fun way. The Foire aux Sorciers is held on the first weekend of August. It starts with a mass, followed by a large procession of *birettes*, and then nocturnal celebrations with ghostly apparitions.

# TOURS

THE GARDEN OF FRANCE

NICKNAMED THE GARDEN OF FRANCE, TOURAINE IS A LAND of both good living and good eating. It is also said that this is the region where the best French is spoken. So it is only right that it should have been the native land of Rabelais and his truculent character Gargantua, as well as other poets and writers. Its capital, Tours, stretches out along the right bank of the Loire River. This old trading city has retained its magnificent private houses—both Renaissance, (beneath their dark, clay-tiled roofs white tufa stone and half-timbering are combined) and classical. It is a little-known fact that in the fifteenth century, with Louis XI's help, Tours was one of the leading producers of French silk.

Of the royal castle built by the Plantagenets, only two towers remain standing. And two towers of the Renaissance grace the St. Gatien Cathedral, in which the evolution of all the Gothic styles from the twelfth to the sixteenth centuries may be traced. A few miles west of Tours, St. Cosme Abbey houses the tomb of the poet Pierre de Ronsard, a great lover of roses. In the nineteenth century, Honoré de Balzac had more down-to-earth preoccupations. "The rillons and rillettes of Tours formed the main element of our meal which we took in the middle of the day, between breakfast in the morning and dinner at home . . ." are words that he writes for the hero of his *Lily of the Valley*. He even describes *rillons* as "fried scraps of pork, resembling a cooked truffle." They were slow-cooked over a wood fire and served with an aperitif, or as a salad or even as an entrée.

Today these succulent cubes of pork are prepared in the same way as rillettes. A slightly shorter cooking time allows them to retain their shape, while imparting the delicious taste of meat preserved by the confit technique. The most delicate pieces of pork, shredded with a fork, are reserved for the famous Tours rillettes. Balzac called rillettes "the brown preserves of pig." Tours rillettes are brown and are less fatty than those of neighboring areas. Cut into strips, the lean pork meat is steam-cooked in its own fat for four hours. It is browned on a high heat during the cooking process, which gives it its characteristic color. The end product is rich in pieces of meat and meat fibers—while the proportion of fat varies according to the producer (it should never exceed half). Rillons and rillettes are eaten on their own and are sometimes included in the preparation of local specialties: *fouaces* (a kind of focaccia) and *tarte Tourangelle* (Tours tart), among others.

A wine cellar in Vouvray, just outside Tours, that produces a range of whites.

*facing page*
Rillettes is made from chopped pork slow-cooked in seasoned fat and then mashed into a paste; it is spread on bread or crackers.

The most famous vine-growing area of Touraine is one of the oldest, believed to date back to the seventh century. According to legend, Saint Martin introduced the grape variety and pruning method still used to this day on the left bank of the Loire. Vouvray's Chenin vineyards rise above the river, benefiting from good exposure to the sun. The white wines produced are dry, sweet, or sparkling, the latter accounting for two-thirds of the production. The sweet wines can be kept for an impressive ten to forty years. The cellars where the wine ages at a constant temperature are dug directly out of the hillside.

According to some sources, Sainte-Maure goat cheese may be thirteen centuries old. More of this goat cheese is consumed in France than any other, with 1,260 tons of it produced every year outside the village for which it is named. It is shaped like a log and left to drain before being removed from the mold. After it is removed, a piece of rye straw is inserted through the middle; the straw aerates the cheese and stiffens it during maturation (the straw has the producer's name and identity code on it). The whole is lightly salted, then dusted with wood ash. Maturation takes a minimum of ten days if it is consumed fresh; it can be extended to a month for those who prefer a drier cheese. This "little cheese bolster" has been protected by an AOC designation since 1990.

Baked in salt, or prepared with fresh morels or with Vouvray wine, the chefs of Touraine do not lack for inspiration when it comes to cooking géline, an unusual fowl. Long the pride of the Touraine farmyard, and also called "the dark lady," the géline experienced its heyday during the 1920s; at that time it was among the chief specialties in the region. There were about 750,000 géline at the time, and it was around Loches, where they originated, that they were reared; After World War II, the breed all but disappeared in favor of others that were easier to produce and more profitable (the breed needs to be reared for 120 days). Thanks to the efforts of breeders and gourmands, Touraine géline was saved in the 1980s; in 2001 it even obtained the first "Label Rouge." Black, ruffled, and free-ranged Touraine géline rarely weighs over two pounds; its flesh is tender with a strong flavor. It can be cooked in the tradition of great Touraine chefs, but it is also delicious spit-roasted over a wood fire.

*above*
Vouvray wines are produced from the Chenin Blanc grape variety only. These grapes thrive in a chalky or silica-rich clay soil.

*right*
A label for Vouvray, which has been a DOC wine since 1936. These wines vary from very dry to very sweet.

*far right*
A night scene of the the illuminated town hall and fountain on Place Jean Jaurès.

73

# VALENÇAY

## IMPERIAL CHEESE AND EXCELLENT WINE

VALENÇAY CASTLE IS ONE OF THE JEWELS OF RENAISSANCE ARCHITECTURE. Geographically, it belongs to Berry (indeed, George Sand found it very pleasing), but the date of its construction and its similarity to the Chambord Château clearly connect it with Loire Valley. In 1540 the original manor house was razed to make way for the existing castle. Subsequently, an entrance pavilion—a keep flanked by four towers and crowned with a parapet walk—was added. Later a new wing was constructed on the main courtyard, marking the beginning of classicism in the region. What makes Valençay special is that the whole castle, from the grand reception rooms to the private apartments, and even the offices and kitchens, still contains its original furnishings. And then there are the gardens, both French-style gardens and vast English-style parks.

Valençay Castle had many residents: wealthy nobility, farmer-generals (pre-revolution tax farmers), and even a financial adventurer named John Law. At the request of Napoleon, Talleyrand was one of the owners of Valençay, which he transformed into a residence for distinguished foreign guests. He even installed a theater with seating for 150, for the entertainment of the exiled princes of Spain who were welcomed in Imperial France. At that time, Valençay comprised about 100 sumptuously furnished rooms, half a square mile of parkland surrounded by an estate, and woodland of 73 square miles. It extended over 23 districts of Indre county.

Talleyrand, an astute strategist and diplomat, survived every regime, royal and imperial, to serve the king once more after the fall of Napoleon. He is said to be responsible for the actual shape of Valençay cheese. As result of some incident that occurred during a banquet at which Napoleon Bonaparte was present, he supposedly sliced the top off what was then a pyramid-shaped cheese with a cut of his sword. This non-pasteurized goat cheese conceals a pure white texture beneath a rind with a bloom. It is sometimes dusted with wood ash that gradually fades with aging to allow a blue-gray mold to come through. The cheese remains in the cellar for at least 10 days, but may be aged for up to five weeks. A young Valençay has a fresh citrusy flavor; aged longer, it develops a slight nutty taste. Valençay cheese has benefited from an AOC designation since July 1998.

Valençay Castle was built in the sixteenth century and belonged to Talleyrand. It has been remodeled over the centuries.

Valençay is the only place name in France that refers to two different AOC-designated products: cheese and wine. Vine growing is believed to date back to the sixth century, but Talleyrand also had vines planted at the foot of the château. Valençay's vines are planted on slopes overlooking the Cher River and its tributaries. The soil is a silica clay that gives the wine its flinty bouquet, and in some places it's a soft chalk that has made the reputation of Touraine and Anjou wines. Four grape varieties are blended to make reds: Gamay, Cot, Pinot Noir, and in a lesser quantity, Cabernet. These wines go well with poultry. For the whites, Sauvignon is the dominant grape. These are delicious with grilled fish or shellfish—and Valençay goat cheese.

With its many rivers and lakes, Berry is a region of water and abundant supplies of fish. The lakes are drained roughly every two years, which encourages wonderful fishing. In the lakes of the Brenne, there are carp, pike, pike-perch, river lamprey, *grenouilles* (frogs), including the tree frog, and, in the past, crayfish, which are now practically non-existent. It is hoped that salmon will return. Carp is often stuffed with meat or braised with red wine. One word of warning: choose your fish carefully; if it is too old, it will likely have a lot of bones.

*facing page*
Valençay goat cheese, with its distinctive flat-topped pyramid shape, and the disk-shaped Selles-sur-Cher, are both soft cheeses coated in ash.

# R E I M S
CHAMPAGNE–
ARDENNE
# T W I C E   R O Y A L

REIMS NO LONGER GIVES KINGS TO FRANCE, BUT IT DOES CONTINUE to give pleasure to the whole world. Once Clovis was baptized here by St. Rémi, nearly all French kings came to the capital of Champagne to be consecrated. The town came to be identified with royalty. Reims Cathedral, on whose facade stands the smiling Angel (above the left-hand porch), has stained-glass windows by Chagall. These were installed in the apsidal chapel in 1974. Next to this edifice, which was constructed in the thirteenth and fourteenth centuries, is the Palais du Tau, where the kings resided when they came to be consecrated; it houses the cathedral's treasures, including the famous talisman of Charlemagne. Made in the ninth century, this large, clear sapphire mounted in gold, and adorned with filigree and precious stones, contains a fragment of the Holy Cross.

It is said that Clovis was baptized in champagne. That may be so. But what is certain is that the earliest royal consecrations were not celebrated with the kind of champagne drunk today, whose corks pop to mark special occasions. The divine beverage dates only as far back as the seventeenth century. If legend is to be believed, it is to a Benedictine monk of St.-Pierre-d'Hautvillers Abbey, the famous Dom Pérignon, that we owe its invention. By design or by chance, he made the discovery of fermentation in the bottle, which was later to be called the "méthod champenoise." Just as wealth begets wealth, this same monk is also credited with being the first person to improve his wines by blending different grape varieties.

Champagne is a white wine made mostly from black grapes, which is why the grapes are harvested entirely by hand. Specialists distinguish four types of champagne: powerful, structured, and full-bodied Pinot-dominated champagnes; generous and warm Pinot Noir or Pinot Meunier champagnes; delicate but vivacious Chardonnay-dominated champagnes; and, finally, gold-colored, rare-vintage, soulful champagnes that are composed of a special or distinguished blending. But champagne is a matter of personality. Everyone chooses according to taste and circumstances. Champagne is drunk chilled, never ice-cold, at 46- to 50-degrees F. To reach this ideal temperature, the bottle needs only to be left in an ice bucket for twenty minutes.

The thirteenth-century Gothic Notre Dame de Reims Cathedral has been a UNESCO World Heritage site since 1991.

Reims ham is like the jambon persillé of Dijon. In the past it was eaten only at Easter, but today it is consumed throughout the year. Of great delicacy, it is made with deboned pork shoulder and blade. It sits in brine for four or five days, after which the meat is cooked in a flavorful stock. The ham is then set in a terrine and covered with breadcrumbs; it is consumed with a glass of white wine, preferably a Pouilly-Fuissé, a Mercurey, or a Saint-Romain.

"A little powder on a pink cloud . . ." is a lyrical description of Le Biscuit Rose (pink biscuit, also a pink champagne biscuit) of Reims. It is probably one of the last biscuits to warrant this term—biscuit meaning twice cooked; it is baked very slowly after an initial fast bake in the oven. As for the color, this cookie was white when first created. In the seventeenth century Champagne biscuit makers wanted to flavor their cookies with vanilla. But the vanilla made stains. To mask these they used cochineal, a red coloring. Though the recipe is a secret, the ingredients are known: flour, sugar, eggs, vanilla flavoring, and a pinch of coloring. Twice as long as they are wide, these hard cookies are able to absorb their own volume in liquid. In the past it was the custom to dip the cookie in champagne or a wine from Champagne. The glass of wine used for this purpose was not drunk. Some locals, who cannot conceive of champagne being consumed in anything other than its pure state, recommend dipping the cookie in port or a vin doux naturel such as Banyuls (these are sweet wines made by the mutage method, with the addition of spirit during fermentation).

facing page
Champagne takes its name from the region. Vines have been cultivated in the area's clay-poor soil since Roman times.

76

It was in the eighteenth century that Champagne began to specialize in the cultivation of mustard seed. Today there is only one local company still producing mustard. Straw-colored, with a smooth, homogenous texture, Reims mustard has a distinctive though slight aroma of wine. This is because of the addition of Reims vinegar, which is made from sedimented wine removed in the making of Champagne. Known under the brand-name Clovis, founder of the Frankish dynasty who was baptized in the Champagne capital, Reims mustard is widely exported; much of the exported mustard comes to the United States.

*right*
The entrance gate to Maison de Pommery Champagne.

*below*
Champagne vinegar and spices are used to create the unique flavor of Reims mustard.

*far right*
Reims biscuits— twice-baked cookies as the name implies—are a specialty of the area.

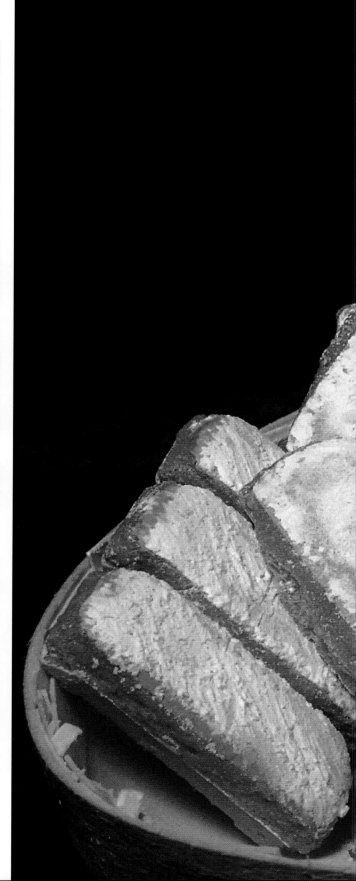

# TROYES

## HOME OF ANDOUILLETTE

CHANCE CREATED THE CONTOURS OF THIS TOWN, BUT WHAT A COINCIDENCE! The outline map of Troyes, capital of Champagne, is exactly the same shape as a champagne cork. Of course, Reims and Épernay are names much more evocative of the bubbles of this noble wine. But it should be remembered that a few Aube vineyards, in the vicinity of Troyes, also produce champagnes of character, some of which easily rival those of the Marne Valley. However, it is for another specialty that this town has entered the French culinary pantheon: the andouillette, which was invented by Guillaume Andouillette, the abbot of St. Loup. If this legend is accurate, the holy man fully deserves to be remembered for all time.

The recipe has remained the same for five centuries, and a gastronomic association, the AAAAA (Association Amicale des Amateurs d'Andouillettes Authentic), zealously protects the tradition. This delicious comestible is made with pig *chaudins* (intestines) and stomach, which is cut into long strips, packed into a casing, and seasoned with salt, pepper, and onions; white wine or champagne is added. It is slow-cooked for several hours in an aromatic broth. Genuine Troyes andouillette is tender, has very little fat, and preferably carries the AAAAA label.

A display of handmade andouillettes de Troyes, consisting of pork intestine and stomach seasoned with onion, pepper, and salt.

There are other reasons for visiting Troyes as well. Beautifully preserved and intelligently restored, the largely vehicle-free historic center has an exceptionally rich architectural heritage, a reminder that between the fifteenth and seventeenth centuries the town was one of the great artistic centers of the West, and that the Troyes School had an enduring influence on the European Renaissance. Crowding the quaintly named medieval streets—the rue des Chats (cats), de l'Eau-Benite (holy water), Corne-de-Cerf (hart's horn)—are half-timbered houses, Gothic and Renaissance private residences, chapels and churches. Among the latter, St. Pantaléon (from the sixteenth to seventeenth centuries) and its extraordinary statuary, St. Madeleine and its flamboyant Gothic rood screen, and St. Jean and its Renaissance choir are must-sees, as is St. Pierre et St. Paul Cathedral, which owes its façade to Martin Chambiges, one of the great masters of religious architecture. But the absolute masterpiece of Troyes heritage is without a doubt St. Urbain Basilica, regarded as one of the most perfect Gothic buildings in the world. Finally, art lovers will be thrilled by the wealth of the works displayed in the Musée d'Art Moderne, housed in the former episcopal palace.

The winegrowers of this lovely village—it holds the record in France for the number of historic monuments per resident—produce a natural rosé made exclusively with the Pinot Noir grown in this area; oenologists class them among the best in the world. There is a special art to making this wine. A short maceration is halted as soon as it acquires the famous "Riceys taste," a combination of hazelnut and violet, that gives it its distinctive character. After fermenting in vats, the wine is aged for at least a year in oak barrels; the result is a distinguished wine with a subtle taste and generous bouquet. It may be stored for three to ten years. Unfortunately, Rosé des Riceys is rare, since the vine growers only produce the wine in especially good years (more often than not most of their grapes are used to make champagne).

Pays d'Othe, to the south of Troyes, is the realm of apples. Countless varieties of apple, some of which are almost impossible to find elsewhere—the rambour or calville, for instance—are cultivated here in "orchard reserves." In addition to apples for eating, an artisanally produced cider—extra-dry, naturally sparkling, and non-pasteurized or sterilized—is the specialty of this Normandy-like region of Champagne. The producers continue to make the cider using traditional methods, pressing only select and often very old varieties.

*facing page* Half-timbered houses are now landmarked buildings much-appreciated for their charm.

# CORSICA

## ITALIAN SUN, FRENCH CUISINE

CORSICA HAS BEEN FRENCH SINCE 1768, WHEN LOUIS XV bought it from the Republic of Genoa. Previously it had been occupied by the Romans, Goths, Lombards, Saracens, Berbers, and many others, so it's not surprising that Coriscans have identity issues. This is also the reason why this mountain jutting out of the sea has never had a maritime vocation. Its inhabitants feel safer in the forests or the scrubland. With cragged coves, red rocks standing in turquoise waters, vertiginous cliffs, and deserted beaches, the Corsican coast has been zealously preserved, while the interior of the island presents villages perched on the heights, a labyrinth of forest tracks, and a network of paths climbing a mountain not always easily accessible. The rambling route GR 20, which crosses the island from one end to the other, is one of the most beautiful in France, but also the most difficult.

It is said that wine is the lifeblood of Corsica, which has vines growing along nearly the entire length of its coastline. The most interesting wines are produced around Ajaccio and Patrimonio, an appellation that has almost become in itself a guarantee of the quality of the island's wines. In the region of Ajaccio, between the sea and the forests, the vines exist on the mountainside along with olive trees. Red wine is primarily produced, from one specific grape with a strong character—sciacarello—along with some others. Although it does not give wines a deep color, it does make them tannic and spicy. Sheltered from the winds at the foot of Cap Corse, and overlooking the bay of St. Florent, the vineyards of Patrimonio extend over about one and a half square miles, in the island's only chalky-clay zone. The reputation of Patrimonio wines dates back centuries. Wines of character, they are made from particular grapes: Nielluccio (also known as Sangiovese, which has made a name for Italian chianti) for the reds, which may be combined with black Vermentino; and for the whites, white Vermentino exclusively. The generous, spicy reds combine notes of red and black fruit; they pair well with game and red meat. The whites, all subtly nuanced, present floral and fruit notes, and go very well with fish, shellfish, shrimp, lobster, and crab. The fresh, bright rosés, at once spicy and fruity, are an invitation to discover Mediterranean cuisine. Patrimonio wines were awarded an AOC designation in 1968.

*facing page*
Corsica grows more than thirty varieties of local grapes, of which three are noble and provide Corsican wine appellations.

*below*
Charcuterie and cheeses are the most typical expression of Corsican gastronomy.

There is a definite "chestnut culture" in Corsica, and for a long time, almost a monoculture. Flour made from chestnuts was the staple food of the island's inhabitants. Today the majority of chestnut producers are in Haute Corse, where the total yearly production is 1,325 tons of chestnuts, 85 percent of which is turned into flour. Dried in a wood-fired oven for twenty days, then shelled and sorted, the chestnuts are completely dehydrated before being milled. Corsican chestnut flour has an AOC designation.

Pigs roam free in the undergrowth, at altitudes where holm oaks and chestnut trees grow—it has always been this way on Corsica. It's in the scrub that pigs find their food: chestnuts, acorns, roots, and fruit that has fallen from the trees. From their meat, nourished with the flavors of nature, skilled charcutiers, who have inherited their expertise from their ancestors, produce unusual and appetizing meats. *Prizuttu* is a ham cured in salt for forty days; it is then washed and scrubbed, dusted with pepper and chili, and left to dry for at least eighteen months. *Coppa* is larded blade of pork put in a natural casing before being smoked with beechwood and then dried. Made in exactly the same way, *lonzu* uses tenderloin of pork. Both are served with fresh onions. Other charcuterie specialities include *panzetta*, pork belly that is smoked and dried, and eaten fried with eggs or as an accompaniment to dishes with a sauce; and *machetta*, smoked, dried, and rolled pigs' cheeks. But the most typical Corsican charcuterie product is *figatellu*. This sausage is made with pork meat and liver, though in some parts of Corsica solely with pork liver. Figatellu is dried and eaten raw, or, in winter, grilled over a wood fire.

Niolo and *bruccio* are the two best-known Corsican cheeses. Niolo, or *niulincu*, as the Corsicans call it, takes its name from the small area of Haute Corse where it is made. It is a soft cheese with a natural bloom. It is made from ewe's milk, or a mixture of ewe's and goat's milk. Cube-shaped with rounded corners, and weighing 18 ounces, it is matured for at least three months—even as long as a year—in a humid cellar where it develops a strong peppery taste. Bruccio, created from a mixture of ewe's and goat's milk, is the equivalent of brousse from the south of France. After being curdled with rennet and salted, it is put into a mold and eaten the day after it is made. It is cut into slices like a cake, and it is eaten fresh with tomatoes and prizuttu. Many Corsican dishes also incorporate this cheese.

*above*
*Brocciu*, made from the whey of goat's or ewe's milk, is consumed fresh without aging. There is also a *brocciu passu*, or *sec*, which is aged for fifteen days.

*right*
A stall at Ajaccio market where cheeses made with goat's and ewe's milk are sold.

*far right*
A lovely view overlooking Bonifacio Bay.

# ARBOIS

## THE REPUBLIC OF WINE

IS IT REALLY A CLICHÉ TO SAY THAT IN FRANCE EVERYTHING—OR VIRTUALLY EVERYTHING—revolves around the love of wine? Take the case of Louis Pasteur. Would this great scientific genius, who demonstrated the existence of microorganisms, invented vaccines, promoted the importance of sterilization, and developed the technique (pasteurization) for preserving fermentable liquids, have flourished had he not lived in Arbois? It was while conducting experiments on a grapevine that he proved the ridiculousness of the theory of "spontaneous generation."

Situated in the heart of the Jura vineyards, with the bell tower—the tallest in the Jura—of St. Just Church, the sixteenth-century Tour Gloriette, and the imposing Château Pécauld rising above it, Arbois is an elegant and affluent small town. It exudes bourgeois prosperity, so it is surprising that it chose to declare itself an independent republic in 1834 in a gesture of solidarity with a rebellion of Lyon silk workers.

The vine-growing area from which its wealth is derived and created was already famous in the sixth century BC, since its wines were exported to Phocaea (ancient Marseilles). Twenty centuries later these wines were served at the tables of François I and Henri IV. This vine-growing area would reach its zenith in the middle of the nineteenth century, before phylloxera, wars, and competition from the wines of southern France almost led to its demise. Only the determination of the vine growers, and, above all, the quality of their work, saved its wine-producing industry.

Arbois is a mecca for tourists who are drawn to its food, wine, and heritage.

Today, the Jura vineyards cover an area of almost eight square miles, and extend over about 60 miles, between Salins-les-Bains and St. Amour. Of the 40 or so grape varieties that used to be grown, five have been retained for AOC classification: two whites, Chardonnay and Savagnin, and three reds, Pinot Noir, Poulsard, and Trousseau. 105 communes share six AOC designations, four of them geographic—Château-Chalon, Arbois, L'Étoile, Côtes du Jura, and two "created" products, Macvin and Crémant de Jura.

There is no better way to become acquainted with the Jura vineyards than to follow the well-marked wine trail (information is available at all tourist offices). Running between Salins-les-Bains and St. Amour, over a distance of 50 miles, it passes through wine villages and small towns that are surrounded by an enchanting landscape of slopes and valleys dotted with castles and abbeys. With a few detours, you can see the stunning and unspoiled reculées, high-altitude valleys that cut into the hillside, terminating in a dead-end referred to as "world's end." At Arbois, a visit to the home of Louis Pasteur and to the remarkable Musée de la Vigne et du Vin, housed in Château Pécauld, are not to be missed. Finally, an event to remember is the Percée du Vin Jaune (when the first cask of yellow wine is tapped), held every year during the first weekend of February.

After two or three years in the barrel, the Chardonnay whites acquire a characteristic smoky taste. Combined with Chardonnay, Savagnin produces a dry wine with a nose of the terroir. While the pure Poulsard reds are quite rustic—this grape variety is often combined with Pinot Noir—Trousseau wines are warm, lingering in the mouth and developing red-fruit fragrances. Finally, this region also produces various types of sparkling wine, as well as Macvin, a liqueur made from grape must muted with marc.

One of France's greatest chocolate makers has his headquarters in Arbois. Édouard Hirsinger, heir to four generations of confectioners, has been given the rare and coveted title "Best Artisan in France." He is an artist of the palate, both an upholder of tradition and a tireless inventor. Only if you have tasted his *palets à la gentiane* (gentian-flavored almond-paste nuggets coated with chocolate), or his *chocolat noir aux noix et au curry* (walnut-and-curry-flavored dark chocolate) is it possible to understand that greed is the most pardonable of the seven deadly sins.

*facing page*
The vin jaune (yellow wine) of the Jura is a dry sherrylike wine produced from a single type of grape: Savagnin.

1989
Vin Jaune
Côtes du Jura
Appellation Côtes du Jura Contrôlée
Mis en bouteille à la propriété par
Baud Père et Fils
Vignerons Le Vernois 39210 France

The two finest products of the Jura's viticulture are inarguably vin de paille and vin jaune. Vin de paille is made from a blend of Savagnin, Poulsard, and Chardonnay. Grapes are picked early, then left to dry in a well-ventilated room, either hung from the ceiling or laid on straw. They are not pressed until Christmas, at which time they are wrinkled and dried out but filled with sugar. The juice obtained—221 pounds of grapes produce between four and five gallons of must—is put in small barrels to age. Once bottled, this near-relative of Sauternes, sweet and with a high alcohol content—14.5 to 17 proof—can be kept for at least fifty years.

Vin jaune, which is found nowhere else in the world but the Jura, is regarded as one of the best white wines on the planet. Made from Savagnin, it is also called *vin de gelées* (wine of the frosts), and is often harvested after All Saints' Day. Aged in barrels for at least six years, it is put in 21-ounce bottles, called clavelins, and can remain in the cellar for 100 years without going bad. Little known today, even by the French, the vineyards of the Jura are worth visiting for this reason alone, but also because they're in a region of spectacular beauty.

# MORTEAU

## WHERE SMOKING IS NOT A VICE

THERE ARE CERTAINLY MORE POETIC WAYS OF BECOMING FAMOUS than by associating your name with sausage. But what a sausage! This flavorful miracle is made in Morteau, a small town in Franche-Comté. One of the most peaceful stretches of the Doubs River—with its lazily meandering course, flooded fields where herons wade, and fishermen dozing over their fishing rods—runs through the Val de Morteau. This is no doubt the reason why some Benedictine monks in the twelfth century chose to build a priory here around which the town grew. While Morteau doesn't boast a wealth of monuments—few were spared during a devastating fire in 1865—it has many other sources of pride; for example, it is a famous watch-making center. From as early as the seventeenth century residents, whose dexterity was legendary, turned themselves into rural industrial workers, manufacturing mechanisms for watches and barometers at home during the long winter evenings. But it is for its famous sausage that Morteau is known.

Traditionally, twice a year—on St. Martin's Day and during Lent—every farm used to kill a pig. This provided stocks of charcuterie and meat that were smoked in the *tuyé*, a vast 325-square-foot well-ventilated room surmounted with a huge pyramid-shaped canopy rising through the house to a tall chimney on the roof. Slowly burning in the hearth of the *tuyé* was a mixture of timber—spruce, pine, juniper—used to smoke the sausages, which were suspended over the wood ensuring their preservation while imparting a unique flavor different from any other smoked sausage.

Though many of the striking-looking farmhouses with the *tuyé* still exist around Morteau, family production has almost died out. But some twenty producers, who have joined together to form an association of manufacturers of genuine *saucisse de Morteau* (Morteau sausage)—the Association des fabricants de la véritable saucisse de Morteau—continue to use traditional artisanal methods and have a registered label to guarantee an authentic, quality product. Genuine Morteau sausage comes in two forms: the *jésus*, a short, lumpy sausage, and the *suivant*, a long, smooth sausage. They are smoked for at least forty-eight hours, are recognizable by their brown, amber-tinted, slightly shiny appearance, have a wooden pin that seals them at one end, and have a green-and-white label. When you have tasted these sausages, served warm with potato salad, for example, you will agree that Morteau can be justifiably proud to have given its name to a sausage.

Like Morteau sausage, the Montbéliard sausage is also worthy of mention. Made throughout France, it is too often associated with the menus of marginal bistros and school cafeterias. Thanks to the Confrérie des Compagnons du Boitchu, which takes its name from a knife used in the past by charcuterie butchers, it is regaining its reputation. The true Montbéliard sausage is made from Franche-Comté pigs' meat, 90-percent lean and 10-percent fat, which is roughly chopped to give it texture, and seasoned with salt, pepper, and spices. This mixture is stuffed into one-foot-long casings, which are then braised and smoked over wood. While the Montbéliard sausage may not yet have an AOC designation, the Compagnons du Boitchu's seal guarantees authenticity.

*facing page*
Morteau Church dominates the pastoral scenery.

*below*
These smoked pork sausages are made from locally raised pigs.

Morteau and Montbéliard sausages are not the only glories of Franche-Comté charcuterie. *Jambon du Haut-Doubs*, weighing at least twenty-two pounds, is smoked in the *tuyé* after its excess fat and some of the rind have been removed. *Jambon de Luxueil* is steeped in red wine and rubbed with salt. After it sits for a month, it is smoked over wood before being left to dry for seven to eight months suspended from poles in a well-ventilated room. *Brési* is a piece of dried smoked beef served in thin slices.

# PONTARLIER

## THE GREEN FAIRY

*facing page*
Raclette de Morbier
is a semi-hard
cheese with a line
of ash running
through it. It is
excellent melted on
local bread and
accompanied with a
glass of Jura wine.

*below*
Pontarlier was the
world capital of
absinthe until it was
banned in 1915.

IN THE NINETEENTH CENTURY PONTARLIER AND PARIS were the most famous cities in France. Strolling the quiet streets of this modest capital of Haut-Doubs, you might well wonder why. Certainly Pontarlier does have a few claims to fame. At an altitude of approximately 2,750 feet, it is one of the highest towns in western Europe, set in the heart of a glorious wild landscape. It is close to the fortress of Joux, Franche-Comté's most spectacular military construction that for close to 1,000 years has guarded a narrow valley through which, from the days of the Roman Empire, all commercial traffic between Italy and Flanders had to pass. And despite a particularly eventful history—the numerous fires, pillagings, and epidemics to which it has fallen victim—it retains a few fine monuments from its past: the St. Bénigne Church, built in the seventeenth century, with its splendid stained glass by master glassmaker Manessier; the eighteenth-century Porte St.-Pierre; the Annonciades chapel; the Capuchin monastery; and a number of significant houses, including one that was the residence of the French revolutionary Mirabeau, who, although a prisoner at the Joux fortress, was so leniently treated by the governor of the prison that he was allowed to live in town.

However, it is not to this heritage that the town once owed its immense celebrity, but rather to its reputation as the world capital of the "Green Fairy." In 1805 a certain Henri-Louis Pernod settled in Pontarlier to exploit the recipe for a liqueur that until then had been consumed for therapeutic purposes: absinthe. He went on to enjoy extraordinary commercial success with the spirit. But its effects were devastating—inexpensive and at 65- to 72-proof, it was said to be filling the asylums with the deranged. It was banned in 1915 due to pressure from temperance and moral organizations and, concerned about their own businesses, the vine-growers who were unhappy about the way the Green Fairy was competing with red wine in the hearts and throats of drinkers. At that time twenty-six distillers in Pontarlier were producing nearly 1.85 million gallons per year. There are many in Franche-Comté who have been fighting ever since for the rehabilitation of absinthe. By making a few compromises, most importantly a lower alcoholic strength of 45-proof, some distillers have created aperitifs with a similar taste, among them the famous Pontarlier Anis. But nostalgia for absinthe remains so strong that an active and well-known contraband trade has been established with Switzerland, where its production is still allowed.

On August 11, 1901, a fire started in the Pernod distillery, and to avoid a serious explosion the vats had to be emptied into the Doubs River. Pontarlier residents rushed to the river, filling every available receptacle, while firemen and soldiers drank this free aperitif from their helmets. Two days later the source of the Loue River was green, which proved the connection between the two rivers. Thanks to the Green Fairy, alcohol and science for once combined to take a great step forward.

Its rich pasturelands are grazing territory of the famous Montbéliard cows, and this has contributed to the Pontarlier region's wealth of cheeses. Among the most well known is Comté, which is pressed into molds that can hold 88 to 110 pounds of milk; the contents are salted and stirred daily then matured in cellars for several months. Mont-d'Or comes with a band of spruce bark that gives it a unique flavor; it has a golden rind and a creamy interior, and is often eaten with a spoon. The ivory-colored, mild Morbier, with its creamy texture and a thin horizontal charcoal-colored layer running through the middle, is another fine example. Lesser known but equally delicious are the bleu de Gex, a blue cheese with a slightly bitter taste, and the Concoillotte, a strong-smelling, jarred cheese to which garlic is sometimes added.

# MEAUX

CULINARY SECRETS

THE MARNE VALLEY WAS FOR A LONG TIME THE FAVORITE COUNTRY retreat for the powerful in France. Countless ministers, parliamentarians, and courtesans built châteaux and sumptuous residences for themselves. But times have changed. Today, established in the heart of this region, is Disneyland® Resort Paris. The regional capital, Meaux has preserved its imposing St. Étienne Cathedral and its episcopal palace, occupied notably by Bossuet, masterful orator of the late eighteenth century. Meaux is also one of France's mustard capitals. The antiseptic and digestive virtues of this condiment have been praised from earliest times. Distinct from Dijon mustard because of the addition of vinegar, the less refined Meaux mustard is made with crushed or whole mustard seeds, and it is described as *moutarde à l'ancienne* (mustard made the old way). Although usually considered a strong mustard, this preparation gives it a certain sweetness.

Mustard has ancient origins. The plant was cultivated by the Chinese more than three thousand years ago, and has long been appreciated by gourmets and epicures. Charlemagne recommended the cultivation of this plant in all his domains, including the gardens surrounding the monasteries close to Paris. This is no doubt why, for a very long time, the manufacture of mustard was solely done by the monks of Meaux abbey. In 1760 a dignitary of that religious order shared the secret of this original mustard, which had officially graced the royal table since 1632, with the Pommery family. The Pommery company first established itself in the shadow of the cathedral, then later in the outskirts of town. It continued to operate until 1925, when the last descendant sold the business, the brand name, and the secret. To this day it is packaged in its distinctive earthenware pot with wax-sealed cork stopper, making Meaux Pommery Mustard instantly recognizable. Its recipe is unchanged: Meaux mustard contains black mustard seed (*Sinapis nigra*) crushed with water, vinegar, and flavorings. Also among the ingredients are white mustard seed, the mustard seed integument (seed coat), and spices. Understandably, the holder of the recipe still refuses to give any information about how it is made.

Brie, a soft cheese with a bloomy rind, takes its name from a natural region of which Meaux was the most important town. The name of the valley? Brie de Meaux.

It was in 1238, on his return from the Crusades, that Thibault IV, known as the *chansonnier* (songwriter), and count of Brie and Champagne, brought back from the Holy Land a red rose that has continued to be cultivated in Provins. In the Middle Ages the *Rosa gallica* was much sought after in all the major markets for its curative properties. Provins rose-petal jam was traditionally offered to leading figures and French monarchs who came to Provins: from Joan of Arc to Louis XIV, Catherine de' Medici, and Henri IV. Today, rose-petal jams are appreciated above all for their delicacy and fragrance. This specialty continues to be produced by the last of the town's jam makers. The petals are gathered at the end of the summer, before being sorted, washed, blanched, and cooked in large copper pots, using a recipe and methods that are age-old and still secret.

At Moret-sur-Loing in 1638, Benedictine nuns seeking to alleviate the suffering of their patients developed a sweet made of cane sugar flavored with barley; the addition of vinegar prevented crystallization. This barley sugar was a great success at the court of Louis XIV. Because it soothed sore throats, it was appreciated by the best orators. The nuns continued to make these sweets until 1970 when they entrusted their secret to a confectionery company. The site where the sweets used to be made has been preserved. The former convent retains its shop sign and now houses a museum that traces the history of this product.

*facing page*
The Gothic St. Étienne Cathedral was built between the twelfth and sixteenth centuries.

# PARIS

## CAPITAL OF THE BAGUETTE

FROM AFGHAN OR MADASCAN RESTAURANTS TO CHINESE TAKEOUT, the hamburger stall to the pizzeria, every type of cuisine in the world, to fit every budget, can be found in Paris. Sample the cuisine of the Auvergne, Brittany, Corsica, Alsace, or Provence. If you prefer home-cooking that is also easy to arrange. Every neighborhood has a covered market and once or twice a week the streets are taken over by the stalls of the market gardeners of the Paris region, who sell their fruits and vegetables; the poultry sellers, with their eggs and hens; and the fishmongers, with a fresh catch from the nearest fishing port.

Notre-Dame Cathedral is one of the greatest masterpieces of French Gothic architecture.

But what food specialty can Paris boast? In the past, Paris was famous for its mushrooms, which used to grow in the city's cellars and ancient quarries, but have now been exiled to the banks of the Loire. Striving to come up with something, but with no convincing historical proof, some writers credit the Paris region with inventions such as *hachis parmentier* (a kind of shepherd's pie with beef and mashed potato), *sauce gribiche* (a cold hard-boiled-egg-yolk, vinegar, and oil sauce served mainly with fish), or *blanquette de veau* (a veal stew with an egg and cream sauce). Practically the only gastronomic item that still bears the epithet "*de Paris*" (of Paris) is *jambon*—ham, from a pig that almost certainly comes from elsewhere. In the end, the only truly Parisian specialty is the baguette. Perhaps it is no accident that Frenchmen are commonly caricatured wearing Basque berets, rarely worn in the city, with baguettes under their arms. Wonderfully crusty, the Parisian baguette is the pride of real bakers, who still make their own bread in their own ovens, and it is the joy of their customers, who are happy to line up at their favorite bakeries.

One baker in Paris was as good with his flour as he was at marketing, and he succeeded in giving his name to a bread product. Poilâne bread is now an international brand-name. In 1932 Pierre Poilâne opened

Vines covered the hills of the Paris region in the ninth century. Suresnes wine was served at the table of the kings of France, from Henri IV to Louis XIV. Until the seventeenth century it was considered one of the best wines of the Île-de-France. The last surviving vineyard in this area today extends over three acres; its 5,000 vine stocks are planted within view of the Eiffel Tower. A blend of separately produced Semillon and Chardonnay wines, Suresnes wine, of which 5,000 to 6,000 bottles are produced per year, is pale yellow with a subtle fruity taste. More of a quaint eccentricity, the Montmartre vineyard was planted in 1929 by the cartoonist Francisque Poulbot, creator of the little Parisian urchin to whom he gave his name. With an exposure facing due north, the 2,000 vines of Gamay and Pinot produce 1,800 bottles a year; these are generally auctioned for charity.

a bakery in the St.-Germain-des-Prés neighborhood, where he made bread in a unique way: he used mill-ground flour, leavening the dough naturally with yeast, and baked the bread in a wood-fired oven. In the 1970s his son Lionel took over the business, using the same production methods. His baking artistry became known throughout France and abroad. Lionel Poilâne was killed in a helicopter accident in October 2002. His daughter, Apollonia, picked up the reins, following in the footsteps of her father and grandfather.

*facing page*
A display at the nearly 150-year-old Ladurée patisserie, which is most famous for its macaroons, almond meringues with a ganache filling that come in many flavors and colors.

These almond macaroon cakes, two of which sandwich a ganache of cream and chocolate, are the same as they were at the beginning of the nineteenth century. Every day Ladurée pâtissiers carefully weigh out the almonds, eggs, and sugar, with an authentic and secret pinch of expertise. It is only forty-eight hours after the macaroons have baked and the filling added that they are put on sale. They come in summer flavors: green lime and basil, icy mint, or violet; winter flavors include licorice or chestnut; and flavors available year-round are pistachio, raspberry, lemon, and Java pepper, among others. The color of the macaroon is also important. At Ladurée, deliciousness is synonymous with beauty.

# AUBRAC

## COMFORT FOOD

AT THE FOOT OF THE MASSIF CENTRAL, THE AUBRAC'S VOLCANIC SURFACE reaches like fingers down to the banks of the Lot River. This is another universe, a mineral world perched at an altitude of over 3,000 feet. When the winds chase the clouds, set the wire fences whistling, and flatten the close-cropped grass, this basalt plateau, wind-blasted for 3 million years, gives the impression of underpinning the sky. Against a background of *trucs* (mountains) and *puys* (volcanos), stonewall-enclosed pastures disappear into the horizon, beyond the curved surface of the track-crossed land.

Winter is so much in its element on the Aubrac that it lingers for a while. The arrival of spring is always impatiently awaited. Once a handful of flowers manages to break through the patches of snow betrayed by the first rays of sunshine, a few weeks is all that is necessary to cover the Aubrac with a multicolored carpet. From the snow-drop to the martagon lily, gentian, and the narcissus, botanists have identified approximately 2,000 species of plants on these deceptively unbroken expanses. This is a restorative place: the ozone-rich air on the plateau is thought to induce euphoria. These vast serene expanses are occasionally punctuated by the changing waters of a lake reflecting a few clusters of trees or by the glimmering of a peat bog.

In the heart of this mineral world, people shelter under the roofing stones of a *mazuc*, or *buron*, the isolated huts the shepherds have built into the contours of the land, where cheese and creamy milk are obtained. It is with the fresh Laguiole Tomme cheese that *aligot* is made. The recipe for aligot was invented by the monks at the Aubrac hospice, who served this hearty dish to pilgrims on their way to Compostella. The preparation of aligot begins with a potato purée, on which the fresh Tomme (made two to five days ear-lier) is placed. According to personal preference, this is the point at which the finely chopped garlic is added, although it can also be put on the table and added according to taste. The cooking pot is then placed on a low heat and the purée worked with a stick or spatula. It should be lifted up from below with a twist-ing motion. The tomme slowly melts and forms threads—*l'aligot file* is the expression that describes what happens at this stage. As the aligot gradually acquires elasticity, the spatula should be raised higher and higher. When the tomme is completely melted, the aligot is ready. All that remains is to serve it by letting it *filer* onto the plates.

*Aligot* is a potato purée blended with butter, cream, the local Tomme cheese, and often garlic. It is carefully stirred to create its unique, stringy consistency, and is served with Aveyron sausages.

Because they acquitted themselves well during a battle, Napoleon I conferred on the knife makers of Laguiole, a village on the Aubrac plateau, the privilege of using the imperial emblem. This is why Aveyronnais knives are decorated with a bee. Pierre-Jean Calmels is credited with having created the *laguiole* knife at the beginning of the nineteenth century. With its crooked horn handle and strong, sharp blade, the laguiole may also have a spike that peasants used, a *pique-boeuf*, or "cattle-prick," (it was used to puncture swollen bellies of cattle or to pierce holes in straps). Some have a corkscrew, used universally for one purpose. The laguiole was given new life at the end of the 1980s when the designer Philippe Stark came up with a knife entirely made of steel. At that time, Laguoile was only selling knives made elsewhere, but since then forges and workshops have reopened in the village.

*Tripoux de St.-Chély* is prepared based on ancient recipes. This three-tripe dish is composed of veal and lamb rumen (tripe) finely chopped and seasoned, and wrapped in a mutton-rumen container. It is then sewn by hand. The three tripes are slowly simmered with fresh vegetables, a calf's foot, and a few other zealously guarded secret ingredients. The tripe are served warmed up in a bain-marie or in a casserole on low heat. They can also be baked au gratin and are usually served with boiled potatoes.

*facing page* Aubrac cattle are highly prized and are bred in the region for which they are named.

# CASTELNAUDARY

## DIVINE CASSOULET

WAS THE EMBLEMATIC DISH OF SOUTHWEST FRANCE, CASSOULET, invented in Toulouse, Carcassonne, or Castelnaudary? This is a serious issue in the region, as is everything relating to the pleasures of eating. The cassoulet war has been going on for so many centuries, and such is the passion that each camp puts into claiming this exquisite dish as its own, that it would be risky, especially for an outsider, to take a position.

So the prudent definition found in Elizabeth David's *French Provincial Cooking* will have to do. It quotes Prosper Montagné, the culinary authority who compiled the monumental *Larousse Gastronomique* and was born in Castelnaudary, as stating "Cassoulet is god in three persons. The Father is that of Castelnaudary, the Son that of Carcassonne, and the Holy Spirit that of Toulouse."

What is certain is that if you were only to eat a cassoulet once in your life, it is in Castelnaudary that you should try this unforgettable gastronomic experience. It remains unknown when the recipe for this Provençal stew was created, but its origins can certainly be traced back to the Middle Ages. The rules governing its preparation are now immutable: in an earthenware vessel, the *cassoulo*, pork rind, andouille (chitterling sausage), pork fat chopped with garlic, and blanched lingot haricot beans (white beans) are simmered with a pig's knuckle, sausage, and preserved goose. The pot is then put into the oven to cook slowly for four or five hours. The dish may seem simple, but the quality of the local ingredients as well as the cook's skill are the only guarantees of its success; it is actually an incredibly difficult dish to perfect.

Cassoulet is so largely responsible for Castelnaudary's renown that the town's other attractions might almost be forgotten. It is worth taking a stroll around the town's old section, where classical-style private residences line the streets. Major monuments to visit include the Gothic collegiate church of St. Michel; the chapel of Notre-Dame-de-la-Pitié and its eighteenth-century gilt paneling; the Présidial, a citadel dismantled in the fourteenth century that was reconstructed to serve as a law court and prison; St.-Jacques Hospital, whose pharmacy has a rich collection of faïence and porcelain; and finally the Moulin de Cugarel, the last surviving windmill of the 32 the town once had. First off, stroll around the Grand Bassin, an 18.25-acre stretch of water dug out in the seventeenth century, which made Castelnaudary the main port of the Canal du Midi, one of the greatest achievements of the reign of Louis XIV and now registered as a World Heritage site.

Cassoulet is a classic French dish made with white beans, preserved goose, garlic, sausage, pork rind, and mutton.

It was in the sixteenth century that the haricot bean, brought back from America by the conquistadors, began to be cultivated in southwest France. The fat, thin-skinned variety grown in the Castelnaudary region is theoretically the only kind allowed in the preparation of an authentic cassoulet. Some cooks, however, occasionally dare to break this sacrosanct rule by using broad beans, reinventing the medieval recipe that predated the discovery of the New World (and therefore the introduction of the haricot bean).

Covering nearly 116 square miles, the vine-growing area of Languedoc-Rousillon is the most extensive in France. But it is not the most highly renowned, despite recent improvements achieved by vine growers tired of producing "rough red," which is losing popularity in France. To the northwest of Castelnaudary, between the Black Mountain and the Canal du Midi, the small wine area of Minervois—17 square miles—is one that does credit to Languedoc's viticulture. The well-structured reds, the vivacious rosés that preserve their quality, and the elegant, dry, fruity whites are perfectly capable of holding their own. An excursion to the Minervois vineyards is highly recommended and is made all the more enjoyable because of the stunning beauty of this region, with its limestone plateaus and gorges, steep valleys, vine-covered slopes, and ancient villages.

*facing page*
The Moulin de Cugarel is one of Castelnaudary's last surviving windmills.

# COLLIOURE

CATALAN COOKING

GREAT PAINTERS HAVE IMMORTALIZED THIS SMALL CATALAN PORT. Matisse was the first to be seduced by the Mediterranean light that would alter his way of painting; then came Derain, Dufy, Picasso, Chagall, and many others. Nestled slightly inland along the Vermilion Coast, so called because of the warm colors of the rocks in the rising and setting sun, Collioure lies at the foot of a hillock dominated by an ancient castle of the Knights Templar. Below, beside the port, stands the Château Royal, built between the thirteenth and fifteenth centuries, and the architectural jigsaw of Notre-Dame-des-Anges Church, whose bell tower, constructed in the Middle Ages, served as a lighthouse for the port.

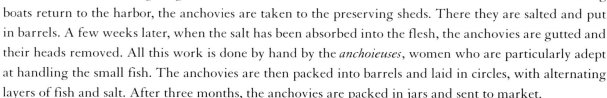

A view of Collioure, at one time a fishing village and today a popular tourist destination.

The Port of Collioure has always specialized in fishing and preserving anchovies. In the eighteenth century this activity was so important to the economy that Louis XIV exempted the people of Collioure from paying the *gabelle*, or salt tax. This small, blue fish spends the winter in the deeper waters of the Mediterranean and approaches the coastline at the beginning of spring. The fishing season begins in April or May, and ends in September or October. Anchovies are fished at night, with nets and a *lamparo*, a bright light mounted on the boat to attract the schools of fish. As soon as the fishing boats return to the harbor, the anchovies are taken to the preserving sheds. There they are salted and put in barrels. A few weeks later, when the salt has been absorbed into the flesh, the anchovies are gutted and their heads removed. All this work is done by hand by the *anchoieuses*, women who are particularly adept at handling the small fish. The anchovies are then packed into barrels and laid in circles, with alternating layers of fish and salt. After three months, the anchovies are packed in jars and sent to market.

Collioure anchovies come in three different forms: salted, fillets in brine, and fillets in oil. Collioure produces 441 tons of anchovies a year. However, in the 1930s there were thirty salting companies in the port; today there are only two. The Collioure anchovy is appreciated for its red-brown color and slightly nutty taste. It is said to stimulate the appetite and ease digestion. The Catalans eat anchovies plain, with the salt removed, on slices of toast, or in salads with chopped garlic, parsley, boiled eggs, and grilled bell pepper and topped with a vinaigrette of olive oil and Banyuls wine vinegar.

Generous, rich, and robust, Banyuls fortified wines are known for their aromatic richness and color palette. Primarily made from the Grenache grape, Banyuls is a vin doux naturel, the result of a process called *mutage*, during which fermentation is slowed by the addition of a small amount of alcohol. This allows the wine to retain a considerable amount of the grapes' sugar and natural aromas. Banyuls is stored in oak barrels. Depending on the methods of elaboration and aging, it comes in various types: *demi-sec* (medium dry), *doux* (sweet), *fruité* (fruity), and *rancio* (aged outside in the sun in barrels that are not filled to the the top, which allows oxidation and gives the wine a distinctive character).

Cultivation of the almond tree is also a Roussillon speciality. The almond may be eaten simply as a dry fruit with Banyuls wine, but it is used in a thousand ways. In the past, Languedoc cooks would fry it after removing the skin and dipping it in sugar. It is still widely used in sweets and lends flavor to pastries. *Croquant* is a dry almond cake made every morning in Collioure, at Le Croquant à l'Ancienne patisserie, under the gaze of the curious and the appreciative.

*facing page*
Delicious Colliure anchovies are famous because of the traditional artisanal methods used to prepare them—it is work still done by hand.

# LIMOUX

## BLANQUETTE BUBBLES

FOR A LONG TIME THE ECONOMY OF THIS SMALL TOWN AT THE FOOT OF THE PYRENEES was based on weaving and tanning, where hides imported from Spain were treated. In the thirteenth century the town already was exporting its woolen cloth to the remotest parts of Italy, and its wares filled the regional fairs. Today the town is better known for its festivities and its wines.

Limoux's carnival runs longer than any other in the world. For ten weekends, groups of revelers (each district is represented by its own group) parade through the streets; the origins of these carnival traditions go back to the fourteenth century. Musicians play the same piece repeatedly, while masked revelers in Pierrot costumes dance the *fécos* (a very slow dance) and wave their *carabénas* (a kind of wand), in time to the music. They egg on spectators, who whisper ribald jokes and risqué remarks in their ears; the spectators become the actors in an edgy improvised play. Carnival, which is subject to strict and unchanging laws, traditionally ends with the Nuit de la Blanquette (Blanquette de Limoux is a sparkling white wine). A stuffed dummy representing Carnival is tried and condemned to be burned on a pyre in the public square, while corks pop and blanquette flows.

Blanquette de Limoux was the world's first sparkling wine and the first Languedoc wine awarded AOC status.

Blanquette de Limoux first saw the light of day by accident, in 1531, in the cellars of the St. Hilaire Benedictine abbey. A monk discovered that the wine he had bottled and carefully corked was forming bubbles, as if a second fermentation were underway. Long before champagne, the world's first bubbly was born. By the seventeenth century the English had succumbed to the charm of this sparkling wine, of which it was said at the time that it "sparkled like the clever remarks of a man of wit."

The Limoux vineyards cover an area of 30 square miles, 2,000 of which qualify for AOC status. Most widely grown is a traditional grape, Mauzac, the dominant grape in blends (10 percent Chenin or Chardonnay is permitted). After the blending, a second fermentation is activated by adding a *liqueur de tirage* (sugar dissolved in reserve wine). It is then that the wine develops its effervescence. It is left in the bottle on the lees for nine months. The sediment in the wine is brought into the neck of the bottle, then the neck is frozen. Sediment trapped in this ice plug is then removed. Before the bottles are finally corked, a *liqueur d'expédition* (a dose of sugar and reserve wine) is added that will make the sparkling wine a brut, sec, or demi-sec (determining how dry or sweet it is). The Blanquette will then be aged for another nine months in the cellar, and enjoyed two or three years later.

In the past, chickpeas were used as currency in the upper Orb region. They have been cultivated on this plateau for millennia—seeds dating from 7000 BC were found in a nearby cave. Three growers account for the total production. Planted during Holy Week on the day of a full moon, the chickpea is harvested in July. Traditionally eaten on religious holidays, on All Saints' Day, and during Holy Week, in soup or salad, or puréed, today the "pale-yellow pearl" is eaten throughout the year.

In this area the turnip is described as "the black gold of a poor village." Black on the outside with a white interior, these turnips are sweet, tender, and delicate and grow on a cool, damp plateau some 25 miles from the sea. Pardailhan black turnips have been appreciated for their quality for a long time—even in the nineteenth century they were tinned or bottled. Turnip seeds are planted at the beginning of August. In the autumn, rain and mist encourage the plants' growth; it is said that the turnip "drinks in the mist through its leaves." The local variety, the long-rooted black Caluire, has a hazelnut or pine nut flavor. These turnips are served cold with a vinaigrette, or hot, glazed, and fried in goose fat. They should be cut lengthwise, in the direction of the grain of the fibers.

*facing page*
Chalky, clay-rich soil, the type found in the Limoux region, is well suited to the cultivation of white wine grapes.

# NÎMES
## COD FISHING

BOTH ROME AND SPAIN CLAIMED IT, AND, AS A RESULT, NÎMES has retained the one within its walls and the other in its heart. Nîmes-la-Romaine is a perfect triangle. In one corner stands the Maison Carrée, one of the finest temples of antiquity, preserved practically intact—in the twenty centuries of its existence it has served as a temple, town hall, stable, church, and museum, but was all too often neglected. The Porte d'Auguste is the second corner of the triangle. Beneath its arch is a statue of the emperor that marks the starting point of one of the countless roads that led to Rome. The Arena completes this Roman trinity. With its double row of arches and austere decoration, this amphitheater is the best-preserved example in France. Whether it is sunny or cloudy, the amphitheater is always full when French Rome turns Spanish. Nîmes has two delightful outbursts of frenzy, during the Feria de Pentecôte and during the grape harvest. But this temple of sport has served longer as a shelter than as a place of entertainment. From the fifth to the fourteenth centuries the Arena fulfilled the role of fortress and was completely inhabited until 1809. The arches, floor, and steps of the Arena actually constituted an entire quarter of Nîmes, with its castle, houses, and churches. The bishops who valued its coolness kept their reserves of Châteauneuf-du-Pape there.

In the shade of the Arena, *brandade à la Nîmoise* (from the word *brandado*, which means "stir" in Provençal) celebrates the marriage of cod from the north with olives from the south. This cold-seawater fish found favor at the foot of the Cévennes because of the *terre-neuvas* ("new worlders") who came to the Camargue in search of salt to preserve their fish. There are indications of its existence as early as the end of the seventeenth century, but it was not until 1830, when the chef presented this dish to the Archbishop of Alès, that it officially came into being. To prepare a good brandade, care must be taken to remove the salt from the fillets of salt cod before it is broken up in a mortar. The fish flesh is then blended with garlic. Olive oil is added a drop at a time, until a creamy paste is obtained; this is then cooked over a gentle heat with the addition of a little fresh cream and eaten hot or cold. Brandade is served with croutons or in little boat-shaped pie-pastry packages. A sliver of fresh truffle is a final touch.

*facing page*
The Arena, a first-century amphitheater, where bullfights and other events are staged to this day.

*below*
Costières de Nîmes wines, most of which are reds, are produced from grapes grown in the Rhône Valley.

The Musée du Bonbon Haribo is a magical place. Housed in a former licorice factory, it has three floors dedicated to delighting young and old alike. With a décor featuring vintage advertising posters and candy wrappers of the past, you will discover all of the secrets of producing sugar-coated sweets, fruit gums, and more—all those tastes associated with childhood. The best part: free samples can be enjoyed at the end.

From the ports of the Camargue to the spurs of the Cévennes, the Costières de Nîmes wines have the advantage of an appellation contrôlée. They come from terraces carved out long ago by the waters of the Rhône River, which left deposits of gravel and pebbles carried down from the Alps. With plenty of sunshine and a favorable exposure, allowing the soil to absorb heat during the day and returning it to the vines during the night, this terroir produces red, white, and rosé wines that are supple and fruity. Whites and rosés are drunk young, while the reds may be kept for four to five years.

# PERPIGNAN

## CATALONIA'S SOUL

ROUSSILLON HAS ITS FEET IN THE WATER AND ITS HEAD IN THE CLOUDS. This land of tradition that abounds in marvelous sites strung out at the foot of the Canigou Mountains has over the course of time forged a strong personality for itself. Sometimes inhabitants even prefer to call it French Catalonia. Salvador Dalí, one of the most famous and eccentric Catalans, discovered one day that Perpignan Station was the center of the universe.

Catalonia's second capital has other more tangible attractions. Crowned with a weather-vane in the form of a caravel sailing ship, recalling its original maritime focus, the Loge de Mer in the heart of town is reminiscent of the splendors of Venetian architecture. On the neighboring square, a statue by the sculptor Maillol, a native of the area, looks less worried than the one of the Mediterranean, which Maillol depicts as a seated woman, in the court-yard of the Hôtel de Ville.

Above the old town and its narrow streets rises the high-walled palace of the Kings of Majorca, a reminder that in the thirteenth and fourteenth centuries, Perpignan was the capital of a short-lived empire. All that remains of the fortifications that previously sur-

Castillet was the old gateway in the ramparts, once used as a prison and today housing the city's museum of Catalan folk culture and traditions.

rounded the town is the Castillet, an old gateway with crenellated walls, surmounted by a pinnacle bellcote. This elegant red-brick monument houses the Musée des Arts et Traditions Populaires du Roussillon. In St. Jean Cathedral, a composite building housing under one roof a fine eleventh-century Romanesque door, a fifteenth-century carved-wood gilt retable, and a sixteenth-century chapel, is an extraordinary statue, the Dévot Crucifix, which is carried during Holy Week processions—a ritual that has continued for centuries.

Perpignan is true to its symbols and traditions. Touron, a nougatlike confection, is a traditional Catalan sweet deriving from the sugar-syrup or honey confections made during the Middle Ages with pistachio, pine nuts, and walnuts. Its name supposedly comes from the word *torrere*, which means to grill, or from a Catalan confectioner of the seventeenth century whose name was Torro. Touron is semi-hard when full of hazelnuts or almonds and soft if made with pine nuts; it contains 40 to 50 percent dried fruit and 15 percent honey. It is customary to eat touron at Christmas festivities, when it is served along with other traditional holiday desserts. On the night of Christmas Eve, Cata-lan families conceal touron, sweets, and toys in small tree trunks. Singing children find them by tapping very hard on the trunk. Touron is used as an ingredient in numerous desserts, and it can even be served as an accompaniment to meat and poultry.

This "Mecca of Cubism"—the town played host to Georges Braque, Pablo Picasso, Juan Gris, and the Catalan sculptor Manolo—also celebrates a little round red fruit. The first fruit of spring, the Céret cherry is the earliest, most brightly colored, and sweetest in France. It is also called the red gold of Vallespir. The red bigarreau was once a very productive tree, whose thin foliage made its fruit easy to see and harvest. Every peasant farmer had one of his own—the tree thrived in the poorest soil. With improved transportation came an unprecedented rise in the consumption of fresh fruit in the 1930s, and Céret became "the Cherry Capital." Today acres of orchards extend over both banks of the Tech River, and in the Vallespir Valley new varieties—hâtive and burlat—have been developed. They fruit just as early and are just as much appreciated.

A delicacy enjoyed by the kings of Majorca, the rousquille is a soft, cakelike cookie in the shape of a ring (it looks like a mini-doughnut). It derives its name from the word *rosca* (Catalan for "crown"). A light, lemon-flavored meringue coats the rousquille. It also comes in flavors such as orange, anise, or chocolate. This artisanal product is made using a secret recipe and preparation handed down through generations. Amélie-les-Bains, a nearby town, makes the best rousquille, along with the somptueux, a dense cake of almond paste and yéma (an egg-yolk jam), and cooked with rum.

*facing page* Famous Céret cherries are a sweet variety cultivated in France's southernmost cherry-growing area.

Emballeur · Expéditeur · Export

COOPÉRATIVE AGRICOLE

**Céret - Primeurs**

CÉRET (Pyr.-Or.) France

Tél. 69 et 156

*right*
In the heart of the city sits the Palais des Rois de Majorque (Palace of the Kings of Majorca), a fortified palace built in the thirteenth century.

With one of the most ancient cuisines in Europe, this region, with its exceptional geographical location between mountain and sea, has a rich culinary repertoire. Even the simplest, tradition-based Catalan dishes are sophisticated. There is *boles de picoulat*, meatballs made with pork and beef and served with a spicy olive sauce, and pork cheeks that are slow-cooked in the oven or in a casserole with tomatoes and herbs. Guinea fowl à la catalane is cooked in rancio wine with garlic and bitter orange or lemon. Made with ham, black pudding, and cabbage, *Ollada* is a hearty Roussillon soup best eaten in winter. *Cargolade*, roasted snails, is a heavier dish as well, but it inspires conviviality and is often the high point of a Catalan "barbecue." Snails are cooked over charcoal made from pruned vine stems, along with sausages, black pudding, and lamb cutlets. Even religious festivals have their own cuisine. Since the thirteenth century, no Easter can be complete without *coque*, a bread garnished with vegetables or fruit.

*left*
An essentially Catalan cuisine is prepared in the city and its local markets are veritable institutions.

*right*
Céret's much-beloved cherries are honored each year at the beginning of June with a major festival.

# SÈTE

## LANGUEDOC'S VENICE

WHAT IS THE EXPLANATION FOR SÈTE'S INFINITE CHARM? Compared with its lovely neighboring rivals, Sète offers neither the prestige of a long history, nor the splendor of exceptional monuments. In a region where the smallest village can claim a history of thousands of years, the "Venice of the Languedoc," founded in 1666, is something of a new town. It was because of the gradual silting of the ports of Agde, Barbonne, and Aigues-Mortes, and the desire of Louis XIV to give France a powerful Mediterranean port, that Sète came into being. Perhaps this is its secret: the last of the Languedoc harbor towns to be established, it has the colors, gaity, and freshness of youth. Do not expect to see amazing churches or stunning private houses in Sète. Its strengths lie elsewhere: in its smells of the sea and the garrigue (scrubland), in its light, in the constant party atmosphere on its quayside, in the unbelievable beauty of the landscapes around it, and in the poignant charm of the coastal cemeteries where Paul Valéry and Georges Brassens are buried. If Sète is a town of poets, it is because the town itself is a poem.

Situated between the Mediterranean and the Étang de Thau (Thau Basin), Sète has based the originality of its cuisine on a particularly inventive use of fish and shellfish. Incomparable specialties include Bouzigues oysters, from the oyster beds in the Étang de Thau. These oysters owe their unique flavor to the breeding method used, which is adapted to the lack of tides: suspended in water for 24 hours a day, they feed on the nutritious waters of the lagoon and reach maturity in 12 or 20 months—a year faster than oysters from the Atlantic or the English Channel.

Mussels, which are also bred in the lagoon, are prepared *à la Sétoise*, with a sausage-meat stuffing that includes eggs, tomato paste, garlic, and white wine; aïoli (Provence's garlic mayonnaise) is served alongside. But Sète's most iconic dish is without a doubt the *tielle*, a tart filled with diced octopus, chopped tomatoes, and onions, and dressed with olive oil, garlic, and hot pepper. Every day, when the catch is brought in, sea bass, gilt-head bream, mackerel, and sardines are sold on the quayside before reaching the kitchens of the restaurants that line the harbor. There they can be oven-baked, baked in salt, or simply grilled and seasoned with a drizzle of olive oil.

*facing page*
Renowned Bouzigues oysters, cultivated in the Étang de Thau, are more rustic in taste than those of Brittany and Normandy but are wonderfully tender and fleshy.

*below*
Lovely seaside towns Frontignan and Sète share tourism and some industries.

In the past, wine was often transported by boat in barrels placed on the deck and therefore exposed to the wind, sun, and water. Surprisingly, this natural fortification seemed to improve it. In 1813, Joseph Noilly decided to re-create this process artificially and thus developed the first formula for French dry vermouth. Light and fruity white wines are first stored in large oak casks, then transferred to outdoor oak barrels. The wines are transformed after being exposed to the elements for a year. To mellow the dry, full-bodied nature of the white wines, a dash of grape juice blended with alcohol and fruit essences is added. Then about twenty plants and spices are left to macerate in the wine giving Noilly Prat its unique flavor.

There is no better accompaniment to Bouzigues oysters or *tielle* than the wines made from vines grown by the sea or the Thau lagoon. Once kept mostly to produce vermouth, today these wines are drinkable in an unfortified form and quite tasty. To end a meal on a delicate, sweet note, make sure to order a *pastissou*, a cake of green olives flavored with anise, or *zezettes*, crisp shortbread cookies made with oil, rosé wine, and vanilla sugar.

# BRIVE LA-GAILLARDE
## PRIZED PIG

A SONG BY GEORGE BRASSENS MADE THIS TOWN'S MARKET SO FAMOUS that it was eventually renamed to honor him. It is an indisputably excellent place to discover regional specialities. A Limousin breed of cattle, the hardy red cow with ivory horns, is renowned for its meat. Also bred in Limousin is a type of pig called the *cul-noir*, or black bottom. Previously known by the name "porc de St.-Yrieix," and originating from west of the Massif Central, this breed was already known in the sixteenth century. Without the determination of a few motivated hog farmers, these pigs would likely not be around today.

The cul-noir is a hardy animal that matures slowly, which at one time justified replacing them with faster-growing animals. There were more than 100,000 in the 1930s; by the 1980s there were little more than sixty breeding pigs. Of average height, with a broad, round, stocky body firmly planted on slender legs, this pig has a conical head, with a long narrow snout; its eyes are shaded by thin ears that point forward; its black bottom is the reason for its somewhat unusual name.

Extremely bright and alert, used to foraging for itself in natural surroundings, the cul-noir devours chestnuts and acorns found in the undergrowth in autumn. During the rest of the year, it is fed a natural diet of Jerusalem artichokes, beetroots, potatoes, or cereals. The fattened pig is slaughtered after the chestnut season, from November to December. It is then eighteen months old and can weigh from 375 to 500 pounds.

This animal, nicknamed the "Rolls-Royce of pigs," is a favorite product of butchers and cooks, appreciated for the quality of its meat and fat. Its marbled red meat is exceptionally delicious. Its white, flavorful fat with a slight hint of hazelnut, is firm and melts easily; it can be up to seven inches thick. The hams are tender and for people who enjoy traditional cuisine, the lard is as unctuous as you could hope for.

At St.-Yrieix-la-Perche, where the cul-noir originates, Chef René Maury is an ardent advocate of this Limousin pig, the official name of the breed. He serves it as ham, prepares the liver with truffles, and escaloped with porcini mushrooms and foie gras. Thanks to this former cooking teacher, the cul-noir has truly regained its status.

Once a breed that nearly died out but today is protected, the Cul-Noir de Limousin pig is famous for the quality of its meat.

*facing page*
Chestnuts and the local *vin bourru*, a white wine that is drawn before it is fully fermented.

*Marigoule* and *bouche de Bétizac* can be found in terrines or sausages, accompanying meat and poultry, or turned into cakes and liqueurs. What are they? They are Limousin chestnuts, as Limousin is the land of the chestnut tree. For a long time the chestnut was the food of the poor and of animals. Not until the mid-nineteenth century, with the arrival of the potato, would its use decline. Long winter evenings on Limousin farms used to be spent removing the chestnuts from their brown shells. Most were destined to feed the pigs, while those intended for human consumption needed blanching (to remove the inner hairy layer of skin) before being eaten with a winter salad of lamb's lettuce or escarole seasoned with a clove of garlic. Today, the chestnut is used in *boudin* (blood sausage) d'Uzerche or *boudin de Pompadour*, in soup with garlic and croutons, and as a garnish with braised loin of pork. In Corrèze, it is traditional to make chestnut sausages when a pig is killed in the autumn, and to grill chestnuts over the hearth in a perforated frying pan.

Called the "fairy in the purple dress," the local sweet and spicy violet mustard first became popular in the fourteenth century, thanks to Pope Clement IV, who was from Corrèze and possessed of a certain nostalgia for the dishes that used to be prepared for him. Very much in vogue during the Belle Époque, this mustard gradually fell out of favor before being rediscovered in the 1980s. Updated for the modern palate by the maker of Denoix liqueur in Brive, it is made with black grapes picked off the bunch, cooked, and sieved. Mustard powder and a masterful blend of vinegar and flavorings is added to the grape must. Violet mustard is the perfect accompaniment to *magret de canard* (fillet of duck breast), grilled beef, all forms of veal, and even black pudding.

# BAR-LE-DUC

## "SWEET CAVIAR" PRESERVE

PERCHED ON ITS PROMONTORY, BAR-LE-DUC BECAME PROSPEROUS in the thirteenth century when the counts of Lorraine held sway over the king of France. Some time later this Lorraine town was to be the birthplace of two marshals of the Empire—Oudinot and Exelmans—and the tenth president of the French Republic, Raymond Poincaré. In the fourteenth century the counts of Bar were obliged to surrender their privileges to the king of France. In exchange he granted them the title of duke; today, only the town now bears this title.

It is during this same period that in some anonymous cauldron a little marvel first saw the light of day and still excites the admiration of gourmands. Mary Stuart, the wife of Francis II, compared them to "a ray of sunshine in a pot" and, according to legend, Alfred Hitchcock would only stay in hotels where they were served at breakfast. The Bar preserve is a seeded red- or white-currant jam—"sweet caviar" is not too exalted a description. This gourmet delight dates back to the fourteenth century, a time when, being a genuine luxury, the jams were offered by noblemen as gifts to presiding judges when they won their court cases. In the sixteenth century the preserves had acquired world renown: it was obligatory for kings and queens to present samples of the preserves in crystal goblets to eminent guests.

Five centuries later production methods are the same. The currants continue to be seeded by hand with the aid of a goose feather by skillful young women called *épépineuses* (seeders). The seeders pick up the currants individually, holding them between their thumb and index finger; then, with the aid of the bevel-edged goose-feather quill, they cut into the flesh below the stalk in order to extract the seeds—there are about seven per fruit—without damaging either the skin or the pulp. The nick simply has to be covered over with the skin flap so as to preserve the fruit's crunchiness and flavor. A good worker can seed up to nine pounds of currants in a single day.

But why go to such lengths to seed the fruit? This is done so that the acidulous fruit retains all its original consistency after it is dropped into the boiling sugar syrup, a process that retains the currant's flavor and bright color. The distinctive mark of the very best quality preserves, guaranteeing an authentic product, is that the stalk remains visible as a black speck in the jar.

Some of the production is exported to Germany, Britain, the United States, and as far away as Japan. Bar-le-Duc has even set up a consortium to promote its distinguished product: the Ducale et Tastépepineuse Sénéchalerie des Gousteurs de Groseilles, which organizes courses in seeding and an annual Seeding World Championship.

*facing page*
According to legend, Commercy madeleines are either named after a local waitress who invented them or a girl who offered them to pilgrims on their way to Santiago de Compostela.

*below*
The historic center of the upper town.

Before World War II, six pastry makers shared the madeleine market. Some 2,500 were made every day, most of which were sold on the platforms of Commercy's railway station to passengers traveling between Paris and Nancy. Today there are only two producers: Jean-Pierre Zins makes artisanal madeleines under the name La Boîte à Madeleine; the Bahlsen company, which inherited a local recipe, makes 5,500 tons a year and distributes throughout Europe.

The madeleine, the "little scallop-shell of pastry," as Marcel Proust called it, owes its fame to Stanislas Leczinski, king of Poland and father-in-law of Louis XV. In 1755 he happened to discover this treat made by a peasant named Madeleine, hence the name, but there are many other stories of how the madeleine came into being. The Commercy madeleine is made with flour, butter, eggs, sugar, and lemon essence—not to mention the pastry-maker's special touch, which will always remain a secret.

# NANCY

## IN PRAISE OF THE GOLDEN FRUIT

ITS NAME COMES FROM LATIN AND MEANS "LOVELY TO BEHOLD." The mirabelle, a variety of golden plum that comes from the East, was introduced into Lorraine in the fifteenth century by Duke René d'Anjou. From the Woëvre to the Xaintois, from the gates of Metz to the slopes of the Vosges, the mirabelle is delicious everywhere it's grown. An emblematic fruit of the region, it is to Lorraine what the olive is to

A basket of prized mirabelle plums grown in the Lorraine region's Nancy and Metz.

*facing page*
This grand entrance leads to the monumental Place Stanislas, built between 1751 and 1755.

Provence, as Jean-Marie Pelt put it. Every Lorraine family has inherited a recipe for mirabelle tart. And no one would exchange it for the world. From the time it was first planted, mirabelle took to this terroir—it grows well in clay and damp soil—but its real renaissance only dates back to the 1950s.

There is a distinction between the mirabelle de Metz, a smaller variety with a thin, red and yellow skin (used for the best jams), and the mirabelle de Nancy, a larger plum with a thick yellow skin. Today, Lorraine accounts for 80 percent of the world's production of a fruit that has been awarded a Label Rouge, guaranteeing that the picking and sorting have been done by hand. While there are larger, more well-organized orchards, the mirabelle tree, a key element of the Lorraine landscape, graces the fields as the apple tree does in Normandy. It is the pride of small gardens and even grows wild beside roads and trails.

In mid-August, when the mirabelles of Lorraine reach maturity and attain their best flavor, locals happily shake the trees to loosen the fruit. Fruit-picking extends over six weeks but no longer. The "fruit of gold" harvest provides the opportunity for village festivals or much bigger celebrations, such as those held in Metz in the middle of August. At the end of the summer, the mirabelle is eaten as a fruit, but can also be appreciated year-round, and particularly on special occasions, at the bottom of a glass. Not before winter does the mirabelle go into the still, giving the best of itself one last time. This golden fruit also has its place in the pantry of every self-respecting Lorraine household. The bottle may be bought or, more often

Bergamot is a pear-shaped citrus fruit grown in southern Italy, notably in Calabria and Sicily, where the dukes of Lorraine ruled for two years. The fruit is unpalatable, but it produces a delicately scented oil that the dukes brought home with them. In 1850 a confectioner in Nancy by the name of Lillig added bergamot essence to cooked sugar. He gave his sweet a square shape and that was the beginning of a tradition that continues to this day. The sugar is cooked, mixed with the flavoring, poured onto an oiled marble slab, then cut by hand with a cookie-cutter. This technique preserves the integrity of the flavor and the yellow-amber transparency of the true Nancy bergamot. Many Lorraine pastry makers and cooks also use bergamot to make iced mousses, soufflés, desserts, ice creams, and sorbets. Bergamot has digestive and laxative properties.

than not, come from a relative or friend. Everyone is careful not to advertise the source of his supply. But never mind the shape of the bottle, or the label—in fact, sometimes the latter is reduced to its simplest expression: just a date stuck on the bottle is enough to loosen tongues even before the stopper is removed. Mirabelle is both a miracle and a secret.

In Nancy, Saint Epvre is first and foremost a basilica that stands in the heart of the old town. Completed in 1871, it is a neo-Gothic-style building financed in a manner worthy of mention in the category "Precursors of Europe." The man behind it, Monsignor Trouillet, had the idea of creating an international fund—raising money from Poland to Austria by way of Italy—to pay for it. To commemorate the completion of the construction in 1895, a pastry maker from the neighboring square created a cake. Round and pale yellow, dusted with icing sugar, the Saint Epvre is a soft cake consisting of two disks of almond macaroons filled with vanilla butter cream and crushed praline. Understandably, the recipe is a secret. Pâtisserie Adam, in the shadow of Saint Epvre's bell towers, is the only source of this delight.

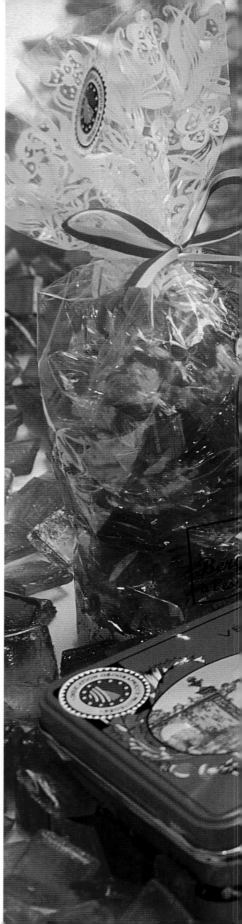

Though the color varies from year to year, dark, almost black fir-tree honey has a tinge of green or red and is produced in the mountains of the Massif des Vosges. The production zones extend from St. Dié in the Vosges to Remiremont, and in the Moselle from Sarrebourg to Sarreguemines. Depending on where it comes from, fir-tree honey may have a mint, blackberry, or heathery flavor. It is used to make the famous Bonbon des Vosges sweet. In other parts of Lorraine equally sought-after honeys are produced on the plains. Rare and original, black-alder honey is collected near St. Avold and used to make gingerbread, which is typically consumed at the beginning of December. It would not be the feast of St. Nicholas in Lorraine without the distribution of St. Nicholas gingerbread bearing an image of Lorraine's patron saint.

*above*
Ninety percent of the mirabelle plums harvested become jams, brandies, and liqueurs.

*right*
Vosges fir-tree honey comes from the black pines on the Lorraine side of the mountains. It has a malty flavor and balsamic aromas.

*far right*
Nancy bergamot, caramelized sugar candy infused with the essence of bergamot, is a local specialty.

# T O U L

## LORRAINE'S WINE CAPITAL

BETWEEN ALSACE AND CHAMPAGNE, THE WINE-PRODUCING REGION OF LORRAINE could not hope for more prestigious neighbors. Moselle's dry, fruity whites have already found their way onto our tables, and other vineyards are displaying a similar ambition.

With its little valleys and thick forests, the Côtes de Meuse region is charming. Its narrow country roads run in a straight line through the woods and you can drive between Hattonchatel and Verdun, above the Lac de Chavine, without passing a single house. Villages nestle at the foot of a line of hills bordering the Parc Naturel Régional de Lorraine; most have added "sous-les-côtes" to their names. The vineyards are here, climbing up the slopes behind these market towns. Over a nine-mile-long area, six winegrowers continue a tradition dating to the Middle Ages, when vines were planted in the direction of clergy. Auxerrois, Chardonnay, and Pinot Noir are all classified as "vin de pays." Around Toul, it all goes back to Charlemagne, who owned land and vineyards in the region. The town rejoices in St. Etienne Cathedral, with its flamboyant facade and a cloister from the thirteenth and fourteenth centuries, one of the largest in France.

St. Etienne Cathedral is a masterpiece of flamboyant style.

*facing page*
Vin de Pays de la Meuse wines—reds, whites, and rosés—are fresh and lovely.

Since 1998 Côtes de Toul wines have ranked as the only AOC-quality wines in the province. This classification applies to eight villages to the north and south of town. The vines covering these sunny slopes sheltered from the damaging west winds, are Gamay, Auxerrois, and Pinot Noir. At Mont-le-Vignoble, south of Toul, no vines have grown for a very long time, but there is a charming cooperative wine cellar, supposedly the smallest in France. The Toul region is famous for its vin gris, also called blanc de noirs because it is made from Gamay, the Beaujolais grape. With its refreshing hint of acidity, this wine comes fully into its own at summer barbecues, but it is also excellent with white meat and quiche Lorraine. This area is enjoying a full-scale revival thanks to young viticulturists who want their villages to embrace their original vocation: producing wine—preferably good wine. It has been a long time since the vine growers gave poor vintages the name of some loathed individual. In the last century Cabooural, a murderer, Garibaldi, and Bismarck had the honor of being on such labels.

Despite its rich architectural heritage, notably the magnificent Lorraine-Gothic St. Etienne Cathedral, Metz is still marked by its past as a fortified town at the gates of the German Empire. Unfortunately, it has retained the reputation of being a garrison town. Its long military history was bound to take some culinary form, and it has been, with the boulet de Metz. In its size, shape, and outward appearance, this pastry-shop specialty suggests a cannonball. Created by a local confectioner, it is a ball-shaped pastry filled with frangipane and chopped hazelnuts, and dipped in dark chocolate.

Almonds, sugar, and egg whites: these three ingredients are all that are needed to create half an ounce of soft, sweet joy. The Boulay macaroon was created in 1854 and its recipe has not been altered since; even the red box in which the macaroons are packaged remains the same. The Alexandre family, heirs of the creator, hold the secret to how these cookies are made. Each ingredient is meticulously weighed out, and the cookies are molded with a spoon before being placed into the oven from which they emerge perfectly glazed. They contain no artificial colors or preservatives.

# VERDUN
SUGARED ALMONDS

FROM JOAN OF ARC TO THE SOLDIERS IN THE TRENCHES OF THE 1914–18 WAR, Lorraine has paid in flesh and blood for an eventful history. Long the symbol of the most dreadful carnage in the history of the world, Verdun has chosen a vocation as capital of peace. From fort to citadel, from cemetery to ossuary, the region's memory is nothing but a terrible wound. And yet Verdun has had a taste of sweetness. It is the home of a confection whose story is little known: the sugared almond.

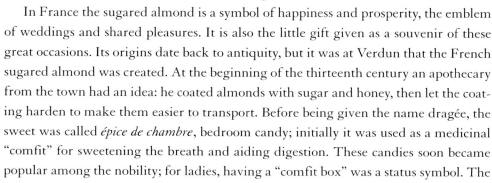

In France the sugared almond is a symbol of happiness and prosperity, the emblem of weddings and shared pleasures. It is also the little gift given as a souvenir of these great occasions. Its origins date back to antiquity, but it was at Verdun that the French sugared almond was created. At the beginning of the thirteenth century an apothecary from the town had an idea: he coated almonds with sugar and honey, then let the coating harden to make them easier to transport. Before being given the name dragée, the sweet was called *épice de chambre*, bedroom candy; initially it was used as a medicinal "comfit" for sweetening the breath and aiding digestion. These candies soon became popular among the nobility; for ladies, having a "comfit box" was a status symbol. The

A tranquil scene on the Meuse River, which flows through the town where one of the bloodiest battles of World War I was fought.

*épice de chambre* originally was a praline. It was not until the seventeenth century that it would take on the appearance it has today, with a hard, smooth coating that preserves the shape of the individual nut. In 1660, Jean-Baptiste Colbert, the soon-to-be minister of finance, wrote to the king: "At Verdun there is a great trade in sugared almonds."

These candies became popular with the lower classes as well and soon they were consumed throughout the kingdom. Louis XIV even ordered them to be distributed among schoolchildren during New Year celebrations. The quality of the dragée depends on the almonds used. The best and nicest looking ones are flat and tapered at one end. Only regular-shaped almonds allow a uniform distribution of the layer of sugar, so confectioners must ruthlessly select the best ones. Avolas are the most highly prized type of almonds. Long, flat nuts that taste fruity and keep well, they grow on the sunny slopes of Sicily near Syracuse. Spanish almonds, such as valencias, also retain their freshness. The quality of a sugared almond depends too on the fineness of the layer of sugar coating.

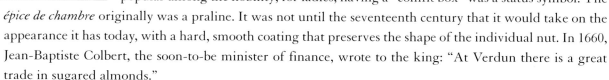

The amber-colored beverage with foam that is consumed today at the *stammtisch*, or *table d'hôte*, likely has nothing in common with the drink brewed by monks at the end of the eleventh century. It is said that in the 1900s Stenay locals could each consume as much as 46.25 gallons of beer per year! In homage to these dedicated drinkers, the Musée Européen de la Bière was set up in this small village on the Belgian border; it is the largest museum of its kind in the world. Placed under the protection of the patron saint of brewers, St. Arnould, this is where to find everything about the history and production of the drink with the highest consumption rate in the world.

Sweet-toothed as they are, the people of Lorraine also find room for savories. Quiche first made its appearance at the end of the sixteenth century. If the accounts are to be believed, Duke of Lorraine Charles III ate it regularly. Originally, it was a bread dough with an egg and cream topping. Today there are many recipes and countless variations. Purists exclude cheese in their quiche Lorraine; their short pastry, or possibly puff pastry, base will have nothing but lean smoked bacon, eggs, and fresh cream. The choice of this last ingredient, a thick cream of high quality, is essential to the flavor of this dish, which should be served warm.

*facing page*
Pastel-colored dragées, sugared almonds, produced by the long-established Braquier confectioners.

# VITTEL

CURATIVE SPRINGS

ITS WATERS AND FORESTS ARE THE MAIN ASSETS OF THE VOSGES REGION. Set in locations with idyllic green vistas, the spas here were known for attracting a wealthy clientele; guests came to take to the waters because it was fashionable more so than for health reasons. Later, the spas would provide relaxation for the affluent on a country break, and then assist in training programs for top-level athletes before major competitions. Vittel's waters were familiar to the Romans, who have left a few precious remains. But the history of this spa town really began in 1854 when a lawyer from Rodez bought the Gérémoy Fountain, whose waters had restored his health. He began by setting up the Société Général des Eaux Minérales, and the following year, with state authorization, he opened the Grande Source Spa Resort. A modest venture, the spa at that time had three bathing cabins and a shower room. But the virtues of Vittel water were already considerable and well-known: it was good for gout, gravel, diabetes, and other ailments. Bottling the water began in 1857; first used was a square-shaped hand-thrown stoneware container with a porcelain stopper and a rubber ring to seal it.

From the start, people who created Vittel had an original concept for the development of the resort, which was to combine curative treatments, relaxation, and entertainment. Charles Garnier, who had just completed the Paris Opéra, drew up plans for the casino, the baths, and the renovation of the Grand Hotel. Other eminent architects, such as August Bluysen and Fernand César of the Nancy School, would later modernize the resort in the art nouveau style, assisting in the restoration of hotels, the construction of new pavilions, the swimming pool, and even a racetrack. The quality of this architecture, conceived of as part of a development project for the town as a whole, was popular with an international clientele attracted by the waters and the social scene equally. Today, the curative treatments offered—patients are ministered to a few times daily usually for three weeks—are not in vogue. But the resort now caters to people who come for physical rejuvenation. More Vittel water is consumed elsewhere than here: 1,800 bottles of this water, rich in both magnesium and calcium, are consumed every minute worldwide.

*facing page*
At one time this famous spa town specialized in treating kidney and liver ailments; today guests focus on relaxation and rejuvenation.

*below*
Rhubarb wine, made from the fermented plant, is a local specialty of the Vosges.

In 1760 a doctor named Bagard informed the Académie de Médecine about the virtues of Vosges water for the treatment of obesity, and liver and kidney diseases. Not until the arrival of the railway, more than a century later, did patients taking the cure come flocking to the spas that bubbled up in the recently erected pavilions. Though it had previously attracted the crowned heads of Europe and elsewhere, the two world wars proved fatal for this spa town. Only in the 1980s did the fashion for health cures and weight-loss treatments help Contrexéville rediscover the good taste of its water.

A few miles from Épinal, fields of rhubarb stretch out on the edge of a forest. The Moine family is reviving the local Vosges tradition of making rhubarb wine. In the past it was made by women and served only at family meals or among friends. By adapting the old recipes to modern oenological methods, the Moines have created some original products that have already been recognized by the most distinguished sommeliers and leading gourmands. At the end of May the stalks are picked by hand, then washed, crushed, and pressed to extract the bright red juice. Depending on the process used, once "vinified" the juice produces a sweet wine, Crillon des Vosges, which accompanies foie gras or a strong-flavored cheese, or a dry wine, Blanc des Vosges, a perfect match with fish.

# A L B I

## THE LEGEND OF PINK GARLIC

THE HEART OF ALBI IS AN ISLAND. THE FICKLE STREAMS THAT ONCE USED TO SURROUND the old town have been filled in with broad boulevards, but the old town itself is still curled round the cloister of St. Salvi like a snail in its shell. Along the narrow, winding streets, the courtyards of the brick-and-wood houses interlock like the pieces of a jigsaw puzzle. Their facades, whether plain or adorned with curious characters (a naked man on the half-timbered Pharmacie des Pénitents, or grimacing faces such as those on the front of the Hôtel Reynès), are evidence of a period when fortunes made with woad (the plant from which a blue dye was extracted) were displayed for all to see.

Albi was the capital of the famous "Pays de Cocagne" (Land of Plenty, in this case the region between Albi, Carcassone, and Toulouse, made rich by pastel). It is also mindful of its troubled past. A "grim fortress the color of the dried blood of Albigensian heretics," St. Cécile Cathedral illustrates the doubts and fears of a Christianity that in the thirteenth century had just crushed the Cathar rebellion. With its red walls warmed by the early southern sun and bathed in the green waters of the Tarn River, Albi was certainly a place where a talented painter could have grown up. Henri de Toulouse-Lautrec's work is honored at the Musée de la Berbie, housed in the former episcopal palace. There the artist's love for his mother and his passion for boats, horses, and dogs are revealed. Later came the cynical portraits, the bitter Parisian scenes of a disillusioned artist.

The artist's distant ancestors came from the medieval village of Lautrec, whose pink garlic has contributed to its fame. Legend has it that pink garlic appeared in the region in the Middle Ages when an itinerant seller stopped at an inn and, not having any money, paid for his meal with the pretty pink cloves. The innkeeper planted these cloves in his garden and not long thereafter pink garlic spread throughout the region. Already by the early 1800s the markets of Albi, Castres, and Mazamet were redolent with the smell of the bulbs. The cloves are planted in the cold season, during December or January. At the end of spring the flower stem is removed to prevent decay. The harvest takes place at the end of June or beginning of July, and the pink garlic reaches the market around July 14. Garlic is traditionally sold *en manouilles* (woven into braids). Lautrec's pink garlic, which is extremely sweet, keeps very well. The pink garlic festival is held in Lautrec on the first Friday of August (Friday is the local market day).

A picturesque view of the arched Pont-Vieux over the Tarn River that leads to the "pink town."

*facing page*
Lautrec's pink garlic is sweet and delicate, a prized product of this small town a few miles outside of Albi.

Butcher shops in Lacaune specialize in dried products—for both historic and geographic reasons. The salt route passes through this high-altitude region, and the dry climate is favorable to this type of meat production. Worthy of special mention is *jambon sec*, which undergoes a long process of salting, then is left to rest, warm up, and age. In total, it takes at least nine months for the ham to fully develop its distinctive flavor. Numerous other products, such as various types of fresh and dried sausage, are a tribute to human ingenuity and the local terroir. Two original specialities are made here: *melsat*, a white pudding made of meat, bread, and eggs; and *bougnette*, made with the same ingredients as melsat but served fried.

Every year, at the beginning of September, Albi organizes a patisserie festival. According to tradition, in 1629 Cardinal Richelieu was welcomed by the people of Albi with a procession in which a fattened ox's horns were adorned with pastries. During the festivities, *gimblettes*, ring cakes flavored with grated lemon and orange-blossom water, are served as are *navettes*, made with sugar, flour, butter, and eggs, and little anise-flavored *jeannots*. Approximately ten local pastry makers gather on the banks of the Tarn River during the festival with hundreds of pounds of pastries that are consumed by sweet-toothed locals and visitors alike.

# CAHORS
## WHERE THE WINE FLOWS

WITH ITS SIX LARGE GOTHIC ARCHES AND ITS THREE SQUARE TOWERS, the Valentré bridge spans the Lot River 130 feet above the water. Completed in 1378, and the symbol of the town of Cahors, it is the best preserved of all European medieval bridges and the most significant example of the military architecture of the Middle Ages. Discouraging all assailants, it was never attacked by anyone. Surrounded by hills, including Mont St. Cyr, which offers a superb panoramic view of the town, Cahors is neatly contained in a loop of the river.

The fourteenth century was the city's golden age. At that time, it was one of Europe's most important banking centers, and it had enough influence to impose a pope from the city—John XXII, son of the city's merchant class—on the Catholic Church. The Romanesque St. Étienne Cathedral is crowned with two cupolas, and its ornate sixteenth-century cloister is a fine example of Gothic style. In the Daurade district, there are many lovely old houses: the thirteenth-century Maison du Bourreau; the fourteenth- to fifteenth-century half-timbered and corbelled Maison Hérétie; and the seventeenth-century Maison d'Olive.

Water flows through Cahors, as does wine. The sixteenth-century poet Clément Marot called Cahors's wine "fiery liquor," and the priests of Imperial Russia, who had no fear of burning themselves, adopted it as their communion wine. In 1971 vin de Cahors acquired AOC status. The vineyards extend downstream of the town, on the sheltered terraces of the Lot River Valley and the Causse de Limogne plateaus. This relatively dry area enjoys late sunshine that allows the grapes to ripen and reach harvesting without risk of rain. The main grape used, Cot Noir (Malbec), locally called Auxerrois, must constitute at least 70 percent of the blend. It is the Cot Noir that gives Cahors wine its beautiful crimson color with purple highlights, as well as its aging ability. Merlot Noir is added for roundness and bouquet, and Tannat to enhance the unique qualities of the Auxerrois. A Cahors wine can be enjoyed as early as the first year. Slightly tannic, it is delicious paired with foie gras, meats in sauce, and charcuterie. Well-aged maturer wines release more subtle and refined fragrances, and go well with truffles, red meat, game, and porcini mushrooms. Cahors wines have the potential to keep for ten to fifteen years.

Bunches of black grapes from the Auxerrois vineyards.

Its creamy-colored striated rind has a velvety appearance, and the soft cheese has a subtle buttery and nutty taste. In the past it was called *cabécou de Rocamadour* ("cabécou" meaning "small goat's milk cheese" in the Occitan language); since obtaining AOC status, it has retained only the name of its place of origin. It is made with raw, whole goat's milk that is curdled for twenty-four hours, then drained for the same length of time. It is then hand-molded before maturing in the cellar at a constant temperature and humidity. It is small and coin-shaped, almost two and a half inches in diameter and about half an inch high, and each piece weighs about one and a quarter ounces. Rocamadour is matured for at least six days. Its flavor intensifies as it dries.

Lalbenque market, the most important black truffle market in the southwest of France, is held every Tuesday afternoon during the winter months. The *Tuber malanosporum* requires three conditions for growing: the presence of an oak or hazel tree on which the truffles can grow, a chalky soil, and a Mediterranean-like climate. Between 6,600 and 22,000 pounds are gathered in the département of Lot, compared with 440,000 pounds in the early 1900s. The truffle grower chooses between a truffle hound or a pig to assist him in the harvesting of this mysterious mushroom, which takes place from November to March.

*facing page*
An arched bridge with watchtowers, the Valentré is an outstanding example of medieval defensive architecture.

# CONDOM

## THE ELIXIR OF THE THREE MUSKETEERS

CONTRARY TO WHAT MIGHT BE ASSUMED, CONDOM GETS ITS NAME from the Latin *Condatomagus*, which means "the market at the confluence." This has not prevented the inhabitants from good-humouredly exploiting the expected semantic confusion by organizing a show every summer around the popular form of contraception.

With its medieval streets running through the old town, the Gothic St. Pierre Cathedral, the Chapelle des Évêques, and lovely private residences—the Hôtel de Polignac, de Bourran, and de Cugnac, among others—this small, quiet town has plenty of charm. It is Armagnac above all that has made the town famous. This strong yet subtle eau de vie, so typically Gascon that it is inevitably associated with D'Artagnan and his fellow musketeers, paradoxically owes a great deal to the British, who for a long time occupied this region. By preventing the ships of their Dutch rivals from sailing up the Garonne River to load cargoes of wine from upper Gascony, they forced the winegrowers to distill some of their grape harvest for preservation. It was this accident of history that gave birth to "France's oldest brandy." From the seventeenth century, again thanks to the British, Armagnac was exported throughout Europe, mainly to northern countries. At the end of the nineteenth century, phylloxera dealt it a near-fatal blow. It survived thanks to the determination of a few winegrowers, but, like Cognac, is now suffering a decrease in demand due as much to competition from grain spirits as to the continuous decline of alcohol consumption.

Armagnac is obtained from the distillation of white wines made from eleven grape varieties. It is made by a single distillation process, in a still of pure hammered copper. As soon as it is removed from the still, it is placed in oak casks, called *pièces*, that can hold approximately 110 gallons. The new wood gradually imparts its aromas and tannin. It is then transferred to older barrels to complete its aging, in the course of which its alcohol content diminishes through the process of evaporation known as "the angel's share" (the same as with Cognac). When the master distiller deems the aging to be sufficient, he proceeds to the *coupes*, blending the eaux de vie of different origins and different ages. Armagnac is drunk neat, generally at the end of a meal, in a balloon glass with a narrow opening that contains its aromas. In the mouth, connoisseurs detect aromas of violet, hazelnut, quince, plum, and vanilla.

The age given is always that of the youngest eau de vie in the blend. Three stars: Armagnac aged at least two years in the barrel. VO, VSOP, or Réserve: Armagnac aged at least five years in the barrel. Extra, Napoléon, Vieille Réserve, or XO: Armagnac aged at least six years in the barrel. Some old Armagnacs, made from exceptional vintages, are dated. In this case, the year given is that of a single harvest that has reached its natural degree of aging.

With their full-bodied flavor, the wines of Gers provide an ideal foil to the punch of Gascon cuisine. Powerful, deep, and luscious, yet still subtle, Madiran can be drunk young, but is capable of considerable aging—up to ten years—which makes it an excellent wine for storing. It is served with robust-flavored dishes, such as game. The Côtes de Saint-Mont, including substantial reds; elegant and aromatic rosés; and fresh, zesty whites, are drunk young, and go perfectly with any kind of duck dish. The appellation Pacherenc du Vic Bilh produces very perfumed and admirably mellow dry white wines with aromas of candied fruit that perfectly complement foie gras. Finally, white or rosé Floc de Gascogne (*floc* is Gascon for *fleur*, or flower) consists of one-third Armagnac and two-thirds grape juice. Spicy and fruity, these wines are served chilled as aperitifs.

*facing page*
Armagnac is produced from the distillation of dry white wines and is celebrated in the local museum of Armagnac.

*below*
Pacherenc du Vic Bilh wines are mostly sweet and very aromatic, with a citrus bouquet.

# FLEURANCE

## THE LAND OF FOIE GRAS

LOCATED IN AN AREA THAT IS NO LONGER THE PLAINS AND NOT YET THE MOUNTAINS, and endowed with fine weather, the glistening snows of the Pyrenees are often visible on the horizon from Fleurance. Lomagne county resembles a little Tuscany that might have strayed into the Gascone region: with steep, though never precipitous, hills; narrow valleys sometimes opening up to unexpected vistas; summers that are long and hot, though never unbearable; winters just cold enough to make people relish the spring; and autumns so sumptuously scented and mild they evoke the splendors of Indian summers.

But what about the architectural jewels of its *bastides*—the small cities that were built during the medieval golden age? It is generally believed that the development of new towns is a characteristic of modern times. But this is wrong. Bastides are extraordinary examples of planned urbanization. Anxious to attract laborers to their estates, the thirteenth-century lords of the Languedoc launched themselves into real-estate development. Once they determined where to build, they erected a church and a covered market, then offered peasants plots of land on which to construct houses at their own expense. To win "customers," they offered them all sorts of rights, privileges, and tax exemptions. This is how Fleurance was founded in 1272, with its grid layout, covered market set within four statued fountains, and Gothic church testifying to the *bastide* origins of this exquisite little capital of Lomagne.

A view of the medieval town from above.

This is the heart of foie-gras country, and to walk through Fleurance's market in winter, when the farmers set up their stalls featuring geese, ducks, and plump, ivory-colored livers, is an unforgettable experience. Despite the increasingly widespread view that the force-feeding of geese and ducks is cruel to animals—some countries have banned the practice—this procedure exploits what is a natural and totally reversible

Gascon cuisine is not restricted to the great classics: foie gras, confit (meat preserved in fat), and magret (fillet of goose or duck). Local spring chickens, guinea fowls, capons, and roasting hens rival the quality of Bresse's poultry. The Lectoure melon, with its dense, sweet flesh, is comparable to that of the Cavaillon melon. The pipless Auch pear is a delicious rarity any gastronome can appreciate. Crayfish, which are still abundant here, are served pan-fried in duck fat and seasoned with chopped parsley and garlic. A dish that certainly ought to be sampled is *garbure*, a vegetable soup with cabbage, turnips, white haricot beans, and carrots. Simmered in the soup are preserved duck, pigs' knuckles, and Toulouse sausages. Another dish to try, *croustade*, is a delicate confection in flaky pastry flavored with Armagnac and orange-flower water, made from a recipe supposedly brought by the Arabs in the seventh century.

phenomenon characteristic of migratory birds, which store fat in their livers in preparation for the winter migration. Artificial force-feeding, a phase that lasts two to three weeks, is done without causing the animal pain or stress to avoid producing livers and meat of poor quality. The gourmet may rest assured: he can feast on the incomparable delicacy of foie gras without shame or regret.

One of the most important component's of Gascon cuisine is garlic. Just as Lautrec, France, is the land of pink garlic, St. Clar, in the heart of Lomagne, is the capital of white garlic. It is said that Henri IV had a great fondness for it and preferred Lomagne garlic above all others. Every Thursday morning during the summer months at the St. Clar market, white garlic is sold loose, in bunches, or woven into strings, to wholesalers from all over Europe. But ordinary shoppers can also buy it at excellent prices.

*facing page*
Garbure, at one time a staple food of the Gascon peasant's diet, is a soup made with cabbage and local vegetables.

# FOIX
## PEASANT FARE

AN IMMEDIATELY CAPTIVATING PLACE, FOIX'S OLD TOWN IS DOMINATED by a castle whose three round towers point skyward. In the Middle Ages it served as the residence of the counts of Foix; one of the last descendants became king of Navarre and then king of France by the name of Henri IV. Foix is situated in the heart of Ariège county, at the foot of the Pyrenees; it is a wild and underpopulated region whose people are proud of its origins and traditions. Famous caves such as the 30,000-year-old Mas d'Azil or the Niaux grotto, whose walls are painted with a Pyrenees bestiary several thousand years old, are found in the area.

Here, a simple and hearty traditional cuisine can be sampled. Soups are made with garlic, onion, egg, or tomato. A classic local dish, *Azinat*, a stew typical of Ariège, is made here. Each cook has his own way of preparing it—there are likely as many recipes as there are residents. The primary ingredients are cabbage, potatoes, carrots, onions, and pork. Some locals include pork rinds, while others add chicken, ham, or sausage. For special occasions, connoisseurs insist that azinat be served with *rouzole*, a kind of pancake made with sausage, egg, and breadcrumbs that is browned in a skillet and served as an accompaniment to the main dish. Just as filling, *mounjetado*, from the word *mounjeto*, a small dry bean, is also one of the classic mountain dishes and is related to the Ariège cassoulet; it is made with beans (cocos de Pamiers, preferably), salted ham, dried liver sausage, fresh sausages, and preserved duck, and cooks for seven hours.

But dessert should not be overlooked. Croustade is a pie made with flaky pastry, fruit, rum, and sugar. In the past, croustades were special-occasion sweets made by the dozen once or twice a year with leftover fruit. The baker would lend his oven and all those who put their pies in would mark their own with strips of pastry. Everything—even the weighing of ingredients—was done by hand. Each croustade was different, and neighbors would taste-test one anothers' creations with great curiosity. In St. Girons, patisserie-maker Martine Crespo carries on the local tradition. She has improved on the old home recipes and makes croustades with pears, pears and walnuts, and apples and prunes steeped in rum.

Hypocras is a wine-based drink flavored with various spices including cinnamon, and dates back to medieval times.

Hippocrates is generously credited with the invention of hypocras, which had its heyday in the Middle Ages. Appreciated at royal tables, the favorite drink of Henri IV, Louis XIV, and, of course, Gaston Fébus, hypocras (hippocras, in the old English version) has become an Ariège specialty. This herbal-based aperitif experienced a surge in popularity once it was produced according to a patented formula and bottled and sold. A skillful blend of wine, herbs, and spices, discriminating palates will recognize flavors of cinnamon, ginger, cloves, cardamom, and rose petals. Hypocras should be served chilled as an aperitif or at the end of a meal accompanied by a slice of chocolate cake.

The epitome of a rustic dessert, which in the past was prepared when a pig was slaughtered or a fattened goose was turned into *confit* (preserved meat) and its liver into foie gras, *millas* is easy to prepare: boil some milk and water in a big copper pot into which corn flour is poured while stirring with a *toudeilho* (a wooden spatula). When the toudeilho stands upright in the mixture—after cooking for about one hour—the millas is ready. It is left to cool, then cut into squares which are fried in butter and dusted with sugar.

*facing page*
The castle, which looks down over the valley, was once a refuge for the persecuted Cathars.

# MOISSAC

## DROPS OF GOLDEN SUNSHINE

SITUATED ON THE BANKS OF THE TARN RIVER, A STONE'S THROW from its confluence with the Garonne, Moissac has preserved one of the most marvelous works of southern French Romanesque art. St. Pierre Abbey-Church's tympanum, sculpted in 1130 and recognized by UNESCO as a world heritage monument, is one of the finest examples of Romanesque sculpture. Showing Christ in majesty surrounded by his apostles, it depicts scenes from the Apocalypse with figures whose features reflect a remarkable subtlety of execution. The cloister of St. Pierre Abbey, built in 1100, is also perfectly preserved. Its four galleries, approximately 130 feet long, are lined with alternating paired and single columns of rare elegance, with capitals illustrating scenes from the Bible, or carved with decorative nature motifs of animals or vegetation, including vines.

It was in the nineteenth century that Moissac became the capital of the *chasselassiers* (cultivators of the Chasselas grape), when its declining flour-milling industry dictated the need for another activity. The Chasselas grape has long been cultivated in Bas-Quercy, either trellised or trained in arches, as ornamentation. The railroad made a significant contribution to the development of grape cultivation, which the phylloxera crisis soon destroyed. However, cultivation resumed with new plants, and the railroad brought further promotional and marketing benefits. In 1933, to compete with spas, Moissac even created an Uvarium, for the appreciation of the virtues of the Chasselas grape and its juice. From mid-June to mid-September, it offers visitors tastings of grape juice and the visual delight of its fine decorative frescoes.

Chasselas grapes are harvested between September and October, early in the day, when they are fully ripened. The Chasselas de Moissac, which produces golden clusters of small translucent grapes, with a sweet fragrance and a crisp flesh, was the first fresh fruit to attain AOC status in 1971. All the work is done by hand. Techniques for pruning and sorting the grapes, which is done by women, have not changed for decades. Tradition still requires that only the expert hands of the mistress of the house should pack the precious grapes in cases marked with the Chasselas-grower's name.

The canal-bridge of Cacor allows water traffic to continue across the Tarn River along the Canal Lateral de la Garonne.

*facing page*
Chasselas preserves are made from table grapes grown in the Moissac. Grapes have been cultivated there since the eighteenth century.

The *grain doré de Moissac* (golden raisin of Moissac) was created over fifty years ago. Made with Chasselas grapes and chocolate, the specialty was invented by the Pâtisserie Laporte, which continues the tradition to this day. In the autumn the individual grapes are carefully detached from the bunch and steeped in a demijohn of brandy. One year later they are de-stalked and coated in Armagnac-flavored milk chocolate and a layer of dark chocolate. Crunchy, juicy, soft, and flavorful, the grain doré de Moissac is advertised as being a mouthful of sunshine you can eat all year round.

Slopes ideally exposed to the sun, rich clay soil, and an expertise developed over generations are the three reasons for the success of Quercy melons. Quercy's soil is especially water-retentive, which makes it possible to regulate plant nutrition. The clay in the subsoil also helps to replenish the melon beds with the minerals that guarantee a quality product. Thousands of green and yellow globes, full of sugar and saturated with sunshine, reach maturity at the height of summer. Quercy melon is served as an appetizing starter and as a digestive dessert. It is served in myriad ways: fresh, in gazpacho, with walnut oil dressing, as a garnish with a thin slice of duck, or as sorbet.

# ROQUEFORT

## THE SECRETS OF COMBALOU

EVER SINCE A VIADUCT WAS CONSTRUCTED BETWEEN TWO CAUSSES (limestone plateaus) in order to ease congestion, the town of Millau has become world famous. So much so that instead of crossing the viaduct, drivers stop to admire Norman Foster's creation, a line of steel pinned against the sky, but also to visit the town, which has emerged from oblivion because of this structure. Once the capital of glove making, Millau is undergoing a revival, and the twenty-first century looks promising.

The viaduct has boosted the economy of the entire region. Visitors to Roquefort's caves are coming in increasing numbers. And of course, where cheese is concerned, there's a legend attached to every story. This one tells how a shepherd, rushing off to meet his girlfriend, left behind his bread and cheese in the cave of Combalou. When he returned a while later, his cheese was covered with mold. He tried it, and it tasted good. This was the beginning of Roquefort cheese.

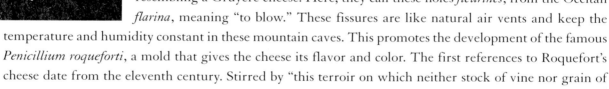

A view of the small town nestled in the foliage.

Separated from the Causse du Larzac by the Soulzon, a little river that has managed to isolate it from the rest of the plateau, Combalou is a rock full of holes, resembling a Gruyère cheese. Here, they call these holes *fleurines*, from the Occitan *flarina*, meaning "to blow." These fissures are like natural air vents and keep the temperature and humidity constant in these mountain caves. This promotes the development of the famous *Penicillium roqueforti*, a mold that gives the cheese its flavor and color. The first references to Roquefort's cheese date from the eleventh century. Stirred by "this terroir on which neither stock of vine nor grain of wheat grows," the kings of France granted privileges to the town's residents and even ruled that those who made imitations of the cheese should be punished.

In the heart of the rock are row upon row of caves, up to eleven, where, after undergoing numerous stages of production, the Roquefort cheese is matured. After innoculating the fresh cheese with the mold, it takes three to four weeks for it to develop. The cheese is wrapped and the *pains* (or loaves, as the young cheeses are called) are aged for four months in the caves on solid oak racks. Interestingly, the appellation includes milk produced in the Pyrénées-Atlantique and Corsica. Every year nearly 19,000 tons of Roquefort cheese emerge from the caves of Cambalou. An important note: Roquefort is eaten at room temperature, 64 to 68 degrees Fahrenheit.

Several regions of France claim the unusual-looking cake, *le gâteau á la broche*, as their own. Some experts maintain that it dates back to the time of the Crusades, while others believe it originated near the town of Rodez in 1890. Whatever the facts, this cake, cooked on a spit in front of an open wood fire, is also known in Austria and the Balkans. A long wooden cone is put on the spit over which the batter is then poured. As the spit turns horizontally in front of the fire, the cone is covered with additional layers of batter, each of which must be allowed to turn golden before the next layer is added. In the past this cake was made for special occasions: weddings, baptisms, first communions, and at Christmas. It is eaten plain, or served with cream or vanilla ice cream.

Near Rodez, the Vallon de Marcillac has been devoted to the cultivation of vines since the ninth century. Today, with 445 cultivated acres, it is one of the smallest AOC areas in France. The vineyards extend over steep hillsides, red clay slopes rising to chalk plateaus, which give this terroir its unusual and distinctive character. Fer Servadou, locally known as mansois, is the primary grape variety and constitutes at least 90 percent of the composition of the wine, which is sometimes blended with Cabernet or Merlot. Marcillac has a purple color with blue tints, and a red-berry nose. Though very tannic when young, it develops roundness with age.

*facing page*
Roquefort is aged in caves in the chalky rock of Combalou Mountain.

# TARBES
BOUNTIFUL BEANS

EVEN THOUGH IT MAY SEEM FAR AWAY, ENGLAND HAS LEFT ITS MARK on the history of the southwest of France, where for a considerable part of the Middle Ages its sovereigns reigned over vast fiefdoms. This was the case with Bigorre; its capital, Tarbes, was occupied by the English from 1360 to 1406 and it did not become part of France again until the beginning of the seventeenth century. The English later returned to inflict heavy damage to Napoleon's troops. However, there is relatively little British influence. In fact, there could be nowhere more typical of the small Pyrenees towns of southern France than this lively and easygoing place, ideally situated at the foot of the mountains. There are winter sports resorts nearby, and it is a short hour's drive from the Basque coast.

While its monuments may not be the most impressive, Notre Dame de la Sède Cathedral, a Romanesque building with a Benedictine layout, is worth a detour for its fine eighteenth-century furniture. Not to be missed is a stroll in the Jardin Massey, considered one of the most attractive gardens of the southwest, which has a cloister dating from the fifteenth and sixteenth centuries. Also worth a visit is the Hussars Museum, with its collections of arms, uniforms, miniatures, and paintings that retrace the history of this light cavalry corps that originated in Hungary at the end of the fifteenth century and was later adopted by more than thirty European and Latin American countries. Finally, horse lovers should not miss the twenty-acre Haras National, the stud farm founded by Napoleon, where a superb selection of racehorses may be viewed, and which organizes high-quality equestrian events throughout the year.

It is to a bean, its hussars, and its thoroughbreds, that Tarbes owes its fame. Imported from America in the sixteenth century, the Tarbais bean is found in Bigorre, with soil and a climate ideally suited to its cultivation. Nourishing and easy to prepare, it rapidly replaced the broad bean in traditional cuisine as an accompaniment to both soups and stews. The Tarbais bean is distinguished from most other beans by its thin skin and light flesh. Credited with a Label Rouge and an IGP (Indication Géographique Protégée) designation, guaranteeing its quality and geographical origin, it is the only bean worthy of inclusion in a cassoulet, whether it be one from Toulouse, Carcassonne, or Castelnaudary.

Haras Park is a lovely place for a carriage ride.

For centuries numerous cheeses have been pressed by herdsmen in the area's mountain pastures. The variety is as great as the valleys are numerous, and each has its own cheese and its own secret way of making it. Cheeses are made with the milk of ewes, goats, or cows, or a mixture of different types of milk, and either cooked or uncooked. Among the most well known are the yellow Pyrenees Tomme, uncooked and made with unpasteurized milk, with a supple texture and a black or pale yellow rind; and the unctuous, semi-hard Bethmale, with a natural, orange-brown rind. It has a slight aroma but it develops in flavor from mild to slightly stronger, even somewhat piquant, depending on the season and the time spent ripening. These artisanal cheeses have not yet acquired the renown they deserve, which is another reason to try them: enjoy before they are seized on by industrial producers.

Still relatively protected from industrial and agricultural pollution, the high-altitude freshwater lakes and mountain streams of the Pyrenees remain some of France's most abundant for fish. Eating a lunch of fario or rainbow trout caught that same morning, and simply grilled or cooked au bleu (in water, wine, and vinegar) is something everyone should try. The firm, tender flesh has a delicacy of flavor that is unequaled, and bears no relation to the soft, pasty flesh of farmed trout. This dish, once the ordinary fare of humble folk, today seems worthy of a king.

*facing page*
Tarbes beans have thin skins that make them easier to cook, and they are prized for their non-starchy taste.

# TOULOUSE

## LA VILLE ROSE

WE VOWED TO AVOID IT, BUT THE CLICHÉ IS TOO STRONG TO IGNORE. Toulouse is indeed the "pink town" as described in the tourist brochures. It is also red when the sky darkens, or mauve in the setting sun, but pink—pink roofs, pink walls, pink light—predominates. Rosy in its reflection in the Garonne River and the canals; pink even under the streetlights. One needs to spend time there, not only to see its monuments—how could anyone ignore the Place du Capitole, St. Sernin Basilica, the Couvent des Jacobins, or St. Étienne Cathedral?—but also to walk around, the only way to truly understand a place.

A picture-postcard nighttime view of the Pont-Neuf over the Garonne River.

*facing page*
Violets, the city's symbol, are featured everywhere—on product packages and in foods and perfumes.

Few towns have such a strong and yet at the same time so ambiguous an identity. In the French imagination, Toulouse is at once quintessentially French, an enclave for natives in their Basque berets, with their love of rugby and cassoulet, whose accents make Parisians smile; but it is also a place of white-coated engineers in high-tech fields who work for Airbus and Ariane rockets. Toulouse is indeed a "futuropolis"; but it also remains the capital of Comtes. It has managed to preserve the best of both roles: it is neither a museum-town—it is too young, too lively for that; nor is it Houston-sur-Garonne—it is too steeped in an ancient civilization for that moniker to make sense. To be there for a few hours is to come up against these two contradictory realities that by a unique alchemy have been rendered harmonious.

There is the picturesque medieval district, the solemnity inspired by the Renaissance mansions, the quiet hidden courtyards glimpsed beyond a gateway, the shady canalsides, the small squares with their babbling fountains, the Garonne that always seems to be rebelling against imprisonment by its riverbanks. But there are also the rowdy terraces of the student bistros, the production lines of Boeing's only rival in the world, and the laboratories where the astronauts work. Intelligent, young, cosmopolitan, full of energy and enthusiasm, laughter and music, Toulouse continues to preside over a land of plenty, whose beauty, prosperity, and culture fascinated Europeans for a long time. This was the case until the repression of the Cathars and the subsequent annexation of the region to the Kingdom of France destroyed an extraordinarily refined civilization. That is why it would be a pity to leave this capital of good living and good food without having sampled all its delights.

A resinous extract from the areca, a plant native to India, catechu was used as a digestive aid when it was first introduced to France. At the end of the nineteenth century a Toulouse pharmacist, Léon Lajaunie, invented a new catechu-based secret recipe, whose other ingredients, apart from the areca extract, are gum benzoin, mint, ambergris, musk, and orris powder. He packaged the cachou pastilles in round yellow tins designed to be slipped into a coat pocket. They were an immediate success—and still are to this day.

It might seem surprising that a flower that symbolizes modesty should be linked with this proud southern capital for which it is the emblem. There is a reason: at one time all violets came from Toulouse. The violet was supposedly brought back from Parma by Napoleon's soldiers. The craze for this winter flower—harvested between October and March—was all the more because the climate is ideal for growing it. Violets were used in many ways: horticulturalists and florists used them decoratively, they were distilled by perfumers, and they were worn on jacket lapels or ladies' hats. Violets also caught the attention of confectioners in an unexpected way. Real Toulouse violets are covered with gum arabic and sugar, then recoated with a mauve-blue coloring. This sugared violet is used for decorating desserts and can also be eaten as a sweet.

Like Lyon and Strasbourg, Toulouse has its own culinary traditions that make it an indisputable shrine of French gastronomy. Foie gras and *confits gascons* (Gascon preserves), lamb from Quercy and Aveyron, poultry from Gers, charcuterie from Rouergue, cheeses from the Pyrenees, garlic from Lautrec or St. Clar, Madiran wines and Armagnac all converge on the "Pink Town" to shape the profile of a strongly flavored, assertive cuisine. At the top of the list of Toulouse's gastronomic delights is cassoulet, Holy Spirit in the trinity that also includes Castenaudary and Carcassonne. It would be difficult to draw up an exhaustive list of these southern specialties; local chefs vie with one another in inventiveness. But the most readily identified with the region include *saucisse de Toulouse*, made with pork knuckle, belly, and leg; *confit de canard* or *confit d'oie* (preserved duck or goose), made from the best parts of the animal and cooked in its own fat, then preserved in pots; *magret*, whole fillet of goose or plump duck breast, eaten grilled or smoked; and foie gras, served cooked, half-cooked, or fried with figs or apple slices. Paradoxically, these heavy, rich dishes do not equate with bad health: the southwest is the region of France with the lowest obesity rates.

*far left*
A docked passenger boat on the Garonne with the Pont-Neuf behind it.

*left*
Violet preserves are a locally made product.

*below*
A pot of cassoulet, made with dried beans and meat. Toulouse, Castelnaudary, and Carcassone all lay claim to inventing this classic French stew.

# AVESNES

## MAROILLES CHEESE

WITH ITS WOODS AND PASTURES, LAKES AND VALLEYS, THE AVESNOIS is a land of vibrant colors. The North has a reputation for being an industrial flatland; the Avesnois is proof to the contrary. This is where the green heart of the North beats. Near the Trélon Forest, the Baives Mountains offer a splendid panoramic view of a landscape so hilly it has been nicknamed "the Switzerland of the North." Suprisingly in these northern parts, Bavay still has a fine Gallo-Roman citadel, constructed around the remains of an impressive forum. Le Quesnoy, a town fortified by French military leader Vauban, has nothing in common with other military strongholds. With its brick ramparts overtaken by greenery, it invites visitors to a pleasant walk around the bastions, among gardens and expanses of water. Stretching away from the gates of the town is the Mormal Forest, one of the largest in northern France: nearly 36 square miles of continuous woodland. Around the forest, the edges of the pasturelands are lined with hawthorn hedges.

Beneath the apple trees the cows feast on rich grass that imparts its particular taste to *maroilles* cheese, with its characteristic delicate orange rind. "Neither town, nor village am I, but Maroilles, Queen of the Meadows," is the motto of Maroilles, surrounded by meadows covered with buttercups in the spring. It claims to be the capital of "the finest of strong cheeses," and of *flamiche*, a tart made with the same cheese and eaten during *Les Ducasses*, a traditional northern festival. Locals definitely like to celebrate. Many villages have bandstands and dance floors ready to welcome brass bands and folk dancing.

Francis Lévêque also has a motto: "Good pasture, good cellar, good cheese." He has for many years been defending the virtues of the maroilles AOC. With references to this cheese found in twelfth-century sources, this is one of France's most ancient cheeses. Lévêque's cheeses are made from untreated milk and matured in a cellar beneath his house. Carved into the floor of this brick-vaulted cellar are *goulottes*, channels with constantly flowing water (as is often the case in this area, the house is built above natural springs). The ambient humidity has covered the vaults with microscopic mushrooms that permeate the atmosphere and give this soft cheese with its washed rind a unique flavor. Cheese lovers should know that the best maroilles is sold at the beginning of summer and from October to Christmas. Also based on maroilles, but with added salt, pepper, and basil, is another local cheese made in the same cellars: boulette d'Avesnes, which can be eaten plain or rolled in paprika.

*facing page*
Maroilles village gives its name to a soft cheese with a washed rind that has been popular since the Middle Ages.

*below*
St. Nicolas Collegiate Church was built in 1534.

Bon pommier, court-pendu, belle fleur, reinette de France: all of these varieties of apple flourished in the orchards of the Thiérache region during the nineteenth century; the Nord département was the leading producer of edible apples. At Liessies, around the imposing Benedictine Abbey founded in the eighth century, is a vast park of meadows and orchards. While walking around the grounds one can see a variety of birds: herons, buzzards, and sparrowhawks. There is also a conservation orchard on the estate, where many types of apple trees are grown. The baguette is one among numerous hardy varieties cultivated by the monks; it flowers late and is resistant to frost. Tasting is allowed, but note that while the residents of Liessies are allowed to collect apples that have fallen from the trees, they are not permitted to pick them.

Napoleon's soldiers were sickened by the lead they swallowed after using their teeth to tear off ammunition caps when they loaded their guns. They chewed tobacco to help them spit out the poisonous metal. The soldiers' wives had a better idea: they concocted a sweet made of sugar, syrup, and sweet mint capable of getting the lead out of their husbands' mouths in the same way. In 1875 a confectioner "invented" the *chique de Bavay* (the Bavay plug), made according to a recipe that remains secret and is now in the possession of Christian Kamette. The only innovation is that the chique de Bavay now comes in three flavors: mint, coffee, and apple.

# BOULOGNE
## SUR-MER
### WHERE HERRING IS KING

EVERY MORNING ON THE QUAI GAMBETTA MANY VARIETIES OF QUIVERING, bright-eyed fish are laid out on the fishmongers' stalls. The fish could not be any fresher: the boats have just returned with the previous night's catch. Located where the waters of the English Channel meet those of the North Sea, Boulogne is one of France's most important fishing ports. There's a lovely view of the port from the Sailors' Calvary, the blue and white chapel above the town, whose silhouette suggests a grounded vessel. The Maison de la Beurière, in the old fishermen's neighborhood, reconstructs the way the seafarers of the past used to live. In the upper town, which retains its thirteenth-century ramparts, the castle has been turned into a museum, while the town hall has a twelfth-century belfry, the city's most ancient monument.

Boulogne is also France's most important center for processing fish. There are still salting and curing businesses there. The Port of Boulogne's history is closely linked with that of one fish in particular: herring. "To each his bread, to each his herring," as the local saying goes. This small, blue-skinned fish was a significant part of the city's economy from the time of the Middle Ages. The herring is ancient; Caesar imported it to feed his soldiers, and it was regarded in medieval times as the fish of the Church. A staple of fast days, it was eaten during Lent and, during the rest of the year, on Fridays. The disputed right to fish herring has even been cited as one of the causes of the Hundred Years' War between France and England.

Herring live in shoals, at a depth of up to 650 feet. The white flesh contains extremely fine bones that can be eaten. Fresh herring is no longer seen much at fishmongers' stalls, except on the quays of Boulogne. Herring is salted, smoked, or preserved in oil, and it goes by many different names: kipper, bloater, pilchard, or rollmop. Red herring is salted and smoked, and comes in fillets. A kipper is split in two before being wood smoked; as a rule, it is not as salty. Less common is the bloater, a smoked herring left whole to preserve the unctuousness of its flesh. A rollmop is marinated in vinegar and herbs. Finally, connoisseurs particularly appreciate *craquelot*, a type of herring, generally not gutted, that is salted for four to five hours, and then smoked for about twelve hours. It is served fried, or grilled, which makes it crunchy—hence the name (*craquer* meaning "to crunch").

*Flamiche au Maroilles* is a savory pie made with the famous cheese.

*facing page*
Herring of all types—salted, smoked, filleted, or whole—reign supreme in this city.

La Gainée Boulonnaise is a fish soup that is to Boulogne-sur-Mer what bouillabaisse is to Marseilles. Originally, *gainée*, from the word *gain* (profit or earnings), was the fisherman's share of the catch. This culinary speciality, which is served at the restaurant in Nausicaa, Boulogne's large marine center and aquarium, was created for the opening of the center in 1991 by the Association des Chefs de la Côte d'Opale. It is a hearty soup of cod, angler fish, whiting, and mussels, to which leeks, turnips, and the ratte du Touquet potato are added; all are cooked in a *fumet* sauce (a concentrated reduction of stock) made from shrimp and fish.

The origins of the ratte du Touquet, a small, difficult-to-cultivate potato, are uncertain. It is a low-yield crop, averse to extreme heat, and it would have come close to disappearing had it not been for the pains taken by a groups of gardeners anxious to preserve it. The temperate climate of the Picardy Coast is particularly suitable for growing the ratte du Touquet. It is planted in April, in sandy or alluvial soil, and harvested in September. Its distinctive chestnut flavor is highly prized and esteemed by great chefs such as Alain Passard and Joël Robuchon. It is delicious served with a pat of butter.

# CAMBRAI

## A SWEET MISTAKE

CAMBRAI WAS THE FIRST TOWN IN NORTHERN FRANCE To be designated a "Town of Art and History," a sweet reward for a city that was devastated during World War I and was rebuilt in its original style. Under Charles V, Cambrai was a Spanish possession, and vestiges remain of a fortress built by the ruler on whose vast empire the sun never set. The Château de Selles, which forms part of the fortress, has seen many invasions and rebellions, and its dungeons are covered with graffiti left by Dutch and Spanish prisoners. The Maison Espagnole, where the tourist office is located, is one of the town's last surviving half-timbered gabled houses; it dates from 1595. Cambrai also has one of the last beguine convents in France—a place where pious women, either unmarried or widowed, live together in a community and lead celibate lives. The convent is still inhabited, as it has been since the sixteenth century.

Situated at the heart of a vast agricultural region, Cambrai makes several special cheeses. Tomme de Cambrai is made on farms from unpasteurized milk, using a maroilles paste matured with beer. Boulette de Cambrai is a soft cheese, hand-molded, similar to Boulette d'Avesnes. It is not aged, but seasoned with pepper, tarragon, and parsley. Cambrai is also home of a confection, whose name is known to all French chil-

Flemish-style houses line the Grand Place.

dren, even those who haven't tasted it: the *bêtise* (literally "bungling" or "foolishness"). the bêtise has been one of the town's prized products since the 1860s, and there is a story behind it. *"Tu n'es bon qu'à faire des bêtises"* (All you're fit for is doing stupid things!), complained the mother of young Émile Afchain, an apprentice in his parents' confectionery business. The scatterbrained boy had yet again made a mistake with a sweets recipe. The result, as it turned out, was not a disaster, since the customers who tried this surprising new mint-flavored confection came back for more. The veracity of this story is uncertain and some believe the bêtise de Cambrai dates back to the thirteenth century. Whatever the case may be, the Maison Afchain has been producing this little treat for a long time. The bêtise is made of boiled sugar flavored with mint, and a caramel strip is placed on top to sweeten the taste. And blessings are heaped on the name of Émile and his clever stupidity.

Cambrai andouillette was supposedly invented by Elisabeth Martin, the first wife of the Cambrai-born painter Louis Joseph Nicolas St.-Aubert. The andouillette appears on Cambrai's official menus from 1791, and Diderot and D'Alembert's *Encyclopedia* dedicates a whole chapter to it. Whereas other andouillettes use pork meat, the Cambrai andouillette is made exclusively from calves' mesentery encased in beef intestine. It is warmed in the oven, fried, or grilled, but it is cooked slowly, so that it heats completely. Mustard and shallot sauce is served alongside, and beer is the typical beverage accompaniment.

France is the world's leading producer of endives, and the Nord-Pas-de-Calais region alone accounts for 80 percent of the total national production. Here, the endive is called *chicon*, as well as Witloof or Brussels chicory. After being sown in open ground, it takes about four months for the plant to take root, forming a kind of carrot shape that has to be cut and then placed in a forcing unit. Endives are then put in a dark place, where it takes them three weeks to grow and whiten. The leaves make a crunchy, refreshing salad. In the north, endive is used in a popular winter dish. It is eaten braised, au gratin, or plain served with roast meat or poultry.

*facing page*
Individually wrapped Bêtises de Cambrai are mint-flavored candies with a caramel stripe that were created due to an apprentice confectioner's mistake.

# LILLE

## A FLEMISH CAPITAL

CAPITAL OF FLANDERS, LILLE WAS BURGUNDIAN BEFORE IT CAME UNDER SPANISH CONTROL. When it was returned to France in 1667, Louis XIV asked Vauban to construct a citadel there, whose star-shaped layout has not changed since it was built. It took one thousand men three years to lay sixty million bricks. With peace the *franco-lillois* style flourished, the finest example of which is the Rang du Beauregard on Place du Théâtre, a series of patterned facades combining stone and brick. It adjoins the Old Bourse, the town's most impressive building. Erected in 1652, the Bourse consists of twenty-four identical houses constructed around a rectangular courtyard with an arcaded gallery. The courtyard is home to florists and booksellers.

Old Lille has preserved a distinctive atmosphere, with unpretentious grocery stores alongside luxury boutiques. From its Flemish past it has retained a penchant for belfries—the town hall's is the tallest in the region—and for carillons, of which the town has five with the most important being that of Notre Dame de la Treille. Its thirty-seven bells weigh more than 8,800 pounds and are chimed for all civil and religious festivities. Lille is both festive and gourmet. One of the most food-centric streets is undoubtedly the rue Esquermoise, where the shop window of the Leroy Bakery is full of regional sweets: *babulettes* (caramels), *frites de Lille*, and *bêtises de Cambrai* (mints). Or there is the Bon Patûrages cheese shop that sells all the cheeses from the North. Not to be forgotten is the Masion Méert, whose chocolates Lille-born General de Gaulle much appreciated, and which have been famous since 1761. In Flemish, Lille is called Rijssel, and a specialty is still eaten here with a name that most French people find unpronounceable: *pot'je vleesch* (potted meat). Pot'je vleesch comprises three or four types of white meat: chicken, veal, corn-fed pork, and rabbit. The meat should be at least 55 percent of the net weight of the potted product. The recipe appeared in northern France in the fourteenth century, and it is not made or even consumed anywhere else but in this region. The meats are cooked in jelly for three hours, with ingredients that vary according to custom (diced bacon, cloves, juniper berries), before being potted. Pot'je vleesch is eaten cold, with French fries and a local beer.

*Pot'je vleesh* is a cold Flemish dish made of a few types of meat in aspic and served with salad and French fries.

*facing page*
Place du General de Gaulle, otherwise known as the Grand Place.

Two million people overtake Lille during the first weekend in September for the Braderie, France's largest flea market. *Moules-frites* (mussels and chips) and a glass of beer are a must during this event. They are everywhere: in the street, on terraces, and in every café and restaurant. However, there is one place where mussels have been raised to a fine art. In its thirties-era décor, Aux Moules serves mussels prepared in many different ways—among others *à la marinière* (in white wine with onion, parsley, thyme, and bay leaf), in cream, and in beer—and prides itself every year on creating the Braderie's highest pile of mussel shells. This local specialty is not necessarily part of a heart-healthy diet, but progress has been made: in the past the frites were cooked in horse fat.

Rouge d'Arleux, a small garlic, is this region's popular variety, and is planted in March and harvested in July. Once it has been dried, the garlic is tied into bunches of three or six heads, depending on their size. They are then woven into *liens*, or braids, of 45 or 90 bulbs. Liens of 20 individually woven bulbs are also available. Since the sixteenth century, Arleux garlic has been peat-smoked, which gives it a pretty russet color and increases its shelf life. Covered with sawdust and chaff, the fire is stoked up every eight hours over a period of ten days, with the temperature closely monitored. Too low and the garlic would not keep; too high and it would end up cooked. Stored in a dry place Arleux garlic may last for a whole year.

*far left*
This monument, known as the Déesse column, is located on the Grand Place and commemorates the French victory over Austria in 1792.

*left*
There are a variety of locally produced pale ale, amber, and dark beers. Blance de Lille is a blend of pale malts.

*below*
A braid of Arleux garlic, which is grown and smoked using old-world methods. Once it is smoked the garlic will keep for a long time.

To be immersed in the Flanders of the past, open the door of the 'T Rijsel *estaminet* (a small bistrolike establishment typical of northern France). Wooden tables and candles, a fireplace, and a jumble of antique objects create a rustic ambience to match a resolutely traditional cuisine. How can anyone resist these menus penned on pages from a schoolchild's notebook, or those rose- or violet-flavored lemonades? Some of Lille's brasseries are also notable for their cuisine and atmosphere. Savoring a *waterzoï de volaille* (poached poultry with vegetables in a cream sauce) or a *carbonade* (braised beef with onions cooked in beer) beneath the 1830s glass roof of the Alcide brasserie is an experience not to be missed. If you opt for a *choucroute* (sauerkraut), go to the Brasserie André. There you will eat on tables dating from 1924. You will also notice a wooden airplane propellor hanging on the wall, which was left in payment after the last world war by a group of American aviators short on cash. At Les Trois Brasseurs the beer comes gushing out before one's eyes from the vats in which it is fermented. Avoid the noisy terrace and instead head for the much quieter back room. Try the house specialty, *flammekueche*, a pizzalike savory tart topped with crème fraîche, onions, and Speck, with a glass of pale ale.

# CAEN

## OF HEROES AND TRIPE

THE TWO GREAT ERAS OF NORMANDY'S HISTORY COME TOGETHER AT CAEN. In June 1944, Caen, a town devastated by the war, was left in ruins. At the center of one of the most terrible battles of all time, Caen wanted to make its own contribution to peace. The town's Mémorial aspires to be "a place in which to encounter contemporary history and reflect on peace and the present day." The Mémorial traces the terri-

ble progress of war, with its retinue of cruelty, indifference, and distress, which is reflected in the monument as a long chain of suffering embodied by the faces of real men and women.

During the bombardments of World War II, the inhabitants of Caen placed themselves under the protection of the man they have always regarded, even to this day, as a hero. In an attempt to escape death, they sought refuge in the Abbaye aux Hommes. It is here that William the Conqueror, who triumphed over England during the battle of Hastings in 1066, rests in peace under a tombstone. Its place in history assured, the Abbaye aux Hommes, which was founded by William, has also earned a place in anecdotal history relating to cuisine.

These barrels are being used to age Calvados, an apple liqueur made from the distillation of cider.

*facing page*
The impressive St. Etienne le Vieux Church.

It is said that William was fond of tripe, but in his day and for many centuries afterward this dish was bland in taste. It was not until the end of the sixteenth century that Sidoine Benoît, a lay monk in charge of the abbey's kitchens, had the idea of adding cider to the beef tripe. The dish would eventually be known as *tripes à la mode de Caen*. Made with the cow's stomach, not the intestines, the tripe is best in autumn when the animals that graze on the wooded pastures feed on grass and apples. The fruit aromas impregnate the lining of the stomach and develop in a distinctive way in the cooking process. Perfectly prepared, the tripe should be cooked slowly to obtain a soft texture, and should not be crunchy but should melt in the mouth.

According to Benoît, the tripe—that is to say the paunch, reticulum, and omasum, or psalterium, to

"Calvados is like men: as it ages, it mellows and loses its aggressiveness." This is what they say at certain distillers in Normandy. A well-known after-dinner drink, and a typical addition to Norman dishes, Calvados is also consumed during the meal. This practice, almost an institution, is called *le trou normand* (the Normandy space maker). It is customary to pause between courses at lengthy celebratory meals. During these breaks guests are served a glass of Calvados or a sorbet flavored with this apple-based spirit. Calvados stops the secretion of digestive juices, making it possible to continue eating as if you were still hungry. The best brands of Calvados bear the words Vallée d'Auge on the label. As long as they have aged in barrels, the finest are also the oldest. Finally, it should be known that Calvados begins to lose its punch as soon as the bottle is opened.

which a cow heel is added—should be cooked on a bed of bacon rinds, onions, carrots, leeks, garlic, and a bouquet garni laid on the bottom of an earthenware tripe pot. Over this should be poured a glass of Calvados and enough cider to cover the meat; only then may the dish be put in the oven to cook for at least ten hours.

In this region of heavily wooded pastureland, of cows and apple trees, "white gold"—or milk—has been the key to the Pays d'Auge's fortune. Chicken, rabbit, "scallop" of veal, game—the Norman recipes described as Vallée d'Auge are countless. They all have one thing in common: they are cooked with butter and, as could be expected, a nice amount of thick, fresh cream and a generous shot of Calvados. Even Paul Bocuse, whose kitchens on the banks of the Rhône River are a considerable distance from Normandy, was not able to resist the pleasure of creating a recipe for *poulet Vallée d'Auge*. He accompanies it with *pommes en l'air*, sliced apples cooked in a frying pan—with butter, of course.

# CAMEMBERT

A POPULAR CHEESE

PERCHED ON A HILLTOP OF THE PAYS D'AUGE, OVERLOOKING A TROUT-LADEN RIVER, is a little village known worldwide. The whole of Normandy long ago identified its most famous cheese with Marie Harel, whose statue is prominently displayed on a square in the village of Camembert. But how many people know that the statue owes its existence, at least in part, to an American?

In 1926 a New Yorker by the name of Joseph Knirim traveled to Burgundy and talked to whoever would listen about the benefits of camembert cheese, which had saved his life by curing him of a serious stomach ailment. He, among others, would be behind the effort to finance the memorial dedicated to Marie Harel, the inventor of camembert cheese, which was erected near the town church. During World War II the statue was decapitated. A second statue was unveiled in 1956, gifted by the Americans.

During the French Revolution Marie Harel, a farmer's wife, hid a non-juring priest (he refused to take the oath to the Civil Constitution) who was from the district of Brie. The priest passed cheese-making secrets on to her. Blending techniques of Brie with those of Normandy, Marie Harel created camembert, but her tasty invention would not be famous if it wasn't for an even more obscure third hero. Without the genius of a man named Ridel, there is little chance that the reputation of this creamy cheese would have traveled beyond the region. It was Ridel who created the round poplar-wood box that made it possible to transport camembert, which until then had been sold wrapped in straw. In 1863, when Napoleon III came to inaugurate the Paris-Granville railway line, he succumbed to the taste of this unusual cheese and asked for it to be brought to him in Paris; from this point on the reputation of camembert was made.

Every year over 165,000 tons of fake camembert is produced, two-thirds of which is made in its region of origin. Authentic camembert should meet three requirements: it has to be made in Normandy, from untreated milk, and it must be hand-ladled. Unfortunately for the purists, it is now possible to make ladled cheese in a quasi-industrial way. The makers of hand-ladled camembert can be counted on the fingers of one hand. In the town of Camembert, François Durand is the last producer of farmhouse camembert with the AOC Camembert de Normandie. As elsewhere, for reasons of hygiene, it is not possible to visit his premises, so the cheese cannot be tasted on site, however, it can be purchased.

"A dessert without cheese is like a beautiful woman with only one eye," the gastronome Brillat-Savarin declared. In the Vallée d'Auge, where the very best cheeses of Normandy come from, beautiful women are far from being one-eyed. After camembert and Livarot, Pont-l'Évêque is the third cheese to carry an appellation d'origine contrôlée. A soft cow's-milk cheese, with a washed or brushed yellow rind and a minimum fat content of 45 percent, Pont-l'Évêque is thought to have been created in the twelfth century by Cistercian monks. At that time it was known as augelot, since it was made in the Auge. In the seventeenth century it took the name of the market where it was sold, Pont-l'Évêque, between Deauville and Lisieux. A century later it began to be packaged in a square box so it would no longer be confused with the cheese of neighboring Livarot.

Livarot cheese is nicknamed "the colonel" because it is encircled with five strands of rush leaves (the colonel's stripes). In the past, when it had a fat content of only 10 to 15 percent, Livarot was nicknamed "the poor man's meat." Not until the twentieth century did the fat content of this cow's-milk cheese rise to 40 percent. Its rind is an orange-yellow, colored with *rocou* (a South American plant), which protects the pale, soft-textured cheese inside. On tasting, Livarot releases a slight smell of straw promising a pungent flavor. It is best eaten with a glass of local cider, a Gevrey-Chambertin, or a Saint-Joseph Côtes du Rhône.

*facing page*
A round of Livarot, a creamy-textured cheese with the traditional rush leaves tied around it.

*below*
World-famous camembert cheese originated in the small village of the same name.

# FÉCAMP

## HOME OF ALEXANDER LE GRAND

NORMANDY IS THE COUNTRYSIDE OF ONE'S DREAMS, as tidy as an English-style park, with its green meadows and neat hedgerows, thatched roofs out of *Snow White and the Seven Dwarves*, and *Sleeping Beauty* manor houses. But another region lies on the other side of the great barrier of cliffs rising above the sea, a secret, mystical place of mists and phantom abbeys, of low skies and storms that break on the black-pebbled beaches.

Fécamp, confined between two walls of white chalk in a narrow valley that opens onto the English Channel, belongs to the latter region. For centuries the *terre-neuvas*, those intrepid seamen who went fishing for cod in the foggy North Atlantic, sailed to Newfoundland from these quays. Today the cod has almost disappeared, and those fishermen's adventures are now history. Although the smell of the smokehouse no longer hangs over the jetties of this fishing port, every stone in Fécamp is impregnated with the memory of it. Fécamp's sailors continue to climb the *sente aux matelots* (sailors' footpath), making the annual pilgrimage to Notre Dame de la Salut; the facade of the majestic thirteenth-century Trinity Abbey-Church still bears the stone-engraved invocations of cod fishers setting out to risk their lives in the coastal waters off Newfoundland; the small fishermen's houses still huddle together as though to protect themselves from the terrors of the open sea; and even today their memory lives on in the Musée des Terre-Neuvas et de la Pêche, where some superb collections evoke the saga of these extraordinary seafarers.

But Fécamp's most striking monument is without a doubt the Benedictine Palace, the creation of Alexandre Le Grand—yes, Alexander the Great. It takes a lot to survive being born with the family name Le Grand, and then to have parents who show such dubious discrimination as to choose Alexandre as your first name. To judge by the building that was constructed to his own greater glory, the individual concerned had no problem with identity. This astonishing, neo-romantic, Gothic-style edifice, now a museum, could only have been conceived by someone with a healthy ego. It was in 1863 that Alexandre Le Grand began to make his fortune. He discovered an ancient manuscript written by a Venetian monk associated with

Fécamp's abbey, who was clearly a connoisseur of the distillation techniques disseminated by the Arabs. In the manuscript was a recipe for an elixir capable of curing all ills. A wine and spirits merchant, and therefore qualified to understand the recipe, Alexandre Le Grand soon penetrated its secrets, and improved it for contemporary palates.

*facing page*
A view of the Norman-Gothic La Trinité Church.

*below*
Bénédictine is a digestif made from Asian spices and native plants.

For a long time the Fécamp hinterland was the domain of sheep raised for wool not meat; the meat of older sheep was too tough and too strongly flavored for roasting. *Pot-au-feu* was conceived by the housewives of the Pays de Caux as a way to use this meat. In this dish, a piece of mutton, usually a leg, is cooked in a broth made with cabbage, turnip, celery, and leeks, and seasoned with thyme, bay leaf, and onions; it is accompanied with a butter and cream sauce. This hearty and wholesome country dish is back in vogue thanks to a number of chefs interested in regional traditions.

Alexandre Le Grand's deciphered and adapted recipe remains a well-guarded secret. Little is known about the Bénédictine elixir except that is made from twenty-seven fruits, plants, and spices, including apricot, angelica, cinnamon, vanilla, and hyssop. Some of these ingredients grew naturally in the vicinity of Fécamp; others were imported from the Middle East or Asia. Once dried and infused in alcohol, this mixture was distilled and then aged before being enriched with honey and saffron. Only after two years' aging is this precious beverage transferred to those unusually shaped bottles: short and pot-bellied, "like a monk's paunch," and designed by Alexandre Le Grand himself, who, realizing that packaging was an essential element of a product's success, was a marketing genius ahead of his time.

# ISIGNY
## SUR MER

## THE CREAM OF NORMAN TOWNS

IT'S HARD TO IMAGINE THAT THIS QUIET COUNTRY TOWN was devastated during World War II. Though today the name Isigny connotes a place where the art of good living and the pleasures of fine food are appreciated to the fullest, it is located between the two landing beaches of Omaha and Utah, and it is a few miles from St. Mère-Église, the town that symbolized the reason for the D-Day landings on June 6, 1944: it is where the first American flag flew over France and the fight to liberate the country began. Isigny-sur-Mer should have been liberated immediately afterward, but major fighting awaited the Allied armies. Almost 60 percent of the town was destroyed before it became one of the first towns to be freed on June 9, 1944.

In 1066 Robert d'Isigny, who participated in the conquest of England alongside William the Conqueror, settled permanently across the Channel. Over time, his surname evolved—first into Deisigni, then Disney. A branch of the family would later move to Ireland, where the grandparents of Walt Disney eventually immigrated to the United States. Situated on the Aure River, two miles inland from the sea and the Bay of Veys, Isigny was once a busy fishing and trading port. Even today you can admire the Hogues, the area where the fishermen used to live, as well as the quay slip and the tidal gates. Activated solely by the power of the rising tide, these gates prevent seawater from entering the marshes.

In the eighteenth century this port exported butter to America, London, Anvers, and the French colonies. Since the butter was made from cream, it can be surmised that the production of cream dates from just as far back. Isigny butter and cream have had AOC status since 1986. With its low floodplains, this region benefits from regular light rainfall and mild temperatures. Its pastures produce a naturally rich and fragrant milk that makes Isigny butter particularly good for spreading—and it keeps well, too. It is also exceptionally rich in carotenoids that give it a natural buttercup color, remarked on in an edict from 1551. In the eighteenth century, Parisians consumed 880 tons of it per year. Traditional production methods are still used, since the slow maturation process allows the cream to develop its aromas. The butter is churned, washed in plain water, then worked before salt is added.

Isigny's hard caramels are made with cream; its soft caramels are made with milk.

*facing page*
Locally produced butter, a regional specialty, is made from rich, sweet-smelling milk.

"Real" caramel, the kind that sticks to your teeth, is soft; it is the best kind. Invented by the Arabs around the year 1000, it has undergone many permutations, but it is always suggestive of tradition and conveys the flavor of the terroir. The earliest Isigny caramels, called "isicrems" were hard. When they were first made in 1932, they incorporated Isigny cream. Today Normandie Caramel produces 330 tons of caramels a year, and traditional artisanal techniques are still used. Caramel ingredients—whole milk, butter, and cream—are locally produced. A word of advice: according to true connoisseurs, a caramel should first be warmed in the mouth before biting into it.

Delicate sablé cookies were created by Charles Bansard in 1904, in a little shop near Asnelles Church. More than a century later, Antoine Cormier, who grew up with the pervasive, mouthwatering aroma of sablés baking, has taken over the shop and is now responsibile for continuing the tradition. The contents of these shortbread cookies are listed on the packaging: eggs, flour, sugar, and 24-percent Isigny butter, but the recipe and how to make them remain a secret. What is known is that these cookies have eighteen crenulations, measure two inches in diameter before cooking, and are baked for fifteen minutes. The package is sealed with a hot iron.

# MONT SAINT MICHEL

## MÈRE POULARD'S OMELETTE

IT MIGHT ALMOST BE SAID THAT THE MÈRE POULARD OMELETTE is as much a part of Mont Saint-Michel's heritage as the town's famous abbey itself, which is known as "La Merveille de l'Occident" (The Wonder of the Western World). Mont Saint-Michel is a small island close to the border between Brittany and Normandy, sheltered by a bay with the strongest tides in Europe. From certain places along the coast, it is just discernible when the tide is out; it appears as a tiny dot on the horizon in a sandy desert. One of the most visited sites in France, this astonishing place has for ten centuries seen pilgrimage and trade thrive in tandem.

The abbey itself is like a child's construction set. Its superimposed crypts and vaulted rooms are filled with a thousand echoes, and it rests on massive columns and slender pillars. Openings in the stone filter in rays of sun, illuminating the sanctuary with an ethereal light. The church is steeped in semi-darkness and topped with a gilded statue of the archangel that stands out against the sky; the cloister is open to the infinity of the sea. A mix of believers and sightseers, of devout piety and busy commerce creates a unique atmosphere here. Also unusual—and wonderful—is the way in which the abbey affords a magical moment of solitude, especially in the evening, when the crowds have surrendered the abbey to silence and all that can be heard are the mingled sighs of the wind and the sea.

In the nineteenth century, when pilgrims came in great numbers, room and board became problematic. One day an innkeeper had an ingenious idea, very nearly as simple as Christopher Colombus's egg: the omelette. Such a dish posed no problem in terms of stocks of food, and it was a dish of variable proportions that could be suited to all appetites. Since 1888, the date the restaurant known thereafter as Mère Poulard was founded, many tides have passed beneath the archangel's wings, but the savory omelette that made this restaurant famous remains, enjoying a renown duly certified by the establishment's voluminous golden book. It is an omelette that competitors, under sometimes very similar names, take devious pleasure in imitating. For more than a century, gastronomes and the curious have tried in vain to discover the secret of this dish. Perhaps it resides solely in the way the eggs are beaten. The beater's hand movement is remarkable: before the omelette is cooked to a golden brown on the wood fire in a long-handled frying pan, he expertly wields his egg whisk in a round-bottomed copper mixing bowl (called a *cul-de-poule*), to a samba rhythm, and none other.

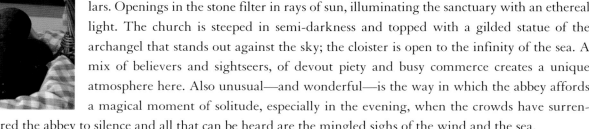

*A display of the area's andouille sausage.*

Genuine *andouille de Vire* is a traditional charcuterie of Normandy. Made with the pig's digestive tract—the large intestine, stomach, and small intestine—its production follows strict guidelines. After meticulous cleaning, the guts are cut into strips by hand, then salted and left to pickle for a week. They are then gathered and bound together at one end and covered with a natural casing of pork intestine. Having now taken shape, the chitterling sausage is beechwood-smoked for a period of three, four, even as much as eight weeks, depending on the individual artisan. Finally, the andouille is left to soak for between twenty-four and forty-eight hours, to remove the salt and rehydrate it; it is then netted and simmered in water for six to eight hours. There are many ways to savor andouille de Vire, but the simplest is to eat it cold with lightly buttered fresh bread.

Before the invention of modern appliances such as refrigerators and freezers, smoking and salting were the only ways to preserve meat in humid areas such as Normandy. Production of the jambon du Cotentin respects this tradition. These hams come from pigs raised on barley meal that are coated with sea salt. They remain in a salting tub for two weeks, while being regularly rubbed by hand. They are then smoked using beechwood or ash for a period of fifteen to eighteen days. Only after another four months' drying are they consumed.

*facing page*
Rising from the sand is the jaw-dropping Mont Saint-Michel abbey, one of the most famous sights in the world. On this day, when the tide is out, visitors walk across the sand alongside the island's still-intact medieval fortifications.

# MORTAGNE

## A SAVORY PUDDING

CAPITAL OF THE PERCHE, MONTAGNE IS A LARGE MARKET TOWN that has retained vestiges of the period when it was the seat of the counts who ruled over the province. The old town has withstood the ravages of time and has preserved its flamboyant Gothic Notre-Dame Church, whose side door is called the Portail des Comtes (the Counts' Door), as well as its ancient grain market and its ramparts, which have been con-

A purveyor of many local specialties showcases a coil of one, *boudin noir* sausage.

verted into a public walk. Mortagne claims two distinctions: it was the birthplace of the philosopher Alain, author of *Propos sur le Bonheur* (Reflections on Happiness), and it carries on a culinary tradition that goes back to the earliest period of France's history. It is possible that *boudin*, black pudding, was introduced to the region by the Moors, who themselves acquired it from the peoples that settled on the banks of the Euphrates. At the time, wild boar thrived in the Norman forests, providing the source of the cooked blood the inhabitants became expert at preparing.

In the Middle Ages Mortagne's boudin was sold in the markets of Flanders and Champagne. This black pudding also graced the tables of the kings of France, and Tsar Peter the Great tasted some when he was a guest at Versailles. Black pudding is made with pigs' meat, fat, and blood, in addition to cream, onions, and herbs. The fat must be evenly distributed, and the quantity of spices expertly judged. The technique is as follows: onions are browned and the fat is placed in boiling water for ten minutes; this mixture is then combined with the cream and blood. After seasoning, the *embossage* (the filling of the length of intestine) begins; all air is squeezed out. As the length of intestine is filled, it is shaped into a ring. The rings are carefully placed in boiling water where they remain for fifteen minutes at a temperature of 194 degrees Fahrenheit. The ring-shaped boudin is then left to cool on a wicker tray or grill. In March there is an annual competition devoted to this triumph of Perche cuisine—and it even garners international attention. The Confrérie des Chevaliers du Goûte-Boudin has the task of selecting the best boudin of some 700 competition entries from around the world (new members of the organization must agree to eat boudin once a week).

In the past it was called *sydre* and came from Biscaye (Spain), where it appeared for the first time in the thirteenth century. "Crush the apples once they are ripe, stack the pulp as regularly as possible, press it hard, barrel the must in well-cleaned casks, and wait until the fermentation is complete and the cider is quite ready before drinking." This was the method for making cider as described by a professor of agriculture in 1878. On the whole, nothing has changed. Normandy is the leading apple-producing region—and the leading producer of cider—in France. The only cider from the region with an AOC designation is from the Pays d'Auge.

*facing page*
A regional product of the Pays d'Auge is its apple cider.

The sablé, which originated in Normandy in the early seventeenth century, was defined as "a kind of sweet that crumbles like sand when eaten." Its success owed a great deal to Parisian vacationers visiting Normandy's beaches. Many bakers created their own versions of the cookie, including Georges Latour, of Lonlay l'Abbaye, who returned from the war and began making a Norman sablé using his wife's recipe. These sablé de l'Abbaye quickly became popular throughout the region—even in Paris. Today this artisanal cookie maker is still a family-run business.

# ROUEN
## CITY OF TASTE

RISING ABOVE THE DELICATELY WROUGHT STONE FACADE, one of the two towers of Rouen Cathedral is called the Tour de Beurre (Butter Tower). Although it was built with stone that might suggest this Norman specialty, it owes its name to the fact that wealthy parishioners paid for it as a way to continue indulging during Lent. At the time, doing penance was beyond the capacity of some parishioners. They bought from a willing Church a right to gluttony. So as not to be deprived of butter, these pious people contributed to the embellishment of shrines that they occasionally honored with their presence.

*Canard au sang à la Rouennaise* (Rouen duck in blood) is a famous local dish.

*facing page*
A street in the old town lined with characteristic half-timbered buildings.

Rouen Cathedral inspired a great painter. Claude Monet depicted it twenty-eight times, at every hour of the day. It was long believed that Joan of Arc was put to death on the Place de la Pucelle (the stake was actually located on the nearby Place du Vieux-Marché). Search through the flowers—the site of her execution is permanently adorned with flowers—to find the spot where the English burned her. Every day for the past eight centuries, the stalls on this square have been supplied with an abundance of Norman butter, cheese and cream, fish and shellfish, and flowers and vegetables.

Poultry, notably the Duclair duck, is also found here. Nicknamed "the lawyer," because of its black plumage and white bib, it has given rise to a curious recipe: *caneton* (duckling) *á la Rouennaise*. Its origin is the stuff of legend. Supposedly, a farmer's wife from Duclair would go to market to sell her free-range ducks. To get there, she had to take a ferry across the Seine. One day when the ferry was full, her duck died of suffocation. When she got home, she decided to cook it. Her *canard au sang* (duck in blood) turned out to be delicious, and the recipe has since become popular: the special characteristic is that the duck is smothered, not bled, so the flesh is of a deeper color and more succulent texture, and therefore more flavorful. As it has been passed down, the recipe for *caneton á la Rouennaise* is attributed to Henri Denise, chef of the

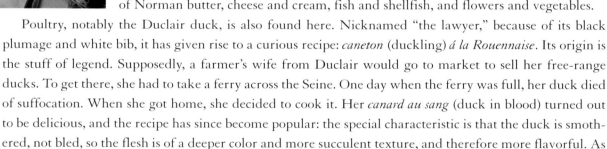

Contrary to what its name suggests, the Petit Suisse is French, not Swiss. It was created in 1850 in a Norman dairy when a Swiss employee (hence its name) suggested adding cream to milk intended for making Neufchâtel cheese. Its history might have ended there if salesman Charles Gervais had not made it his company's most important product. Thanks to a system of distribution by *barouche* (carriage) that extended to Paris, the Gervais company became the largest producer of Petit Suisse, originally sold in a thin strip of paper in little wooden boxes.

Referred to in 1035, Neufchâtel cheese has the distinction of being one of the oldest varieties in France—and the oldest Norman cheese. Its heart shape supposedly dates from the time of the Hundred Years' War and allowed Norman farmwomen to convey their feelings toward the English soldiers stationed in the region. Authentic Neufchâtel, which has an AOC designation, is made with raw milk. This cheese is best in October. It is made with the September milk produced after the cattle graze on the aftercrop, a tender grass that grows back when the first rains water land that is still warm from summer. Neufchâtel is eaten after ripening for three or four weeks. In the past, it was traditional to eat the September cheese when children made their first communion, in June. By then the crust had turned black and the cheese had taken on a strong taste of butter. It was aged in earthen pots and wrapped in nettle leaves. Today's Neufchâtel comes in various forms: the famous heart shape; small sizes in keeping with tradition; or large, which is new. It can also be purchased in a brick shape or a cylinder. Neufchâtel should be cut in triangular portions like camembert.

Hôtel de la Poste at Duclair in the 1920s. Once smothered and plucked, the duckling was roasted for twenty minutes over a wood fire. The slivers of breast were presented rare; the legs and wings were rubbed with mustard and grilled. All were served with a sauce made from the juices of the pressed duckling carcass, the liver, and shallots.

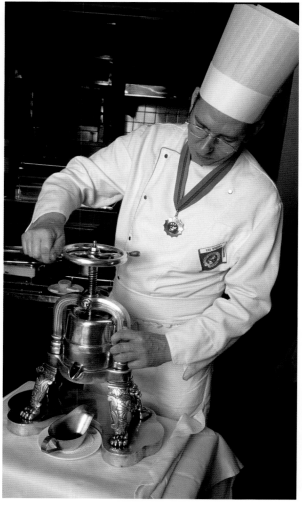

*above, left and right*
To prepare *canard au sang* parts of the duck are pressed to extract juices that are then used as the basis for the sauce.

*far right*
A view of the city from Notre Dame Cathedral.

Apples were plentiful in the surrounding countryside, and sugar was shipped to the port of Rouen, so a sweet based on the combination of the two was inevitable. In the sixteenth century, at the workshop of a skillful apothecary named Pierre Dubosc, this is exactly what happened. Rouen *sucre de pomme* quickly caught on as a medicinal product. With the addition of sandalwood or aloe, it was promoted as a tonic, an expectorant, and even recommended as an antidepressant. But it was not a perfect product and tended to liquify quickly because of the delicacy of its composition. Successful attempts were made to develop sucre de pomme without apples. Today it is a sweet made of boiled sugar flavored with natural apple essence that is rolled into a cylinder. The transparent candy is usually wrapped in paper depicting a monument in Rouen or the Normandy coat of arms.

172

# ANGERS

## A HEARTWARMING DIGESTIF

ANGERS, SET BACK ON A STONE HILL, HAS KEPT ITS DISTANCE FROM BOTH THE LOIRE and the three rivers—Mayenne, Loir, and Sarthe—that converge in the Maine River before their waters flow past it. Bordered by gardens, the seventeen towers of its vast château are a clever mix of shale, sandstone, and granite, looking down on both the waters of the Maine and the old town, whose half-timbered houses adorn the Place St. Croix. The Adam's House, dating to the sixteenth century and decorated with wooden statues, is one of the most remarkable. St. Maurice Cathedral, whose nave and facade date from the twelfth century, is nearby.

Across the river lies the Doutre district, surrounding the eleventh-century Ronceray Abbey; the curious La Trinité Church, with the same lantern structure as the St. Maurice Cathedral, still stands there. At the time of the Renaissance, the nobility took over the higher parts of the town and built their private houses around the Place du Teatre. St. Jean Hospital, founded in the twelfth century, is an example of Plantagenet Gothic art. The Salle des Malades (sick ward) has preserved its dispensary, which holds an impressive collection of seventeenth- and eighteenth-century *faïence* (earthenware), and a curious cupboard of seventeenth-century dressings with their original labels. But, more importantly, it serves as a showcase for the amazing series of "Chant du Monde" tapestries, in which Jean Lurçat tried to give concrete expression to an artist's quest for a little hope and poetry in the chaos of the modern world. This luminous work is on par with the Apocalypse tapestries displayed in the Grande Galerie of the Angers Château.

A bourgeois town, Angers has preserved its traditional cuisine and an impressive body of recipes described as *à l'angevine* (in the Angers style), featuring roasted hen, spring chicken, eggs, fish—with an emphasis on slow-cooked foods with an onion, carrot, and red- or white-wine base. One local recipe used to be a source of embarrassment to some members of the middle class. When doing their shopping, they dared not ask the butcher for *cul de veau* (rump of veal), the part above the top of the animal's leg. Instead they would order *une indécence de veau*, literally "an indecency of veal." The somewhat heavy cuisine of this area does not seem to be especially hazardous. Celebrated French writer Curnonsky saw this region as "the paradise of easy digestion."

*facing page*
Cointreau is enjoyed throughout the world.

*below*
A historic monument, the half-timbered Maison d'Adam is now a Craft Center.

In 1849 the Cointreau brothers set up a distillery to make alcoholic drinks using locally grown fruit. One of the brothers created a revolutionary product in 1875: a transparent liqueur flavored with the peel of sweet and bitter oranges. To distinguish it from their other products, he decided to design a simple bottle, square in shape with rounded corners. Known the world over, the liqueur and its container have not changed, and the secret of Cointreau still lies in the maceration and distilling of an expertly created combination of fresh and dried orange peel.

Clinging to a shale spur dropping into the Loire at the gates of Angers, this 17-acre vineyard is planted with Chenin Blanc and distills a wine about which it has been said: "easier to talk about than to drink, it was so rare." Coulée de Serrant is produced solely by Château de la Roche-aux-Moines, a historic vineyard run by Nicolas Joly, who uses biodynamics to produce the wine. The principle of this technique is to pay attention to the earth and to treat it with respect, and to see that the plant develops in harmony with the support it offers and with the climate. This subtle marriage of mineral and vegetal produces a wine that is both strong and delicate, and always equal to its ambition.

*far left*
Several miles outside of Angers, the landscape of Savennières is dotted with windmills and small farms.

*left*
Workers harvest grapes for the dry white wines of Savennières Coulée de Serrant and Savennières LaRoche aux Moines.

*below*
*Cul de veau a l'Angevin* is a local dish made with veal, carrots, and onions.

177

# GUÉRANDE

## LAND OF SALT

In Breton, *Gwenrann* means "land of whiteness." In the case of Guérande, this "whiteness" refers to the town's famous salt. The primary salt-production region lies just beyond the famous bathing resort of La Baule, but the section covered by the appellation designation includes a less-well-known enclave, the Bassin du Mès, between Assérac and St. Molf, where the salt marshes stretch up through a small green valley. In all, the salt pans of Guérande, Europe's westernmost salt-production area, extend over nearly eight square miles of "sea meadows."

In theory, there is nothing simpler than making salt. All that is required is to direct seawater into a shallow basin and let it evaporate. In practice, it is more complicated than that, and in 2,000 years the methods used have not changed at all. Salt harvesting takes place from the end of May to the end of September, but it is in February that work begins on the salt pans, which require repair after lying unused during the winter. The beds, the levels, and the bridges have to be rebuilt. The seawater travels a complicated route from the sea to the *oeillet*, the small square pan in which it will evaporate and from which the salt will be gathered.

In a job that is 100-percent dependent on nature, and dictated by the sun and the wind, the salt worker can never anticipate production. Harvesting is the most important part of production. It can be tiring work: one salt pan can produce up to 110 pounds of salt each day. The salt-worker's tools have remained the same for centuries, as have his methods, which are passed down from generation to generation. The motion used to collect the salt is elegant and precise: Salt is pushed to the edges of the basin with the *las*, a long, flat rake, and then piled up on the *ladure*, the space between the salt pans. Guérande salt is neither treated nor washed and owes its gray color to the clay that lines the bottom of the pans.

Established in Pradel, in the Salines de Guérande headquarters, the association Terre de Sel promotes understanding of the salt marshes, a protected nature preserve; and it organizes educational trips. The building's terrace, inspired by the ancient *salorges* (salt stores), provides a unique panoramic view of this flat landscape. Approximately 280 species of migratory birds pass through the area each year. It also has a unique vegetation. The strangest of the plants, marsh samphire, virtually grows out of the saltwater. Known for its flavor and health-related benefits, it is eaten raw, pickled in vinegar like gherkins, or cooked like green beans.

Guérande sea salt— sometimes flavored, sometimes not—is an important regional product.

*facing page*
Saturday is the town's big market day and an age-old institution.

"Caviar of the marshes," more commonly known as *fleur de sel*, is a salt with fine snow-white crystals that sometimes tastes mildly of violets. It is a delicate product, usually gathered in the late afternoon in very dry weather, when, thanks to the combined effect of the sun and the east winds, a thin layer of crystal forms on the surface of the salt pans. Because it does not come into contact with the clay lining the bottom of the pans, this layer is not gray. Fleur de sel is carefully collected by the aid of a special tool, the *lousse à fleur*. Slightly pink at the time it is collected, fleur de sel turns bright white as it dries. The special climatic conditions required and the low quantity produced, a little over two pounds per salt pan per day, make this a rare and highly prized product. A pinch of fleur de sel is enough to season any cooked or uncooked dish.

Naturally rich in magnesium and trace elements, sea salt is gray, unwashed, unrefined, and additive free and is employed in all kinds of cooking, including salt-crusted meat and fish. Guérande fine salt is whiter, an unrefined product that is simply dried and pulverized; it can be used for cooking and as a table salt. Flavored salts are also popular. Herbed salts enhance the seasoning of vinaigrettes; seaweed salts are used to flavor fish and shellfish. Flavored salts are also used to cook vegetables and may be added in the final stage of cooking or as a seasoning to sublty enhance cooked vegetables, salads, or crudités.

# LA ROCHE SUR YON

## CHALLANS DUCK

THOUGH IT IS THE MAIN TOWN OF VENDÉE COUNTY, SOME FIND LA ROCHE-SUR-YON somewhat lacking in charm. The town was built by Napoleon in 1804 as a way to establish his authority over the war-ravaged area after the Revolution; it was also a way to develop it. The town was laid out in a pentagon, with rectilinear streets. An enormous square was at its center and there 20,000 soldiers could be deployed; a statue of Napoleon I occupies a place of honor. Apart from this original but rather austere town planning, La Roche-sur-Yon has few curiosities to offer. However, it is situated in the middle of a county that, by contrast, has plenty; it is why the emperor chose it in the first place (according to legend, when he visited the town that at the time bore his name, he was so disappointed by it he didn't stay long before heading to the countryside).

La Roche-sur-Yon is close to the sea, the Marais Breton Vendée to the north, the Marais Poitevin to the south, and the forests that lie to the east, where, unlike Napoleon, the legend goes that the fairy Mélusine was responsible for building pretty towns and delightful castles. La Roche-sur-Yon is also just a stone's throw from the unusual grape-growing area of Fiefs Vendéens. Four tiny regions located around the villages of Mareuil, Brem, Pissotte, and Vix produce wines using the same grape varieties as those used in the Loire Valley: Gamay, Pinot Noir, and Cabernet Franc for the rosés and reds; Chenin, Chardonnay, Sauvignon, and Grolleau Gris for the whites. The terroirs and exposures are varied, and there are even vineyards, such as those near Brem, where it's almost possible to see the ocean. They benefit from exceptional sunshine, comparable with some parts of southern France. Some 100 vine growers share about two square miles of cultivated land among them.

Half the vines and wine production are concentrated in the largest zone, near Mareuil. Since its introduction into the region by Roman soldiers, grape growing in the Vendée has undergone many changes. A source of wealth in the Middle Ages, before long grape growing existed solely for the purpose of local consumption. Cardinal Richelieu, who owned a few acres, gave them to the poor. Today, grouped under the appellation Vins des Fiefs Vendéens, local wine producers work together in the hope that their wines will one day be promoted from VDQS (Vins Délimités de Qualité Supérieur) status and awarded AOC designation. The whites go well with seafood, and the reds with local dishes such as Challans duck or pig's head with cabbage and cream.

Fiefs Vendéens wines from Brem, Mareuil, Pissotte, or Vix consist of a range of whites, reds, and rosés.

A cross between wild duck and ducks brought by the Dutch when they came to drain the Breton Vendée marshes in the seventeenth century, Challans duck is said to have first appeared in the area in 1650. Cross-breeding improved the stock, yielding very large birds. The town of Challans soon became an important poultry center. Ducks were shipped to Paris by train from Nantes (for a while they were referred to as Nantais ducks, but Challans regained its rightful credit). This red-fleshed animal cannot be reared anywhere else but in the Marais, within a relatively restricted area of 19 miles along the coastal marshes and 9 miles in the northern Vendée area. But it was in Paris that the Challans duck obtained its renown. For over 100 years, it has been served at the Tour d'Argent restaurant, where every duck is numbered.

A traditionally cultivated crop in the Bas-Bocage (the undulating, heavily wooded landscape around La Roche), the *mogette* (also *mojette* or *mohjette*), a type of white dwarf bean with a thin, pearly skin, is the iconic food produced in Vendée. This distinctive-tasting legume is cultivated in marshy areas. Mogettes are eaten hot with a thin slice of Challans duck, or cold, in salads dressed with a drizzle of walnut oil. They are served in a classic local dish with garlic, onions, and tomatoes, and accompanied by ham.

*facing page*
Lovely *mogette* beans served with the local ham are a traditional, delicious Vendée dish.

# LE MANS

GOLDEN RILLETTES

SURROUNDED BY PINK WALLS AND FLANKED BY ROUND BRICK TOWERS, Le Mans's old town looks like a ship anchored on the left bank of the Sarthe River. It is one of the best-preserved Gallo-Roman fortresses in France. Rising slopes and flights of steps lead to the foot of the St. Julien Cathedral with its Chartres-inspired portal and unfinished bell tower. The medieval town, where the facades of its patrician houses combine stone, *tufa* (limestone), and timber frames, has often been used as a location for historical films. Le Mans has a long history: its most ancient monument, a menhir known as "the navel," bears its 7,000 years proudly—but the town first became famous at the beginning of the twentieth century for two very different specialties. Even someone who has never visited Le Mans probably could name at least one.

In June of every year, more than 200,000 car-racing fans, convinced that watching people drive around a track endlessly is a lot of fun, attend the 24 Hours of Le Mans, one of the world's most famous tests of endurance. Rillettes is the other item for which the town has been celebrated for more than a hundred years. Great cuisine can certainly be found in this part of the world, where the pleasures of the table are not overlooked.

Rillettes with its common accompaniments of fresh bread and cornichons. In the past, rillets was made toward the end of autumn, so the meat would keep throughout the winter.

Originally created in Connerré, a large country town some 19 miles to the east of Le Mans, *rillettes* was first prepared by Albert Lhuissier, proprietor of a small charcuterie opened in 1900, who invented a pork-based recipe that soon became famous. Thanks to the railway linking Le Mans to Paris, Connerré quickly became the capital of rillettes. The recipe is very simple: All one needs is good-quality meat, time, and experience. Lean cuts of pork are first browned, then the meat is slow-cooked in its own fat at a low and constant temperature. It must cook for at least five hours. For the best rillettes, which are cooked over a wood fire, small cubes of Perche-reared pork are browned in a cast iron pot, then left to simmer gently for eight hours. This is what gives the final product its pale golden or pinkish gray-brown hue. Three generations of the Després family of Connerré, who succeeded Albert Lhuissier, have made it their sole ambition to maintain the high quality of this local product.

A visit to the Maison Reignier is the best way to sample regional delicacies. Founded in 1885, and located at the foot of the old town, it is also known as La Grande Epicerie. The best rillettes and local charcuterie can be produced here, as well as Jasnières wine. A few steps from this distinguished establishment, the Béline chocolate shop proves this is a place where food is taken seriously. In deference to the car race, this store offers race-related novelties such as the "damier" or the "bugatti." But it also recalls the town's long history with its "Queen Berangaria hearts" and "cathedral paving stones." All confections at the shop are homemade.

*facing page*
A well-preserved Gallo-Roman wall surrounds the old town center.

Long the best-kept secret of the Loire Valley, this little-known grape-growing area extends over the slopes shared by two towns, L'Homme and Ruillé, near Château-du-Loire. Curnonsky confidently asserted that three times every 100 years these few rows of vines could produce the best white wine in the world. Although one of the first wine-producing areas to acquire appellation status as early as 1937, Jasnières almost disappeared in the 1970s. Now flourishing once again, its Chenin vines produce a unique white wine that is imbued with the minerally and flinty flavors of its terroir. These wines are aged for a year in chestnut-wood barrels and should not be drunk for five years. Depending on the year, the wines are either dry or mellow. It is said that they may be kept for a century.

# NANTES

## THE BEST BEURRE BLANC

"NEPTUNE FAVORS THOSE WHO LEAVE." NANTES'S MOTTO was inspired by the god of the sea. First-time visitors may be amazed that such an old town has managed to accommodate such broad thoroughfares without harming the original architecture. But until not so long ago, Nantes was built on eight islands connected by about thirty bridges. For practical reasons, the branches of the Loire River were filled in, but the neighborhoods have retained their original names: Île Beaulieu (Beaulieu Island), Île Gloriette (Gloriette Island), Île Feydeau (Feydeau Island), and so on. The hometown of Jules Vernes, Nantes is associated with travel. In the eighteenth century Nantes was France's second most important port. It then became a port for the slave trade. Shipowners who engaged in this activity amassed great wealth, which is still visible in the classical facades of Allée Turenne, once an embankment, and of the Quai de La Fosse.

Capital of the Duchy of Brittany, Nantes has a Renaissance château and a very fine Gothic cathedral. To discover a more lively Nantes, cross the Loire to Trentemoult. In the 1930s this was the equivalent of the banks of the Marne to the Parisian working classes. People went there to dance in the *guinguettes* (suburban café-gardens that had music), to drink Folle Blanche wine (the ancestor of Gros Plant), and to forget the shipyard or the workshop. Houses in every style, from chalet to art deco, line the quayside, and behind this they are crammed together in a disorderly jumble. Gardens beautify the streets, and terraces are linked by intertwined wisteria. Higher up, beyond the reach of river flooding, are the lovely houses of sea captains.

*Beurre blanc*, a typical sauce in Nantes cuisine, is made with butter, white wine, and shallots, and goes particularly well with fish.

In Nantes the sea and the river combine to serve food lovers. Beurre blanc, the most classic of Nantais recipes, and wrongly claimed by Anjou, is a perfect accompaniment for bass, shad, or pike. Anecdotal history has retained only the Nantais version of this culinary invention, for which we have Clémence Lefeuvre to thank. One day in 1890, she forgot to buy eggs and was unable to make the béarnaise sauce to go with the shad for her employer, the Marquis de Goulaine. So she improvised, creating an eggless sauce. Later, when she opened her restaurant, La Chebuette, in St.-Julien-de-Concelles near Nantes, she served the city's bourgeoisie her revolutionary recipe: pike with beurre blanc. Its simple ingredients consist of finely chopped shallots cooked in Muscadet, which is reduced and thickened with butter over a very low flame.

A white wormlike creature with two big black eyes, the *civelle* (a young eel or elver), elsewhere called the *pibale*, is both a curiosity and a delicacy. The eel spawn hatches in the Sargasso Sea, and civelles are carried by the currents toward the Atlantic coast. In winter they reach the estuaries and swim up into freshwater rivers and streams. They are fished from boats by dragging a net fixed to the end of a rod. A Nantais specialty, civelles are eaten fried or boiled. But this "white caviar" is extremely expensive: it sells for approximately $600 per pound.

*facing page*
This fountain on Place Royale celebrates the relationship Nantes has with the sea and its rivers: the city is situated on the Loire and the river's tributaries, the Erdre and Sèvre.

Thanks to its port, Nantes was one of France's major sugar-production centers in the nineteenth century; this gave rise to several food industries. The LU factory may have disappeared, its tower turned into a museum, but the Choco BN, Petit Beurre, and Paille d'Or cookies live on. A dessert characteristic of the early twentieth century and its colonial trading, Gâteau Nantais is making a strong comeback. Made with sugar, ground almonds, apricot jelly, lemon, and Antilles rum, it is most definitely not a dessert for dieters.

In the sixteenth century, the only grape variety known in the Nantes region was the Folle Blanche. It produced a wine that takes its name from the thick, sturdy appearance of the Gros Plant vine. At that time there was an influx of Dutch people settling in Nantes. Being traders and ship-owners, it was they who started shipping wine by sea. This was how Gros Plant became the first Nantais wine to gain popularity in northern European countries. In the following century, around 1635, the Burgundians moved to the Atlantic seaboard and brought with them a round-leafed grape variety called Melon. Whereas it was ill-adapted to conditions in its native region, here it thrived. South of Nantes, and further up the Loire in the region of Ancenis, the vines extend over sunny slopes that benefit from the coastal climate. The AOC designation for Muscadet applies to three different regions: AOC Muscadet de Sèvre-et-Maine, AOC Muscadet des Coteaux de la Loire, and AOC Muscadet Côtes de Grandlieu. A dry white wine, Muscadet has a fragrance that is floral or fruity (lime, hawthorn, almond), and sometimes mineral, and it is a perfect complement to fish and shellfish. Muscadet can be produced by the usual methods, or *sur lie* (on the lees). In the latter case, after fermentation the deposits are left at the bottom of the barrel until bottling.

*above*
High-priced *civelles* are tiny transparent eels, appreciated for their delicate flavor.

*below*
The best Muscadet de Sèvre-et-Maine is produced *sur lie*: it is left to age on the lees (a yeasty residue) until bottling, which gives the wine a full-bodied flavor.

*right*
La Cigale Brasserie, a landmark, is a masterpiece of art nouveau wood and ceramic decoration.

# NOIRMOUTIER

## THE BONNOTTE POTATO

NOIRMOUTIER ISLAND IS LINKED TO THE MAINLAND BY A CAUSEWAY, the Passage du Gois. This paved thoroughfare is used for about three hours a day at low tide. A strategic route in the past, today it serves the pleasure of those who wish to reach the island without going over the bridge. Despite warnings, every year unwary pedestrians caught by the tide have to take refuge on the beacons and turrets along the Gois from which coastguards come and rescue them.

The other peculiarity of the island is the Bois de la Chaise, on the outskirts of the little village of Noirmoutier. Hidden away in this seaside woodland is a resort town from another era. Houses of every shape and style, concealed by gardens carpeted with pine needles and smelling of resin, and that stand oblivious to one another on either side of sleepy lanes, are reminders of the caprices of a few rich eccentrics at the turn of the nineteenth century. To complete this image of old-fashioned charm, you need only make your way to the Plage des Dames (Ladies' Beach). With its pier stretching out into the water and its brilliant white bathing huts laid out on the edge of the wood, it remains frozen in time.

The Bois de la Chaise is made up of sea pines, green oaks, fine-leaved heath, arbutus, and mimosas, like explosions of sunshine in the month of February, which is bonnotte-planting time. This small, fragile potato arrived in Noirmoutier in the 1920s but did not survive the mechanization of the 1960s. Thanks to the efforts of the Coopérative Agricole de Noirmoutier, the bonnotte made a comeback in 1995. Planted by hand each year on February 2 (Candlemas Day) on a bed of seaweed, the bonnotte is the world's most expensive potato. It is ready for harvest in May, exactly ninety days later. The bonnotte is harvested by hand and sold the same day—immediate consumption is essential if this twenty-four-hour prize vegetable is to be enjoyed at its best. It is simply scrubbed in water and cooked in butter. Limited quantities of approximately 110 tons are exported worldwide. Traditionally, there is a bonnotte festival every year on the first Friday of May at Noirmoutier's Place du Château, where it is enjoyed with sardines caught by fishermen from St. Gilles Croix de Vie.

A large part of Noirmoutier is situated below sea level. Over the centuries its residents have protected their island by constructing dykes with marsh mud. Fifth-century Benedictine monks were the first to do this work. They drained the wetlands and turned them into salt marshes. From the twelfth to the nineteenth century, until the advent of tourism, salt was this area's main resource, transported as far afield as northern European and Baltic ports. Today, one-third of the island is salt marsh, with an annual production of around 1,650 tons. Soft, highly soluble Noirmoutier sea salt has a low sodium content but is rich in magnesium and calcium.

*facing page*
Fleur de sel forms on the surface of the salt marshes and is considered the crème de la crème of salt crystals.

*below*
Salt marshes cover a large part of the island.

The port of Herbaudière, on the west coast, is the second largest fishing port in the Vendée area. In the past sardines were the primary product, and the island had five canneries. Today boats for net fishing and line fishing set out at daybreak to catch bass, cuttlefish, and conger eels, but sole remains the most important local catch. Every year Noirmoutier's fishermen land over 2,200 tons, which puts Herbaudière among the leading French ports for sole. Noirmoutier's numerous restaurants typically prepare sole fried in butter with a sprinkling of the island's sea salt.

# SAUMUR
## FINE CRISTAL

SAUMUR HAS BEEN CALLED "THE PEARL OF ANJOU." WITH ITS CASTLE suspended between sky and river, and its limestone facades and dark slate roofs with bell towers rising above them, Saumur's reflection in the Loire River is one of quiet serenity. The town's spectacular castle has been celebrated for centuries and was used to illustrate the *Très Riches Heures du Duc de Berry*. With its four octagonal towers overlooking the Loire, the castle is one of the rare buildings to have survived with its architecture largely intact. A very fine equine museum recalls one of the things for which the region is most famous. The other can be seen from the towers: the vineyards that extend over the chalky slopes bordering the river.

A white-stone statue at the side of the road that runs alongside the Loire at Parnay was erected to honor Antoine Cristal, who appears to be smiling with satisfaction at the sight of his vines. He attained legendary status by introducing red wines on slopes traditionally dedicated to white wines and is regarded as the father of modern Champigny. The best of Saumur wines, Champigny gained popularity in the 1980s, but it is thanks to Antoine Cristal that it was first taken up seventy-five years ago. A friend of Clemenceau, supplier to the king of England and other dignitaries of this world, this Parisian who came to viticulture late in life managed to produce first-class wines. "Feet in the shade, belly in the sun," was his philosophy as far as vines were concerned. He refused to take the easy way out by resorting to chaptalization (adding sugar during fermentation to increase the alcohol content of the wine); instead, intuition led him to find natural ways to encourage grape maturation.

At the beginning of the twentieth century, after the phylloxera crisis, he built east-west-running walls on his property. He then planted the vine stocks on the north side, and made a hole in the wall above each one. As they grew, the vines came through the wall, with the bunches of grapes finally appearing in full sunshine. This original method of cultivation is still in use today. Better able to retain the heat on one side and humidity on the other, these vines produce grapes with higher alcohol potential than their immediate neighbors, and therefore produce better-quality wines. On the slopes of Parnay, the Clos des Murs, built in 1900, is planted with white-wine grapes. Along highway D406, between Champigny and St. Cyr-en-Bourg, the Clos Cristal, established in 1919, is larger, a single site of twenty-five acres planted with red-wine Cabernet Franc. In 1928, at the end of his life, Cristal bequeathed his vineyards to the Hospices de Saumur, which still run them.

*Poires tapées* are produced by the traditional method: the pears are dried in a wood oven.

Champignons de Paris is a misleading name for these fungi, which were thought to have originated in Versailles at the court of Louis XIV before they were cultivated in the Parisian catacombs. At the beginning of the twentieth century they were removed from the capital's underground due to construction of the métro; the banks of the Loire River became their next home. Today, 70 percent of champignons de Paris come from the Saumur region. Horse manure from Saumur's famous cavalry school (home to the *cadre noir*, the black-uniformed officers of the horse) serves as compost to encourage the *agaricus bisporus* to thrive in the depths of tunnels carved out of white tufa rock. In these underground caves the temperature remains cool (about 59 degrees Fahrenheit) and the humidity constant. Near Montsoreau, the Saut-du-Loup mushroom beds produce large mushrooms. When they are baked in the oven and filled with rillettes, snails, andouille sausage, or cheese, they are called *galipettes*.

Using the apples of Anjou and pears of Touraine, updated techniques of the last century are enjoying great success today. In the past these fruits were flattened but not crushed, making them easy to transport on extended voyages via ship. They were much appreciated by the English as a way to prevent scurvy. After sweating for many hours in an oven, the dehydrated fruits are flattened with a mallet before being stored. To restore their pulpiness they need only be soaked in a local wine with or without the addition of cinnamon.

*facing page*
Tufa cellars are perfect places for aging wines made using the champenoise method.

# CHANTILLY

## THE CRÈME DE LA CRÈME

ON THE EDGE OF ITS FOREST AND CLOSE TO A POPULAR RACETRACK, Chantilly Château stands between an ornamental lake and vast French-style gardens. The festivities held at the gardens created by André Le Nôtre and the buildings designed by François Mansart rivaled those the king himself could offer. The approach from the terrace, which has a statue of Constable Anne de Montmorency on horseback (the man responsible for building the Petit Château around a square courtyard), gives the measure of the place. Enclosed within balustrades, the terrace overlooks the park and the stretches of water on which visitors can go for a boat ride when the weather is nice.

The collections of paintings at Chantilly are said to be the most important in France after those of the Louvre. Admire several masterpieces of Italian art, including Raphael's *Three Graces*; a remarkable series of miniatures by Jean Fouquet; and the manuscript of the *Très Riches Heures de Duc de Berry*, which dates to the fifteenth century. But the fact that the donor's wishes have been faithfully respected makes this collection particularly unusual. He specified in his will that no alteration was to be made to the display of the works. And since nothing has been moved since 1897, it is a museum within a museum to which visitors have access.

Chantilly is known throughout the world as an important center for horseracing (2,500 thoroughbreds are trained every day at Chantilly and nearby), and for its famous whipped cream. According to one legend, chantilly cream was the result of a mistake in the kitchen. As the story goes, the Prince de Condé enjoyed receiving guests in the dairy and thatched cottage of the hamlet near the castle. At one meal, there was not enough fresh cream for everyone. A cook's assistant had the idea of whipping it to increase the volume, so all guests could partake. It is also said that Vatel, the Prince de Condé's chief cook, served a sugar-sweetened whipped cream to Louis XIV and for the occasion called it Crème Chantilly.

Leaving aside its supposed origins, Chantilly cream owed its success to the quality and freshness of the cream. Traditionally, the cream was whipped until it could stand in soft peaks that retained their shape. The dairy was destroyed during the Revolution, but in the nineteenth century the Duc d'Aumale had it, as well as the hamlet, restored; both are now situated in the castle park, where today the famous cream may be sampled. Chantilly cream is served with desserts and cakes, and with fruit, such as strawberries and raspberries; it is sometimes used to make ice cream.

*facing page*
Except for its original sixteenth-century Petit Château, Chantilly Castle dates from the nineteenth century. Its reconstruction during that period was undertaken for King Louis-Philippe's youngest son.

*below*
Sugar and vanilla are used to sweeten and flavor traditional Chantilly cream.

Smaller than Brie de Meaux, and weighing less (about three pounds), Brie de Melun is also a soft cheese made with raw cow's milk. The bloom on its rind is slightly reddish when it has matured. Its ancient origins are unknown, but it could be the ancestor of all Bries. After curdling for at least 18 hours, the fragile curd is molded with a ladle. Maturing takes at least four weeks. Brie de Melun has a strong terroir smell and a fruity flavor. It is used to make regional specialties including *croûte au Brie* (a toasted sandwich baked in the oven) and is best accompanied by a glass of Gaillac wine.

Brie de Meaux is a soft cheese made with raw cow's milk, which has a bloom on the rind and a fat content of 45 percent. This type of Brie has a flat, cylindrical shape, 14 to 15 inches in diameter, and is about one inch deep. It weighs about six pounds and is sold unwrapped on straw. During the cheese-making process, the most important stage is the molding, which is done by hand. The curd is spread in a series of thin layers with the aid of a traditional *pelle à Brie* (Brie scoop). After draining on reed mats and coating with dry salt, the cheeses remain in the maturing cellars for at least four weeks; during this time they are turned several times by hand. Brie de Meaux reaches full maturity seven to nine weeks after it is made.

# SOISSONS

## FLAVORFUL BEANS

PICARDY PROVINCE IS VIEWED WITH A CERTAIN CONDESCENSION in the realm of French cuisine. But its forceful character, rich artistic heritage, long history, and varied landscapes make it one of the finest French provinces. If it is true that a people's cuisine is an integral part of their culture, how could anyone imagine that its inhabitants would not have developed a culinary art as sophisticated as their civilization? Nature's bounty provides people here with the necessary products: game, cattle, pigs, sheep, seafood, freshwater fish, dairy, fruit, vegetables, grain, and even wine grapes.

With these categories a cuisine that is rustic in origin has evolved, but it is one that inspired chefs have succeeded in making lighter and more refined. Soissons is one of those Picardy towns where you can sit down to eat in a brasserie knowing that you will be served food that tastes good. Although one of France's most historically significant towns—Clovis, king of the Franks, made it his capital, and Pepin the Short, father of Charlemagne, chose to be crowned king here—it has suffered so greatly from the depredations of war that its architectural heritage has been largely destroyed, particularly during World War I when three-quarters of it was devastated. Fortunately, two exceptional monuments survived the bombs: the Gothic St. Gervais et St. Protais Cathedral, of which Auguste Rodin said: "There is no time of day in this cathedral, there is only eternity"; and St. Jean des Vignes Abbey, whose towers rise above the city's rooftops in all their flamboyant exuberance. Attractions are far from being limited to these two major buildings. With its spacious, breezy, and green areas—walks in the Jardin d'Horticulture, the Parc St. Crépin, and along the banks of the Aisne are recommended—Soissons is an ideal place for leisurely strolls.

It is thanks to an apparently ordinary product that the town has entered the pantheon of Picardy gastronomy. During the Hundred Years' War, Soissons was ravaged by the plague and bands of mercenaries plundered the countryside. Miraculously, inhabitants of the city found fields full of beans, which saved them from famine. Large and white, they are nourishing with a very delicate flavor. They are eaten uncooked, served in a vinaigrette, or make an excellent accompaniment to slowly stewed dishes, such as *soissoulet*, a delicious version of cassoulet. A bean-shaped confection of flaky pastry with praline celebrates these life-saving beans.

Hearty and filling, Picardy cuisine has a few specialties that will delay any thoughts of dieting. Hunger in surely satisfied with *ficelle picarde* (a crêpe with ham, cheese, cream, and mushrooms), *andimolle* (a crêpe stuffed with cream and cooked in pork fat), *anguille à la picarde* (Picardy eel cooked in an egg sauce), *truite rôtie au poivre bouilli* (baked trout with boiled pepper), *flammiche aux poireaux* (leek tart), *salade au lard* (bacon salad), and *caqhuse* (pork braised with onions and butter). One might follow up this fortifying fare with a sweet such as *gaufres au potiron* (pumpkin waffles) or *gâteau battu aux oeufs* (a brioche cake made with beaten egg whites and served with rhubarb jam).

*facing page*
Large, delicately flavored haricot white beans are harvested and dried using old-world methods.

*below*
The facade of what remains of St. Jean des Vignes Abbey, much of which was destroyed in the nineteenth century.

Picardy's forests, among them Chantilly, Compiègne, Retz, Halatte, and Crécy, are some of France's most extensive and most beautiful, and they abound with game. As a result, deer, roe-deer, boar, pheasant, duck, goose, hare, and wild rabbit have traditionally found a place on the finest of Picardy tables. Canard d'Amiens, boned, stuffed, and baked under a piecrust, is one of those dishes that has succeeded in adapting the rusticity of venison to refined aristocratic tables.

# COGNAC

## WHERE ANGELS DRINK

THIS IS A LAND OF SWEETNESS AND HARMONY, AN ALMOST FEMININE LANDSCAPE with rounded curves, pastel skies, and a mild climate—a land as slow-moving as the rivers that traverse it. Its capital is a sleepy town whose houses hide behind high blind walls, all the higher and blinder—wealth is not flaunted here—for being monied. Behind this apparent serenity and orderliness, Cognac keeps its cards close to its chest: every winter its inhabitants turn into magicians and with the aid of retorts and stills produce Cognac, one of the most perfect spirits ever conceived by man, a nectar identified the world over as the epitome of French sophistication. However, it would be a grave injustice if the product were allowed to obscure the region, if Cognac the drink left Cognac the place completely unknown.

A sleepy town, Cognac is also of a substantial fertile beauty, as might be expected of a place of vine growers with their feet firmly on the ground. The Château des Valois, the Couvent des Récollets, St. Léger Church, and the merchants' houses have the sober elegance of true nobility. Serviceability, durability, but no fancifulness; luxury, but without ostentation. It is a wonder that François I, one of the most flamboyant French monarchs, should have been born in such a respectable town. On the banks of the endlessly meandering Charente—"the most beautiful river in my kingdom," François I used to say—orchards and meadows, neat rows of vines, farms, manor houses, abbeys, keeps, and beautiful villages featuring stone buildings form landscapes of serene charm and unmatched harmony.

"Happy as God in France," is a German proverb. Doubtless the author of it was thinking of this Charentes landscape, where indeed a Biblical vocabulary is used in every context, especially when describing Cognac. Thus, *le paradis* (paradise) is the storehouse where the proprietor keeps his most precious brandies. As for the alcohol lost through the wood of the barrels during the process of evaporation, that is *la part des anges* (the angel's share). These are some very boozy angels, since their subliminal consumption of Cognac represents three times that of the French population. However, those who conceal a *paradis* on their premises do so in vain: *torula*, a fungus as fond of alcohol as they are and that gorges on the brandy fumes, blackens the walls and roof tiles, unfailingly exposing the owners to the customs and tax men.

According to legend, a distracted monk inadvertently poured some grape must into a barrel of Cognac. Put aside and forgotten for several years, the contents of the barrel turned into a sweet golden liquid with an exquisite taste. Thus Pineau des Charentes was born. Today it continues to be made using the same "recipe." A blend of grape juice (two-thirds) and Cognac (one-third), and reaching a strength of 16 to 22 proof, this aperitif wine is drunk chilled, and may also accompany certain cheeses, such as Roquefort and most other blue-veined varieties.

There are seven crus of Cognac, which are determined by the exposure of the vines and the nature of the terrain: grande champagne, which produces the most prestigious brandies; petite champagne; borderies; fins bois; bons bois; bois ordinaires; and bois-à-terroir. The main characteristic of Cognac is the double distillation process: the first *chauffe* (distilling) produces the *brouillis*, which is then cooled before the second distillation. This *bonne chauffe* produces an alcohol from which are taken off *la tête* (head, or top) and *la queue* (tail, or bottom). Only *le coeur* (the heart) is reserved. It is then aged in new oak barrels, from which it acquires its color and aroma, before being poured into old barrels, where it will continue to mature for years, even decades. Unlike wine, when Cognac is bottled it stops aging.

*facing page*
Stills used in Charentes to make *pineau*, an aperitif consisting of wine must and Cognac aged in the barrel.

*below*
A cobblestone street in the medieval section of town.

# NIORT

## ANGEL GRASS

INSURANCE COMPANIES ABOUND IN NIORT, GENERATING A LOT OF WEALTH. Built on two hills, and with the Sèvre Niortaise River running through it, it retains the two solid towers of a fortress built in the twelfth century by Richard the Lionheart. Today, the keep houses a museum devoted to regional folk art. Niort is also known for a multipurpose plant—angelica—that used to grow in the nearby marshes: as a liqueur, it is used in the most imaginative cocktails; and it is eaten creamed, with sorbets, ice creams, and pastries. It is also made into jam, coulis, or preserved fruit. Angelica lends itself to enhancing every type of delicacy.

Angelica is an umbelliferous plant with a long, thin, fluted stalk rich in fibers; it is thought to have been imported from Scandinavia in the twelfth century. In the fourteenth century it was cultivated as an herbal remedy in the monasteries of Central Europe. Believed to have magical powers, numerous medicinal virtues were attributed to it—it was thought to be an aid to digestion, a stimulant, and an antispasmodic. In Poitou, angelica was also said to cure the plague, which is why the cultivation of it was introduced to this region in 1603. It was used to concoct a potion called *vinaigre des quatre voleurs* (four robbers' vinegar), which supposedly warded off sickness. Called Angel Grass because of its "great and divine properties," it was also thought to have life-prolonging properties. In the eighteenth century, so the story goes, some nuns in the town of Niort had the idea to make candied angelica. And so this plant, previously known for its health-related virtues, acquired renown as a sweet delicacy. From then on, it gained a reputation as an aid to digestion.

Niort is still known for its angelica, but fields of it no longer reach to the foot of the keep. Instead, cultivation has moved to its outskirts. The recipe for candied angelica is a secret. The candied stalks, removed from their final immersion in syrup, are split open into thick green strips that are wrapped around various types of molds, mostly representing local flora and fauna. In a fenland area west of Niort and before Marais Poitevin, Pierre Thonnard cultivates his own angelica crops and, using artisanal production methods, has diversified the company's output.

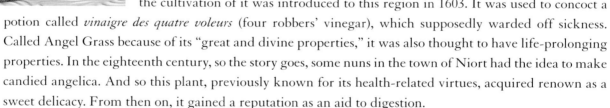

Eels are caught in the Loire River basin, in the Sèvre Niortaise River, and along the Vendée coastline.

The eel, which spends some of its life in saltwater and some in freshwater, has become one of the icons of the Marais Poitevin. The eel lives there for about a dozen years, before returning to breed and die in the Sargasso Sea. Its flesh is edible and highly prized. People have invented all kinds of techniques to fish eel and just as many recipes to prepare it. In the Marais Poitevin eel is eaten *au vert*, with sorrel in red wine, or with bacon and mushrooms flambéed in Cognac.

According to legend, some of the Arabs defeated by Charles Martel in Poitiers in 732 remained in the region with their herds of goats and created a cheese called *cheblis* (meaning goat in Arabic); it eventually turned into the word *chabichou*; this makes it one of the oldest cheeses in France. With an AOC designation since July 1990, its production is limited to the area of Haut-Poitou. Chabichou du Poitou, an ivory-colored cheese made exclusively from fresh whole goat's milk, is somewhat unctuous. It is shaped into a small cone called a *bonde*, and its white crust turns gray-blue depending on the season. It can be eaten young, after three weeks; after six weeks; or when it's drier, after two months.

*facing page*
A footbridge over the Sèvre Niortaise, which flows through the city. The spires of the Gothic Notre Dame Church appear in the background.

# OLÉRON

## HARVESTING OYSTERS

THE COAST BETWEEN THE SEUDRE AND CHARENTE RIVERS CELEBRATES the restless marriage between land and sea. The landscapes are flat, and the vast marine expanses are checkered with oyster-farm grids or quiet solitudinous terrains surveyed by old watchtowers. Brouage, Rochefort, and all the forts along the coast, such as Fort Boyard, the most telegenic of them all, are reminders that the country was for a long time buf-

*Petit-gris escargots* are snails bred mainly in the Charentes-Maritime.

feted by history. Almost half the French production of oysters (the *Crassostrea gigas* Pacific oyster, having largely supplanted the *Crassostrea angulata* Portuguese oyster), comes from this region of Marennes-Oléron. The Charentes oyster farms produce nearly 60,0000 tons of these shellfish every year.

It starts in summer, when the parent oysters that live on protected banks in the open sea release millions of microscopic eggs. Carried by the currents, only a few of them escape the perils of the sea and attach themselves to "collectors." After a year the oyster is about one and a quarter inches long and its shell is starting to harden. At this point it is removed from its support, an operation called *detroquage*. Placed in plastic mesh bags fixed onto steel trestles or set loose in the sea within enclosures marked by tall wooden stakes, the young oysters remain in these beds for six months to a year; the only time they are not submerged in seawater is during the lowest tides. Oyster quality may vary depending on the location of the beds and the richness of the marine environment. Bear in mind that an oyster can filter over a gallon of water an hour! Here, with regular attentive care, the shellfish reach adulthood.

Oysters need to be watched constantly to avoid the silting or crowding that would suffocate them. Oysters also need to be protected from their natural enemies: crabs and starfish, the fish that eat them, and the mussels that compete for their food. At four years of age the oyster has completed its growth cycle. On an ebbing tide, the oyster farmers will run their flat-bottomed boats aground in the beds and start to haul in their harvest. Once brought back to land, the oysters are sorted, then moved to special basins before being distributed for consumption. When should they be eaten? In the past, the rule was that oysters were only edible during months that contained the letter R in their name—in other words, during the colder months—because of transportation and conservation concerns. Although half the total production is consumed during Christmas and the New Year, as long as oysters are fresh, they can be eaten all year, they are just a bit milkier during the summer.

Being left to mature *en claires*, basins in which an algae called *navicule bleue* flourishes, is what distinguishes the Marennes-Oléron oyster, renowned for its nutty taste and excellent pedigree. Claires are connected to the sea by a network of canals. Navicule bleue imparts to the oyster flesh an unusual green hue. True connoisseurs should be able to distinguish three main categories of oyster: *améliorées en claire*, oysters that remain in the basins for a few weeks; *fines de claire*, oysters that remain in the basins for two months, with no more than twenty oysters to 10.75 square feet; and *spéciales de claire*, particularly flavorful oysters left to mature for six months, with only five or six oysters to 10.75 square feet.

Charente-Maritime also specializes in the farming of another shelled animal: snails. There it is called a *lumas* or *cagouille*, though it is, in fact, the *petit-gris*, the common or garden snail, *Helix aspersa*. In the wild, it takes from twelve to eighteen months to reach adulthood; it only takes six months when they are farmed. Before being consumed, snails have to be starved for five to six days. *Cagouilles à la charentaise* are prepared by first sautéing the snails in oil. Then bits of ham are added, and a stuffing is made with onions, tomatoes, garlic, white wine, salt, pepper, and spices.

*facing page*
A popular tourist destination in the summer is the picturesque Oléron Island, where wine production, fishing, and oyster farming are important economic activities.

# POITIERS

## TOURTEAU FROMAGER

FOR DECADES, WHEN FRENCH SCHOOLCHILDREN HEARD THE NAME POITIERS they thought of a battle and a date: 732. That year, Charles Martel, leading an army of Franks, put an end to Arab expansion in the West. Today, Poitiers's "Futuroscope" attracts more visitors than its battlefield. Located on the edge of town, the Futuroscope, created in 1986, was in its day the first theme park entirely dedicated to the image, to multimedia, and to cinematographic techniques. Poitou's capital, with the motto "Holy, healthy and wise," is replete with religious buildings. Notre-Dame-la-Grande, built in the twelfth century, has an exceptional facade in the poitevin Romanesque style. And whereas it is windowless, St. Pierre Cathedral is illuminated by some twenty twelfth- to thirteenth-century stained-glass windows. Lined with old private residences, the rue Grande that rises up the hill from the Clain River is one of the town's oldest streets.

Poitiers is at the heart of a major milk- and cheese-producing region. Among the most famous goat cheeses, Chabichou du Poitou is an institution. Less well known is Mothais sur Feuille, made with unpasteurized whole milk and presented on a plane or

Succulent, sweet, and flavorful Poitou melons account for one-quarter of France's production.

chestnut leaf. Also produced here are the cylindrical bûche de chèvre or truncated cone-shaped goat cheese. A regional goat-cheese-based specialty is derived from a recipe gone wrong. In the nineteenth century, goat-cheese pie was often prepared for family meals. A woman who lived near Poitiers put hers in the oven and forgot about it. When she finally remembered to retrieve it, the pie had expanded and the crust was completely burned. But when it was cut open, the pie turned out to be moist and amazingly delicious. Thus the *tourteau fromager* was born. Called *fromageou*, *fromaget*, or *galette du laboureur*, until the middle of the twentieth century it was served at spring festivals and guaranteed the success of every wedding banquet. It is a cake made with fresh goat cheese on a thin pastry base. Today, cow's-milk cheese is used in place of chèvre, but the tourteau fromager has retained its round shape and black crust. Its appearance is a surprise: a round ball that looks completely burned on top. With a texture like Genoese cake, the tourteau fromager is remarkably fresh-tasting, with good things concealed beneath its black cap: flour, butter, sugar, eggs, and fresh cheese.

For some connoisseurs, Échiré butter is the best in the world. Its reputation is such that it is not even seeking its own AOC designation. It is exported all over the world and is served at the tables of the best restaurants in France and elsewhere. Founded in 1891, the dairy is supplied with milk from within a radius of 19 miles around Échiré village. The milk is collected every day from the 66 members of the cooperative. The quality of this butter is due not to the cows but to the local pasture and to the supply of spring water available to the dairy. The Échiré dairy is exempted from some European regulations, which also helps. It is allowed to use wooden churns made of teak, a dense wood devoid of tannin and rot-proof, and that does not taint the taste of the butter. The most highly prized French butter, it is made with milk used within twenty-four hours of milking, and sold the next day. Unsalted or slightly salted, Échiré butter is molded into 11- to 22-pound blocks, and sold in baskets of poplar wood.

Poitou-Charentes is the third most important melon-producing region in France. In the Haut-Poitou, melons have been cultivated for more than a century. In 1856 a young gardener decided to cultivate them in an open field. These sweet, juicy melons with orange-colored flesh acquired a particularly fragrant and flavorful taste and quickly became popular. Today the most widely cultivated variety is the charentais cantaloupe melon. It is round with a smooth rind marked with stripes and of a light green color that yellows slightly when ripe. These melons are harvested between June and September, but peak production is reached in July and August.

*facing page*
Quaint medieval buildings and shops on Place Charles de Gaulle.

Broyé du Poitou is a specialty of Vienne county. This large, thick cookielike hard cake, which was made on special occasions—weddings, baptisms, first communions—owes its name (*broyé*, "pounded") to an age-old practice: to "cut" the cake, it was laid on a table and punched in the middle. Once broken up, the pieces of the cake were placed in a wicker basket covered with a white cloth and handed out to guests. Made with flour, eggs, and charentais butter, the broyé du Poitou was can also be flavored with spirits.

*right*
Notre Dame le Grande Church.

*far right*
Delicious Charentais *tourteau* cheese along with a variety of goat cheeses of different sizes and shapes.

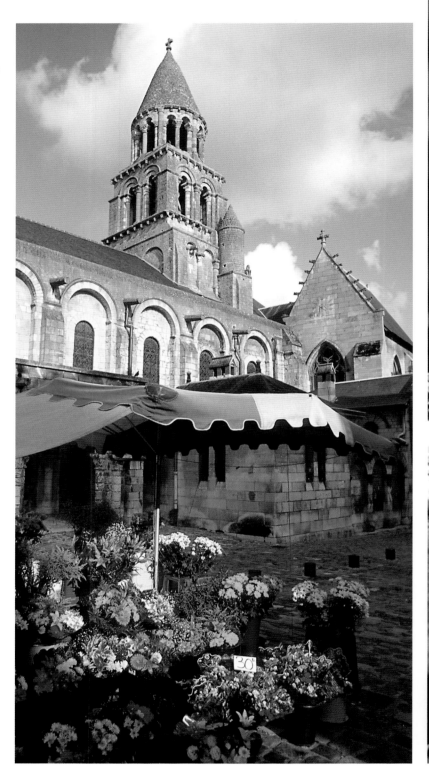

# AIX-EN-PROVENCE

## SWEETS, NUTS, AND MUSCAT GRAPES

"A BLIND MAN THINKS IT IS RAINING, BUT IF HE COULD SEE WITHOUT HIS CANE he would see one hundred blue fountains," wrote the poet Jean Cocteau. Aix-en-Provence owes its name to the waters that spring from beneath its soil. The Romans exploited their virtues by establishing baths here. The actual baths, the Thermes Sextius, are located on the site of the ancient Roman baths. Aix-en-Provence is one of the oldest spa towns in France. Today, the waters, running hot or cold, flow in all four corners of the town, with some 100 fountains scattered throughout the city. This includes the monumental Fontaine de la Rotonde, with its three statues representing Justice, Agriculture, and the Fine Arts, that tower over swans, lions, and water nymphs.

Aix also has a fountain dedicated to Good King René, with a statue of the fifteenth-century monarch holding a bunch of the Muscat grapes he introduced to the region. (He was an important player in the creation of another local specialty as well, described below.) Three fountains, including the mossy fountain that steams in winter, lie in succession along the Cours Mirabeau, the heart of the city, which is lined with plane trees, magnificent eighteenth-century mansions, and café terraces. Cézanne, whose studio in the Lauves district in the northern part of the city has been preserved in its original condition, was a regular at the Café des Deux Garçons, where he would meet his friend Émile Zola.

A little farther on, across the road, is the Maison Béchard, a confectionery shop that has been in business for over 100 years and specializes in a local delight—the *calisson*. This small, diamond-shaped white biscuit of pure sweetness was first made in Aix in 1454 to commemorate King Réne's marriage to Jeanne de Laval. According to legend, the princess never smiled. But when she tasted the biscuit, she could not help but do so. An amazed courtier asked the reason for such a manifestation of joy. "What is it that our queen is eating with so much pleasure?" "Di calin soun" was the reply in Provençal. ("They are coaxers.") And so it was the calisson came into being. Calisson did not change until the sixteenth century, when the almond tree was introduced to Provence. At the beginning of the twentieth century, Aix-en-Provence was regarded as the almond capital of the world. The recipe for the calisson has not changed since that time. It is a subtle alchemy of almonds, freshly blanched to retain the aromas, and then ground, mixed together with crystallized fruit (notably melon), and lavender honey from Provence; the whole is coated with icing sugar. No artificial colorings, flavors, or preservatives are added.

Every year, just before Christmas, Aix celebrates the new batch of olive oil on the Place de la Rotonde. Thanks to the region's Mediterranean climate, the olive tree has thrived in Provence—on its chalky rolling hills that run east to west—for over 2,000 years. The most widespread variety of olive is the *aglandau*. For the most part, it is still green when harvested. This characteristic produces a pungent oil, which is tempered by the sweetness of the *salonenque* and the *cayenne*, a type grown mostly in the olive groves of the Huveaune Valley. The virgin olive oil is obtained solely by mechanical processes; no chemicals are used.

Extending from Durance to the Mediterranean, from Mount St. Victoire (loved by Cézanne) to the Alpilles (celebrated by Van Gogh) are the Coteaux d'Aix vineyards. These vines benefit from generous sunshine and a terroir favorable to the production of great wines. Grenache, Syrah, and Cabernet Sauvignon are used to make the reds and rosés. Robust, with a strong personality, these wines go well with accompaniments and spreads such as aïoli or brandade of salt cod. Fresh and fragrant whites are produced in limited quantities, with Bourboulenc, Clairette, or Vermentino grapes. Worthy of special mention are those remarkable vineyards producing high-quality wines sold under the name of Vins de Palette. Château Simone produces a distinguished wine with aromas of violet and pinewood.

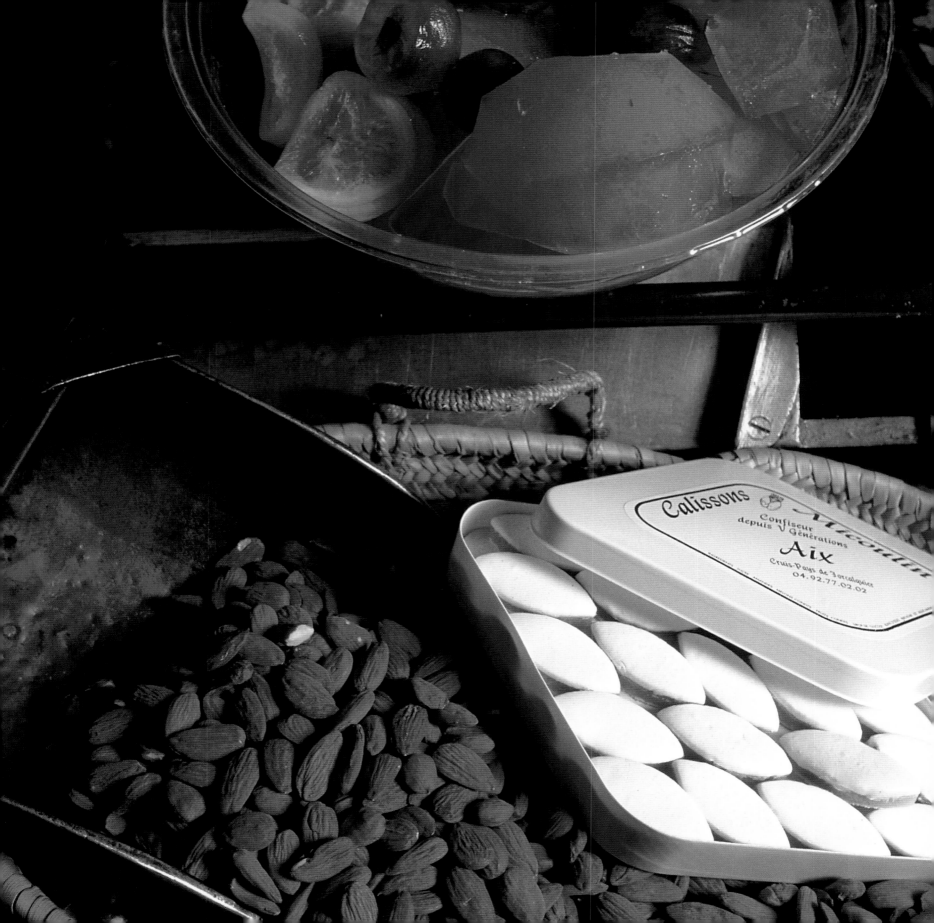

# A P T

C A N D I E D   F R U I T

AT THE FOOT OF THE LUBERON MASSIF MOUNTAIN RANGE, THE TOWN OF APT has laid claim for seven centuries to the title of candied fruit capital of the world (although it is also produced elsewhere in the region, in Saint-Remy-de-Provence). Candied-fruit-making in Provence dates back to the Middle Ages. Initially, the fruits were candied in honey. The technique was improved at the time of the Crusades with the discovery of sugar. Originally, only apothecaries knew how to treat the fruit, which they transformed into jams, jellies, fruits in syrup, and, of course, candied fruits. The popes of Avignon were very fond of these treats, and later Madame de Sévigné would compare the town of Apt to a "jam cauldron." In 1752 the town had six confectioners. In 1868, an Englishman by the name of Matthew Wood came upon this specialty and his compatriots, great lovers of sweets, put the candied fruits of Apt on the map.

Crystallized melon is an essential element in calissons.

*facing page*
A float decked out in lavender, the star attraction during the annual festival celebrating its harvest.

The largest candied fruit factory in the world is located here. It produces 33,000 tons of fruit every year, and 66,000 cherries every day. Artisanal production, although labor-intensive, is more refined than the factory-made product. First of all, the quality of good candied fruit depends on a lengthy process of preparation: the fruit is pricked, stoned, and blanched. Then, after being immersed in a light syrup (of 20-percent sugar), it goes into the *frémie*, a container in which the syrup is brought to the boiling point. This operation has to be repeated numerous times—seven to twelve successive boilings are typical. Depending on the type of fruit being treated, one to four months are needed for the process of osmosis—during which the moisture in the fruit is slowly replaced by the sugar—to take place.

When the fruit has expelled its last drop of moisture, all that is left is the taste, bright color, and firm texture of a perfectly natural product. In Apt and the surrounding area, a few artisans continue to make candied fruits by the traditional method. They use only the *fruits nobles*—the fig, mandarin orange, melon, pear, pineapple, and plum—as not all fruits can be candied. Surprisingly, candied fruits are not as sugary as one might think, but very fruity. The Confrérie du Fruit Confit d'Apt, a candied-fruit consortium, was set up in 1992 to promote this original Provençal product. It organizes annual awards, confectionery competitions, and a confectionery fair. Finally, the town of Apt has been designated "a site of outstanding gastronomic interest," a title conferred by the Conseil National des Arts Culinaires (National Council of Culinary Arts).

The Château de Mille produces one of the oldest wines of the Luberon. At what was once the summer residence of the popes of Avignon, which was built into rock that had tanks carved out of it to store the harvest, tradition has been perpetuated while utilizing modern techniques. Regional grape varieties (Clairette, Ugni, Roussanne) produce a very pale, dry white wine. The rosés, which are pleasant to drink chilled in the summer, have the elegance of the Cinsault grape and the suppleness of the Grenache. Reds are produced from the same grape varieties as Châteauneuf-du-Pape. These wines are aged in oak barrels.

The fragrant flora of the hills is the preferred environment of honey bees. The most prized honey is lavender honey, which is a lovely pale yellow. It has very fine granules and an incomparable scent and flavor. The lavender honey is harvested while the lavender fields are in flower. It is liquid for the first few months, then solidifies into tiny crystals. Provence produces nearly 1,100 tons of lavender honey each year, which represents half of its total honey production; the honeys of Provence account for close to 10 percent of France's total production.

# A R L E S

## THE FAMOUS SAISSISSOL

ARLES-LA-ROMAINE'S MOST IMPRESSIVE SIGHT—THE CRYPTOPORTICUS—IS UNDERGROUND. These vast colonnaded tunnels laid out in a horseshoe shape were built between 30 to 40 BC. They supported the ancient forum of which no trace remains. The town, nestled in a bend in the Rhône River from which it is protected by a huge embankment, was the refuge of Vincent Van Gogh. In complete anonymity, he liked to stroll in the silence and solitude of the Alyscamps Park. Arles has not preserved anything more of its ancient theatre than the grandeur of its location and two columns that give an idea of the magnificent construction.

By contrast, the arena has remained almost intact, and a tradition of bullfighting is very much alive there. In Arles, bulls are found not only in the ring but also on the menu. During the season some specialty restaurants serve an *estouffade camarguaise* or a *boeuf gardiane*; some people enjoy it. Bull meat and Camargue horsemeat were once used in Arles's *saississol*. The recipe for this famous sausage dates from the seventeenth century, according to the research of a charcutier who still makes it in the traditional way. The word's first appearance dates from July 4, 1655. A "chaircutier" by the name of Godart provided the first recorded recipe for it. It was then referred to as *sosisol* and was based on a recipe from Bologna, Italy. At that time the sausage was prepared with beef and pork marinated with herbs. It was smoked in a chimney for two weeks to promote longer storage.

Today lean cuts of pork and beef are first mixed with pork fat. The sausage meat is then seasoned with salt, herbes de Provence (a mixture of rosemary, thyme, bay leaf, and other local herbs), and some spices, to which a shot of red wine is added. After further kneading, the mixture is finally packed into beef casings, then left to dry for about three weeks. Completely natural and authentic, the red color of its meat and its delicate taste make this sausage an outstanding product. The Arles sausage is cut into thin slices and served with a glass of pastis as an aperitif, or on a slice of country bread with gherkins. It can also be good cooked in an omelette with tomatoes and onions. In the *Dictionary of Cuisine*, Alexandre Dumas comments that the Arles sausage had done less for the town's reputation than the beauty of its women. Which just goes to show that a person can be both a gourmet and a cad.

facing page
The Gardians Fête is held on May 1 and commemorates the members of an organization established in 1512: the "cowboys" who work the bulls and horses in the Camargue.

*below*
Various types of rice are grown in the Camargue, France's leading rice-producing region.

South of Arles, the Crau plain is a veritable steppe covered with pebbles. It is merino sheep country. The animals were first bred at the end of the eighteenth century primarily for producing quality wool. But today this animal is renowned less for its fleece than the taste of its meat. The merino of Arles is a sturdy animal, capable of withstanding the summer migration from sea-level grazing grounds to the high-altitude pastures nearly 10,000 feet in the Alps. Most of the lambs are sold for their meat when the sheep return.

Rice made its first appearance in southern France at the end of the thirteenth century. In 1593 Henri IV ordered that it be cultivated in Provence, in the Camargue in particular. While the other attempted sites failed, the Camargue, thanks to its position in the Rhône River delta and its climate, became the leading rice-growing area in France. Rice is sown between April and May, and in June the rice fields look like a vast green carpet. The crop is harvested starting in September, when the heads of grain are plump and golden. The Camargue produces four types of rice: round-grain sticky rice for desserts, medium-grain for paella or risotto, long-grain for salads, and extra-long-grain to accompany meat and fish.

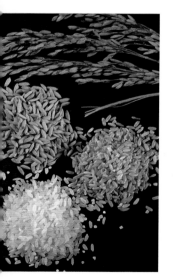

# AVIGNON

CAPITAL OF CÔTES DU RHÔNE

OVERLOOKING THE RHÔNE RIVER AND THE FAMOUS ST. BÉNÉZET BRIDGE (or the Pont D'Avignon), where people have been dancing for centuries, at least according to a rhyme that every French schoolchild has sung, there is a vine and a palace. These two things could very easily sum up the history and economy of a region that has served as a link between Mediterranean countries and northern Europe for centuries. Avignon has

Papalines d'Avignon are small liqueur-filled chocolates.

*facing page*
Dining at the foot of the towering Palais des Papes walls is a pleasant way to spend the evening.

long relied on its history and cuisine to promote what made the fortune of its most distinguished residents, and it is no accident that Côtes-du-Rhône wines are so closely associated with this papal city. From Vienna to the Mediterranean, the waters of the Rhône embrace a fine collection of labels: from Côtes-Rôties to Costières de Nîmes, taking in Condrieu, Saint-Joseph, Crozes-Hermitage, Gigondas, and the famous Châteauneuf-du-Pape. Introduced by the Greeks, and continued by the Romans, vine growing in the valley developed over time. In the fourteenth century, when the popes moved to Avignon, they called on local vine growers to satisfy their needs. Jean XXII, the second of the seven popes that ruled in the city, was responsible for the construction of the Châteauneuf-du-Pape Castle, and under his successor, Benoît II, work began on the Palais des Papes (Palace of the Popes), where he had a cellar built to store his wines.

From as early as the seventeenth century, regulations were introduced to protect the authenticity of the wines' provenance and to guarantee their quality. And in 1737 an edict issued by the king of France ruled that all barrels destined for sale and transportation had to be branded with the letters CDR, the original trademark of a Côte du Rhône soon to assume a plural identity. Inter Rhône, the organization that represents the producers and merchants of Côtes du Rhône, has its headquarters in Avignon.

This region produces an impressive range of wines, from the most prestigious high-end wines to everyday wines served in bars (sometimes these still suffer from a reputation they no longer deserve). The appellation derives its distinctive character from an astonishing diversity of soil, climate, and grape variety.

A pleasure to behold, and tasty to eat, the Monts de Venasque cherry is the product of an exceptional terroir that benefits from 4,800 hours of annual sunshine. It is cultivated on the Venasque Mountains and the slopes of the Ventoux Mountain. Farming the cherry sold under this name—the first-ever trademark for high-quality cherries, which was created in France in 1978—involves some 100 producers spread out over 20 or so communes. The cherry varieties grown include summit, belge des Monts de Venasque, duroni, and burlat. The quality of the fruit is guaranteed by official monitoring carried out by the Syndicat des Monts de Venasque. Every year at the end of May, the Confrérie de la Cerise des Monts de Venasque organizes a major cherry festival that is held in the village that gave the cherry its name, one of the prettiest hilltop villages in the Vaucluse.

Grenache imparts fruit, warmth, and fullness to the red wines, while Syrah and Mourvèdre provide color, spicy aromas, and a structure suited to aging. Cinsault is used to create some very elegant rosés and some fruity primeur wines. As for the whites, they marry fragrance with freshness thanks to expert blendings of Bourboulenc, Grenache Blanc, Roussane, Marsanne, Clairette, and Viognier.

Les Papalines d'Avignon, a little thistle-shaped chocolate filled with an oregano-flavored liqueur, was created in 1960 in memory of the popes of Avignon. The recipe for the liqueur, which was used previously to treat people with cholera, remains a secret. Some 60 plants, gathered on the spurs of the Ventoux Mountain, are required. The liqueur is created through a process of distillation, maceration, and infusion of the plants in selected spirits to which honey is added. Seventy-two hours of mysterious alchemy are needed to produce the papaline, which is made solely by artisanal methods.

# CASSIS

## WINES OF THE SUN

CASSIS IS FIRST AND FOREMOST A PORT, BUT IT WOULD BE NOTHING WITHOUT THE FAMOUS fjordlike inlets along the coastline going toward Marseilles. The best way to see these natural bays is by boat, with one of the regular excursions starting out from the port, or, for the more courageous, by setting out on foot across the garrigue scrubland. The closest one, Port-Miou, is the most accessible; En-Vau is the most beautiful, with its white cliffs plunging into the turquoise waters. These are stunning locations, although to enjoy the pleasures of the sea during the high season, ignore the crowds.

The beauty of this landscape has long been an attraction: at the inlet of Sormiou, an underwater cave was discovered in 1991 whose walls are covered with paintings 27,000 years old. "Anyone who has seen Paris but not seen Cassis can say he has seen nothing," the poet Frédéric Mistral used to declare with a touch of chauvinism. Cassis is located in the shelter of Cap Canaille, whose spectacular 1,400-foot cliffs, among the tallest in Europe, rise above the sea: it is a symphony of green, white, and blue, in which the pines, the cliffs, and the Mediterranean combine to glorious effect. The Greeks loved this coast, and there was at one time a Roman colony, but it never realized its ambitions. A castle was built in the Middle Ages, and for many centuries the village contented itself with its activities as a small fishing port. Cassis had to await the development of tourism to make its name.

After a stroll along the Promenade des Lombards and a visit to the small municipal museum that pays homage to Provençal artists, it will be time to go to the port, which is lined with houses adorned with colorful shutters. It is here, facing the *pointus* (the local fishing boats), that you should try the fruity white wine, with its "fragrance of rosemary, fern, and myrtle," in the words of Mistral. There were vines in this region before the Greeks arrived and founded Marseilles. Unfortunately, they produced only poor-quality wine. The Phocaeans (of ancient Marseilles) brought a new variety of vine, the Ugni, along with their viticulture expertise. But it was not until the twelfth century that the first tangible signs of the Cassis vineyards appeared. Eventually, in the fifteenth century, King René introduced the Muscat vine to Provence. Today the AOC area constitutes 90 percent of the vineyards of Cassis, amounting to 408 acres with a production of 600,000 to 700,000 bottles per year. This is wine to be enjoyed sitting on a terrace overlooking the harbor, caressed by a gentle winter sun and savoring freshly caught seafood.

*facing page*
A picturesque view of the town from the harbor.

*below*
Fruity and delicate dry white wines are the bulk of Cassis production, but some reds and rosés are made as well.

Bandol was the favorite wine of Louis XV and in the middle of the nineteenth century 9,600 barrels were exported every year. Shortly thereafter, phylloxera destroyed the vines; but thanks to the courage and boldness of a few vine growers, their vineyards would enjoy a strong comeback. The late-maturing Mourvèdre is a difficult and demanding grape. At Bandol, where its cultivation has been completely mastered, it accounts for 50 to 95 percent of the composition of red wines, blended with Grenache and Cinsault which add body and a lingering fragrance, respectively. Matured in wood barrels, red Bandol can be opened young, but it is the wine to keep, par excellence. A fifteen- to twenty-year-old Bandol can provide some wonderful surprises. Bandol also produces rosé (the number is increasing), and a few white wines. Learn more about them at the Maison des Vins du Bandol or directly from the producers.

After returning home from Christmas mass, it was traditional in Provence to serve guests the so-called thirteen desserts. Among the desserts are four dried fruits, called *mendiants* (Mendicants) because of their color, which is that of the robes worn by the various monastic brotherhoods; hazelnuts for the Augustines; almonds for the Carmelites; dried figs for the Franciscans; and raisins for the Dominicans. To these were added fresh or candied fruit, depending on local custom: dates, melon, white grapes, mandarins, or oranges. And, finally, sweets and cakes to top off the festivities: dark and white nougat, quince cheese, *pompe à l'huile* (a pancake made of flour cooked with olive oil and orange blossom), and *calissons d'Aix* (a marzipan sweet), each with its own significance and symbolism.

# CAVAILLON

## SLICES OF SUNSHINE

ORIGINALLY FROM AFRICA OR ASIA, MELON WAS KNOWN AND PRIZED by the Greeks and Romans. It has also been associated with the town of Cavaillon for over 1,000 years. First, there was the so-called brodé melon, a very old variety; then came the Malta, or winter, melon, with luscious white flesh. But the melon that has been the glory of town is the cantaloupe (not the same as the American "cantaloupe," which is actu-

ally muskmelon). Cultivated near Rome in Cantalupo, a papal summer residence, this cucurbitaceous plant was introduced to France at the end of the fifteenth century and was named cantaloupe. It was very soon cultivated in Cavaillon, also a papal territory. A luxury product, the melon was offered by the town authorities to visiting dignitaries. Great pains were taken to cultivate it, and it remained rare until the end of the eighteenth century. It was treated as "the caviar of fruit." The arrival of the railroad in the second half of the nineteenth century marked the beginning of a golden age for the cantaloupe, since shipping by train made it possible to get melons to Paris more easily. Local agriculture really began to flourish. The melon reached the most prestigious tables of the capital, and then of the whole world. Many countries requested seeds to grow their own, including Mali, Sardinia, Algeria, and Egypt, among others.

*Provence's melon festival is another opportunity to celebrate traditions of the region and wear period costumes.*

*facing page*
*Tasty Cavaillon melon is an aromatic and flavorful cantaloupe.*

The writer Alexandre Dumas was very fond of melons. In 1864 the Cavaillon library asked if he would donate his works to the town. He agreed on one condition: the town would give him twelve melons a year for the rest of his life. The municipal council eagerly accepted his proposal. The library received his novels, and until his death in 1870 Alexandre Dumas ate cantaloupe. At his restaurant in the town, Jean-Jacques Prévôt devotes a lot of space to the melon. And not only on the plate. He has a collection of more than 600 items: pieces of French majolica from the time of Napoleon I; early twentieth-century tin sorbet molds; lithographs, the earliest dating back to 1771; antiquarian books on gardening; and numerous canvases depicting melons. Prévôt, whose enthusiasm for his favorite fruit is inexhaustible, has even taken up painting watercolors of melons!

Beginning in mid-March, Carpentras strawberries arrive at French markets. Cultivation of the Carpentras strawberry, highly prized for its flavor, developed in this region at the end of the nineteenth century, when the madder-dying and silk industries began to die out. The Pajaro variety accounts for 90 percent of production. Early-fruiting, with low acidity and yielding large, deep-red fruit with a delicate sweetness, the Pajaro is one of four varieties of Carpentras strawberries (the others are Agatha, Ciflorette, and Garriguette).

To the north of Cavaillon, the slopes of Mont Ventoux enjoy an exceptional amount of sunshine: more than 300 days a year. In the vineyards, which are at an altitude of over 650 feet, the rich soil enables the Muscat Hamburg to be cultivated. Grown for more than a century, this variety produces a black table grape that benefits from an appellation contrôlée. This Muscat grows into beautiful bunches weighing a minimum of nine ounces. They are "thinned" (all of the bad grapes are removed) with the aid of special scissors when the grapes are picked, then they are delicately laid on a tray. The grapes should have a bloom (*fleur* or *pruine*), which is a thin whitish deposit coating the fruit. This is the guarantee of a fresh, healthy product untouched by human hands.

How do you choose a good melon? Its weight is important: the heavier the melon, the better it will be. If you detect a slight splitting of the skin, even better. Finally, check the stalk end: if it comes away easily this is a sign the melon is fully ripened.

# DIGNE
## LES BAINS
HOT SPRINGS

TWO CATHEDRALS STAND PROUDLY IN THIS VILLAGE: THE FIFTEENTH-CENTURY ST. JÉROME, which has undergone numerous alterations, and the somewhat older Notre-Dame-du-Bourg, which is considered to be one of the finest Romanesque cathedrals in Provence. Thanks to an unusual microclimate, olive trees grow within close range of snow, and, because of the altitude, the air is pure. Seven 100-degree-Fahrenheit springs gushing from the foot of the St. Pancras cliff create an ideal "spa" experience; the thermal waters are used to treat a variety of ailments. Aromatherapy is also practiced there. This is lavender country, which is celebrated every year in July with a parade. Visitors at other times of the year can see the botanical garden, opposite the municipal museum, which houses 350 species of plants representative of the region's flora.

Explorer Alexandra David-Néel settled in Digne in 1928, where she lived to be over 100 years old. She found Digne to be similar to the high plateaus of Asia, an area of interest to her: At the beginning of the twentieth century, disguised as a man, David-Néel became the first Western woman to enter Tibet. Her house has been transformed into a temple and museum of Himalayan culture. It also contains a craft shop where proceeds help Tibetan children living in exile in India.

However, this region isn't all about austerity. Sisteron lamb, still called César lamb and bred in the meadows of the Haut-Provence Alps, is one of the treasures of the local economy and cuisine. This free-range lamb is fed on ewe's milk. A "Label Rouge" (Red Label) guarantees the meat's quality. Born mainly into the flocks that move to mountain pastures for many months of the year, the lamb can be found at butchers' stalls from November to July. The meat is delicate, tender, and light-colored with little fat. Young lamb has a slight hazelnut flavor; the meat of older lamb, between 70 and 150 days old, has a darker color and gamier taste. Sisteron lamb is cooked with herbes de Provence, thyme, and rosemary. It can be served with many types of vegetables prepared in the regional style such as aubergine (eggplant) gâteau, potatoes, and preserved tomatoes. It is also eaten with vegetables stuffed with a combination of courgette (zucchini), potato, tomato, and aubergine.

Sheep have grazed on the pastures of the Alpes de Haute Provence for centuries. In the past they were an important part of the region's economy; today sheepherders still walk the fields with their flocks.

Fougasse is a style of bread with ancient origins. In the distant past, it was an unleavened loaf of pure wheat flour, cooked beneath the ashes in the oven. Fougasse appeared in Provence in the fourteenth or fifteenth century. At the end of the Middle Ages and during the Ancien Régime, it was regarded as a luxury bread eaten only on special occasions. The shape of the fougasse varies, depending on the baker who makes it. Long, round, or rectangular, the loaves always have one thing in common: slits that are cut into the bread. Fougasse can be found in almost every bakery and may be enriched with cracklings or diced bacon. There are many variations of the recipe: fougasse with olives, cheese, onions, and even flavored with orange-flower water.

Génépi, or wormwood, is an herb that grows mostly in the Alps and is similar to a mountain artemisia. People who live in the mountains use it to make a liqueur of astonishing flavor and exceptional aromatic qualities, based on "secret" recipes and methods that are passed down within families. Every family has its own variations, but the basic recipe is simple: macerate 40 sprigs of wormwood with 40 lumps of sugar for 40 days to obtain a 40-proof green liqueur. Génépi is usually served as a digestif.

facing page Baguettes are pictured with fougasse, a traditional type of bread with slits or holes that is often prepared using a variety of grains.

*218*

# MANOSQUE

## FORBIDDEN FRUIT

NESTLED BETWEEN FIVE HILLS PLANTED WITH OLIVE TREES, THE PANORAMIC VIEW from Manosque extends from the clear line of the Alps to the Luberon, taking in the St. Victoire Mountain and the St. Baume Massif, all places dear to artists. Girded with medieval gates, the town has all the attractions of Provence: winding streets, little squares shaded by plane trees, babbling fountains, and elegant facades of private houses recalling the prosperity of another age.

It was also home to nature poet, advocate of the simple life, and forward-thinking ecologist Jean Giono. The town is one of the gateways to the Provençal highlands, which inspired almost all of Giono's work. East of Manosque, between the Durance and Verdon rivers, stretches the Valensole plateau. In the past, as soon as the first summer sun started to beat down on Provence, large flocks of sheep would migrate from the plains to higher ground. An "ocean of beasts around a few men," in Giono's words, they would cross this vast checkerboard of lavender and wheat, watched over by a motionless guard of almond trees.

The almond tree has grown in Provence since antiquity. It adores the light and the heat, and its flowers, which bloom before the end of winter, announce the arrival of warmer weather. The nuts used to be crushed for oil or almond paste. The princesse almond, the finest, was once much sought-after for pastry making and confectionery—especially used to make calissons and nougat—but because of its fragility more robust varieties are now preferred. But the Valensole plateau remains the most fertile for almond trees, and it still produces nuts of superior quality. The almond can be used sugared or salted, in pâtés or tapenades. It is eaten dry year-round, from the time it is harvested in September, or, at end of June to the beginning of July, when it is fresh and green (it is called an *amandon* at this stage).

When Giono was alive, he opposed as a matter of principle projects for the damming of the Durance, which have made possible the irrigation of previously unfertile land and allowed numerous crops to be grown. The upper Durance River Valley produces other fruit, notably pears and apples, in particular the golden variety. The low humidity and abundant light that come with three hundred days of annual sunshine give these superior fruits a recognizable quality that makes them unique.

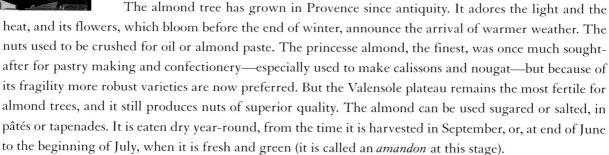

A panoramic view of the town.

*facing page*
Golden Delicious apples, pears, and almonds are cultivated in the Durance Valley.

It is easy to recognize: a small, round cheese about three inches in diameter, wrapped in a chestnut leaf and tied with a strip of raffia. Made from goat's milk, the banon takes its name from an old fortified village set on the fringes of the Montagne de Lure. And it is from these upland meadows that the best milk comes. The banon is also produced in another version flavored with an aromatic herb, with sarriette replacing the chestnut leaf. Both versions are matured for two weeks to two months, depending on whether a creamy or slightly drier consistency is preferred. These two cheeses should be eaten from the end of spring to the beginning of autumn (the artisanal product is best). They go well with a Mont Ventoux or a Côteaux de la Durance wine.

In the Middle Ages gatherers of medicinal plants became peddlers of the distilled herbs they had carefully picked in the Montagne de Lure. In the seventeenth and eighteenth centuries they settled in the region as druggists and apothecaries; in the nineteenth century, some became pharmacists, others distillers. They developed beverages with purgative, tonic, digestive, diuretic, or laxative properties; at the end of the century they specialized in the production of liqueurs and spirits. For more than a century, Distilleries et Domaines de Provence in Forcalquier has continued to live up to its heritage, developing liqueurs with peach, almond, and Provence thyme, as well as herb and spice elixirs, and orange and walnut wines.

# MARSEILLE

## CLASSIC BOUILLABAISSE

PERCHED ON TOP OF NOTRE-DAME DE LA GARDE, THE CHURCH OVERLOOKING MARSEILLES, stands the "Good Mother" with her gaze fixed on the seaward horizon as if she wanted to be sure that all her boats were safely back to port. The walls of this legendary church are covered with ex-votos, symbols of the trust placed in it by the faithful. In Marseilles, whether people are religious or not, everyone believes in the "Good Mother."

On the other side of the harbor is the warren of streets and steps known as the Panier. In this boldly colored former Italian quarter, a few bars and pizzerias recall bygone days. No doubt to exorcize a reputation that clings to the city the way a pastis label sticks to the bottle, carved in stone at the entrance to Old Port is a "borsalino," the felt hat characteristic of the gangsters of the belle epoque, but which is not about to be carried away by the mistral winds.

At once the heart, soul, and symbol of Marseilles, the Old Port, transformed into a pleasure harbor, still shelters a few small fishing boats. Their catches supply the stalls of the fishmongers on Quai des Belges, whose liveliness and verbal exuberance are legendary. They attract customers with their loud voices and unmistakable accents. Fish caught almost in the center of town is used to make bouillabaisse, the city's classic dish. In Marseilles, it is said that there are as many recipes as there are cooks. Everyone is sure that he or she has the only authentic recipe of what was originally fishermen's fare. Some claim that true bouillabaisse requires the inclusion of some forty different types of fish!

Typical ingredients are debated but usually a dozen or more types of fish and shellfish are used: conger and moray eels, and crabs, as well as *rascasse* (scorpion fish), weever, gurnard, and John Dory. A chef's skill level is revealed in the time he cooks the ingredients over a brisk heat, called "bouil" in Provençal, and the moment when he decides to remove his cooking pot from the heat, the crucial phase called "abaisso." Bouillabaisse is eaten with croutons spread with *rouille*, a thick sauce made with garlic, sweet red pepper, and olive oil. Another fish specialty eaten in Marseilles is *bourride*. Unlike bouillabaisse, which is made with shellfish, bourride is cooked exclusively with white fish.

*facing page*
Water-clouded Pastis is a delicious licorice-flavored apertif that is perfect in all seasons.

*below*
A view from the old port.

This is a typical Marseilles specialty, and, as is usual, the recipe varies according to the creativity of the cook. *Pieds-paquets* or *pieds et paquets* are strips of sheep's tripe stuffed with minced ham, garlic, and herbs. These strips are rolled and simmered for up to eight hours in a broth flavored with white wine and with sheep's trotters, lard, and tomatoes. Boiled potatoes are served alongside; a white Côtes du Rhône is the recommended beverage.

An anise-based liqueur that is served with the addition of cold water, pastis is a thirst-quenching, tongue-loosening drink. From ancient times, anise was consumed for its medicinal properties. In 1915 the ravages caused by absinthe led to a ban on anise-flavored alcoholic beverages. Clandestine aperitifs became popular, so the French state, faced with this loss of potential tax revenues, licensed a dozen products in 1932. These were again banned but have been licensed since 1951; today, anise liqueur, its official name, can't be more than 45 proof. The *petit jaune* has become synonymous with sunshine and idleness—in short, vacations. The preparation is easy: pour a few drops into a glass and add a little cold water. Curiously, the earliest consumers of pastis (meaning "mixture" in Provençal) were in northern France and around Paris. Pastis subtly complements other tastes and colors: mixed with mint syrup it becomes *un perroquet* (a parrot); with grenadine, *un tomate* (a tomato); and with orgeat syrup, *une mauresque* (a Moorish woman).

Early on the morning of February 2 is when the festivities begin. It is barely six o'clock when the faithful enter the crypt of Saint Victor Abbey, which overlooks the entrance of the Old Port. They light candles in honor of Our Lady of the New Fire. After devotional observances that take place as the boats are returning to port after a night's fishing, the archbishop who leads the proceedings blesses the town and the sea. After the church ceremony it is tradition for Marseilles residents to go to the Four des Navettes. There they buy little biscuits whose boat shape recalls the vessel that brought Saint Marie to Provence's coast. These cakes, which are kept for the whole year as devotional objects, are the same types of cakes that were distributed in the church in the thirteenth century. They have been made at Four des Navettes since 1871, according to a secret recipe; they can be purchased throughout the year.

*right*
Founded in 1781, the Four des Navettes bakery produces traditional Candlemas cookies.

*far right*
Notre Dame de la Garde in its place of prominence overlooking the city and port.

*below*
A classic French dish, bouillabaisse fish stew is served with garlic-flavored croutons with *rouille*, a spicy saffron-garlic mayonnaise.

# MENTON

CITRUS FRUITS

FEBRUARY HAS AN ACIDIC AFTERTASTE IN MENTON—but this does not set anyone's teeth on edge. Every year during the month, the town celebrates the lemon, its favorite fruit. Eve supposedly brought a lemon when she was driven from earthly paradise by divine wrath. When Adam told her to get rid of the golden fruit she hid it in the shelter of Garavan Bay, which reminded her of Eden. Such is the origin of Menton's first lemon tree.

In the eighteenth century the cultivation of this citrus fruit was the area's main source of income. In the middle of the nineteenth century the town exported 35 million lemons per year to England, Germany, Russia, and North America. Today the flavor of the Menton lemon is still acclaimed, and the fruit is used by famous chefs such as Alain Ducasse, Paul Bocuse, and the Troisgros brothers. Thousands of visitors take part in the annual Lemon Festival and watch the procession of floats with displays made out of oranges and lemons. In total, over 130 tons of fruit (imported from Spain!) are used. This festival provides an opportunity to discover a town that, without quite being Eden, with its 316 days of sunshine each year, has at least retained its spirit, its gardens, and its scents.

At the end of the 1800s, the English brought their love of gardens to Menton. Like Queen Victoria's physician, who came to strengthen his delicate health under the Riviera's sun, there were many that forsook the London fog for what was to become the Côte d'Azur. Returning from the colonies, they brought with them in their baggage exotic trees and plants. They also adapted the art of the English-style garden to the terrain. This produced some stunning parks that embraced the mountainside, overlooked the sea, and, thanks to species originating from the southern hemisphere, were adorned with blooming flowers throughout the year. Some gardens are private, but at the end of the Garavan Bay the public gardens of the Villa Maria Serena contain subtropical species found nowhere else in Europe. Other must-see places to visit include the maze at Val Rahmeh's Botanical Garden; the Serre de la Madone, a garden designated as a historic monument; and the Palais Carnolès, where one can relish the fragrances of grounds that contain a unique collection of citrus trees, including that of the Menton lemon. There is also the superb Jardin des Romanciers. Shaded by fig, banana, and palm trees, it was here that the writer Vicente Blasco Ibáñez, who came to the Côte d'Azur in 1921, had his house. He hoped that his garden would be a tribute to nature and to literature. In Menton, artists have become gardeners, while gardeners are always artists.

Lemons and oranges are honored at the Fête du Citron (Citrus Festival).

*facing page*
The old town with the baroque St. Michel Archange Church.

The pissaladière is a savory tart and a specialty almost impossible to re-create in its original form—with good reason! Its name derives from *pissalat*, a paste that used to be made by salting fish fry. Menton, along with Nice, is one of the four Mediterranean municipalities legally permitted to fish for baby sardines as slender as needles and three-quarters of an inch long. Today, fishing for these sardines is rare and it is difficult to find authentic pissalat. Most pissaladière tarts are made from bread dough on which a purée of anchovies and olives sits atop a bed of finely sliced onions.

A native of Champagne, Marguerite Herbin moved to the south in 1975. She decided to pay homage to the local iconic fruit by making lemon preserves. Her first attempts were a bit like toffee, but it did not take her long to become expert at cooking the fruit. Her successors at the Arche des Confitures still use the same artisanal methods. The preserves are cooked in the old way, in small batches and stirred by hand. And no one has forgotten Herbin's bold preserve combinations: tomato and orange; zucchini and pineapple; or tomato, eggplant, and ginger.

# SAINT-TROPEZ
## PROVENCE TART TROPÉZIENNE

DOES ST. TROPEZ REQUIRE ANY INTRODUCTION? Despite the celebrities and the crowds rubbing elbows on its quaysides, despite the showy yachts of millionaires that have replaced the small fishing boats, this little Provençal port has not betrayed its past—nor its memory. Before it became the refuge of movie stars, St. Tropez had attracted artists and writers. Paul Signac was one of the first to be seduced by the quality of the light, followed by Matisse and many others. Guy de Maupassant saw the cobbled streets glisten "like the scales of sardines." Then came actors, show business, the razzle-dazzle and the parties. Even with the summer invasion of visitors and celebrity-spotters the village has managed to preserve the charm of its little streets. Aside from gawking, sightseers also come to visit the citadel, which in the seventeenth century defended the magnificent bay; and the Annonciade, one of the finest art galleries on the Côte d'Azur.

The local specialty has been nicknamed "the star of desserts, dessert of the stars." One would expect no less of the place. *Tarte tropézienne* has every reason to be proud of its origins, and how it is made is still a carefully guarded secret. Alexandre Micka, a Polish worker, was its inspired creator. He landed in Provence with the U.S. Army before settling down as a baker on Place de la Mairie in what was soon to become one of the most famous ports in the world. He made bread, pizzas, and a cake based on a recipe from his Polish grandmother. In 1955 the beach of Ramatuelle became the location for a film that was also to dominate news headlines worldwide. It was directed by Roger Vadim and starred Jean-Louis Trintignant and Brigitte Bardot. Alexandre Micka catered for the film crew, and served his tart to the technicians and actors; Bardot was particularly fond of it and suggested calling it *tarte tropézienne*. In 1985 Alexandre Micka retired, selling his secrets and his bakery to the enterprising Albert Dufrêne, who was well connected, especially with the world of competitive car racing. Soon *tarte tropézienne* became known worldwide. Today the tart is still made in the traditional way using fresh products (in larger quantities, though): 4,000 eggs, 1,100 pounds of flour, and about 100 gallons of milk per day; 4,400 pounds of butter and 6,600 pounds of sugar per week. During the summer the bakery sells more than 1,000 tarts daily.

A view of the town and the bay from above.

*facing page*
Essential herbs of Provence include thyme, rosemary, bay, savory, and oregano.

There are five herbs that are essential to Provençal cuisine: thyme, gathered before it flowers, is used to prepare grills and marinades; rosemary, which should be used sparingly so its flavor doesn't overpower dishes, can be used to infuse oils (twigs of it may replace skewers when grilling); bay leaves, either powdered or whole, are used in marinades, court-bouillon, and many types of ratatouille; savory, which is excellent for seasoning salads and stews; and marjoram (the wild variety is another name for oregano), which is an ideal seasoning for pizzas and tomato coulis.

Every year in January, St. Marcel is celebrated in an unusual way. A statue of the saint is paraded through the streets to the sound of Provençal flutes, drums, and gunshots. At the end of the procession the participants make their way to church to attend mass. At regular intervals during the ceremony, members of the congregation vie with each other by jumping up and down on the spot. In the past, the success of the festival was judged by the number of chairs broken.

228

# BEAUFORT

## GOLDEN BLISS

A FRUITY CHEESE, BEAUFORT OWES ITS SUBTLE AROMA TO THE VARIETY OF FLORA on the mountain pastures of Savoie. During the summer season Tarine or Abondance dairy cattle graze on the heights of Beaufortain, Maurienne, Tarentaise, and Val d'Arly. Their milk is used to make a cheese that gastronome Jean-Anthelme Brillat-Savarin called "the prince of Gruyères."

To make this fine cheese, a worker bends over a large copper pot. In his hands he holds the ends of a long metal rod slipped into a piece of cheesecloth that a fellow worker, arms outstretched, holds taut. With a deft movement he plunges the cloth into the pot and lifts it out full and dripping with whey. Another cheese has just been caught in the cheesecloth trap. This is the first stage in the making of what will become a 110-pound wheel of cheese. Before this part of the process, no less than 132 gallons of milk will have gone into it—in addition to some hard work and a great deal of patience. To start with, the milk is heated to a temperature of 86 degrees Fahrenheit. Rennet is added to make it curdle. This produces the curd, which would form a solid mass if it were not broken up into small grains with the aid of a curdcutter, a kind of steel-wire comb. Once the curd has been caught in the cheesecloth, it is taken out and carried with the aid of a hoist onto a worktable, then pressed into the wooden mold to shape it. A distinctive feature of Beaufort, apart from its taste, is its concave heel.

The mold will then be turned regularly so that the cheese drains, and every two hours the cloth will be changed, increasing the pressure. After twenty-four hours, the wheel is removed from the press and soaked in a brine bath before being taken to the cellar. There, the Beaufort will mature in a damp environment and at a constant temperature. Every day for six months it will be turned and rubbed with salt. Beaufort benefits from an appellation contrôlée. It can be found at all times of year, but the best cheese is made with the milk of cows that graze freely on the mountain pastures at heights of nearly 10,000 feet. This particular cheese is sold in winter or spring. The very best quality "chalet d'alpage" Beaufort is made by traditional methods twice daily, in a mountain chalet at nearly 5,000 feet. The best way to eat it is with a glass of the local Mondeuse, a quaffable rustic red wine.

*facing page*
Beaufort is a hard, cooked cheese pressed in beechwood molds.

*below*
This small mountain community survives on tourism and dairy produce.

A Savoie specialty, *diots* are small sausages that are sometimes smoked. They are made with pork fillet and pork fat to which seasonings and sometimes local red or white wine are added. In the nineteenth century diots with vegetable soup was a substantial meal. These sausages are served with potatoes or *crozets*, a small, flat, square pasta made with wheat flour and eggs. Crozets are a traditional food of this region and every valley has its own recipe; they are served with butter or au gratin with Beaufort cheese.

Savoie is a land of vineyards on slopes. In the Vallée de l'Isère, the whites of Abymes, Apremont, or Chignin, made from the late-growing grape variety Jacquère, are dry wines, whereas the reds of Cruet and Montmélian, made from Mondeuse and Gamay, are light and fragrant. At Seyssel, in the Rhône Valley, a wine is produced from a grape brought back from Cyprus at the time of the Crusades. Altesse, also called Roussette, which is not found anywhere else, produces a very delicately scented, supple, full-bodied golden white. Savoie whites are best chilled but not served ice cold, and they pair especially well with fish, shellfish, savoyard fondue, raclette, and all Savoie cheeses. Served at 54 to 59 degrees Fahrenheit., the red wines go well with poultry and salted foods.

# BEAUJEU

## WHERE BEAUJOLAIS WAS BORN

IT HAS GIVEN ITS NAME TO A REGION AND, ABOVE ALL, TO A WINE—one known from Oslo to Beijing, New York, and Sydney. Beaujeu, the capital of Beaujolais, is situated in the heart of a wine region that every third Thursday of November causes people throughout the world to rejoice.

The long street flanked with gray houses that leads into town from Villefranche-sur-Saône should not discourage visitors from stopping here. Peaceful, and on better acquaintance, charming, Beaujeu has retained some fine vestiges of its 7,000-year history, especially in the center around St. Nicholas Church, built in the eleventh and twelfth centuries. A few steps away, in a Renaissance house, is the Les Sources du Beaujolais wine center, where the history of wine-making in the Beaujolais region is presented in an intelligent and fun way. A seventeenth-century residence is home to the town hall, the local tourist office, and, most importantly, the Marius-Audin Museum, devoted to local crafts and traditions. Another notable building is the Hôtel de la Tour, on the Place de la Liberté, where Louis XI supposedly stayed during one of his visits to the Beaujolais region. But the town's most iconic monument is unquestionably its hospital, the Hospices, which dates from the medieval period. It was founded as early as 1240, when a canon of Notre-Dame de Beaujeu endowed the parish with a few beds for the sick.

High-quality oils made from nuts—hazelnuts, pistachios, walnuts, and others—are local specialties. These nut oils are produced in limited quantities.

Thanks to numerous donations of funds, land, and vineyards, the Hospices became progressively wealthier and was able to accommodate a growing number of the sick and the poor. It was at the end of the eighteenth century that an important moment in the hospital's history occurred. In 1797 a decision was made to auction off the wine produced from its vineyards. As a result, Beaujeu has the distinction of hosting the oldest benefit sale of this type in France. In 1814 the hospital was partly destroyed in a fire and the rebuilding, which entailed the demolition of almost all the old buildings—with the notable exception of a superb seventeenth-century pharmacy—was not completed until 1868. The Hospices now owns, among other things, 203 acres of vines producing Beaujolais, Régnié, Morgon, and Brouilly, making it the third largest vineyard in the Beaujolais region. The sales, which for more than 200 years have taken place on the second Saturday of December, continue as in the past to contribute to the financing of the hospital.

Beaujolais wines come from one grape, the Gamay. But there is an astonishing variety of wine produced from this single source. All too often it is only the light, crisp, charming primeur wines, ritually put on the market on the third Thursday of November, that are well known, along with the Beaujolais-Villages, which are equally fresh and breezy but can age without losing their fruitiness. It is possibly regrettable that the fame of these two wines should overshadow the ten Beaujolais vintage wines whose names—Brouilly, Chénas, Chiroubles, Côte de Brouilly, Fleurie, Fuliénas, Morgon, Moulin-à-Vent, Régnié, and Saint-Amour—are dear to wine lovers. Complex, noble, elegant, and structured, these great aristocrats can be stored for several years before drinking.

It was by chance that Jean-Marc Montegottero came across an old oil press while rummaging around in a shed on property bought by his father. He restored it and pressed a gallon or so of walnut oil just for fun. He developed a growing interest and set about learning the skills of the trade by working in established oil mills. Today he is recognized as one of the best artisanal specialty oil producers in France, and now many of the best chefs will use only his products, which include almond, hazelnut, pistachio, walnut, pecan, sesame, and poppyseed oils.

*facing page*
Beaujolais vines in the autumn.

# BOURG EN-BRESSE

## RHÔNE—ALPES

## HOME OF KING CAPON AND QUEEN HEN

LOCALS TAKE GREAT PRIDE IN THE FACT THAT FOR A LONG TIME BRESSE was considered impregnable, protected by its heavily wooded pasturelands, hedgerows, sunken roads, and clay soil in which enemy armies became mired. A fiefdom of the duke of Savoy, it was annexed to France by Henri IV relatively late. According to legend, until his dying day the king harbored horrible memories of floundering in the mud of Bresse. Despite its isolation—or perhaps because of it—this small province developed a particularly unusual rural culture. Its architectural heritage is surprisingly plentiful and charming, including Roman churches and chapels, dovecotes, communal bakehouses, windmills, and timber-framed cobwork farmhouses with their spectacular "Saracen" chimneys.

While its capital, Bourg-en-Bresse, boasts a few fine buildings—the collegiate church of Notre-Dame (built during the fifteenth and sixteenth centuries), the half-timbered houses and private residences in the historic city center—it is on the outskirts of the town where one of France's most magnificent religious monuments can be found: Brou Church, flanked by a monastery arranged around three cloisters, is justly considered a masterpiece of Gothic architecture. In addition to its rood screen, stained glass, and very fine stalls, it contains three royal tombs—those of Marguerite of Austria, Marguerite de Bourbon, and Philibert the Handsome—of exceptional craftsmanship. Housed in the monastery buildings is a fine arts museum devoted to French, Flemish, and Italian sculpture and decorative arts from the twelfth to the twentieth centuries. This church alone justifies a visit to Bresse.

But there is another, equally important, reason to go: the cuisine of Bresse, which uses produce renowned for its quality—cheeses, fish from the Dombes, and poultry, among other items—has profoundly influenced French gastronomy. Bresse poultry—spring chickens, capons, roasting hens, and turkeys fattened on grassy pastureland, dairy products, wheat and corn, and raised with care—acquire a succulent, tender, and flavorful flesh unlike any other. Since the early nineteenth century, when two of the most celebrated French gastronomes, Alexandre Grimod de La Reynière and Jean-Anthelme Brillat-Savarin, introduced them to the aristocracy and middle classes throughout Europe, Bresse poultry has had a special place on gourmet tables. Today, the poultry is protected by an *appellation d'origine contrôlée*.

*facing page*
A view of the city's red roofs and its Notre Dame Cathedral.

*below*
Bresse capons are especially succulent and delicious thanks to the careful way they are raised and fed.

While Bresse's vineyards no longer exist, a result of the destruction caused by phylloxera at the end of the nineteenth century and the effects of World War I, neighboring Bugey maintains an ancient viticulture tradition. Though sales of its wines are restricted to about 528,000 gallons per year, still or sparkling white or red Seyessel; white or red Roussette; the sparkling wine Montagnieu; and an unusual sparkling rosé Cerdon, are all worthy of respect.

To the south of Bourg-en-Bresse, the Dombes is "a land of a thousand ponds," most of them natural, but which in the Middle Ages were adapted for fish breeding. To the tune of 440 to 880 pounds per two-and-a-half acres, the approximately 30,000 acres of pools produce tench, roach, rudd, and, above all, carp and pike, noble fish used frequently in Bresse cuisine. Pike with *beurre blanc* (made from shallots and wine vinegar whisked with butter) or smoked fillet of carp are delicacies that are best savored at the inns of the Dombes. To the horror of France's English neighbors, the pools also produce frogs, of which only the thighs were eaten. These frogs are now a protected species in France, but these tasty amphibians are now imported from Turkey, Eygpt, and China.

# GRENOBLE
## MONASTIC LIQUEURS

THE CAPITAL OF THE FRENCH ALPS, GRENOBLE EXTENDS OVER A HUGE VALLEY at the foot of the Vercors cliffs, the peaks of Belledonne, and the Massif de la Chartreuse. Indeed, Stendhal, who knew the region well, saw "at the end of every street a mountain." In the past the town was surrounded by a wall, of which only a few vestiges remain—including the fort of the Bastille, which can be reached by cable car or by climbing 400 steps. At the top there's a panoramic view over the city: the clay tiles of the old parts of town, with several medieval bell towers rising above them, and over the modern town, with its renowned university and technology center. Grenoble is also one of the historic capitals of Dauphiné, a region that, until the French Revolution, remained in the possession of the heir to the throne, the dauphin.

Dauphiné cuisine is famous for four dishes prepared au gratin, although simple dishes were not always in favor here. There are references to local gastronomic history of the sixteenth century, and a recipe for *marmite de Lesdiguières* (Lesdiguières stew), served at a wedding banquet. Among the ingredients were 40 pigs' trotters, two calves' heads, eight good-sized chickens, thirty-three pounds of beef, four gallons of red wine, and a bottle of Cognac. It made enough to serve at least 50 guests. Of the four traditional gratinée dishes, one made with millet is rarely prepared, while the one with shrimp tails has become luxury fare. Gratinéed pumpkin still has its fans, but the dish that is most well known is made with potatoes. It is a reminder that the now very widespread tuber came into France across the Alps from Italy long before it was adopted in other French regions. The famous gratinéed dish is called *dauphinois*. Originating in the Vercors, it is made with potatoes and unpasteurized milk. It is first cooked over a flame, then in the oven in a buttered dish rubbed with garlic. There are as many recipes for gratinée dauphinois as there are valleys in Dauphiné, and the tendency these days is to use fresh cream instead of unpasteurized milk. On the other hand, all the recipes are consistent regarding two ingredients that should not be included: egg, which would strip the dish of its mellow lusciousness; and cheese, whether Gruyère or Emmenthaler, which would alter the taste of the cream.

A romantic nighttime view of the city reflected in the Isère River.

*facing page*
The charming Place Saint Claire market is one of the most picturesque anywhere.

The complicated formula for a life-prolonging elixir was given to the monks of the Vauvert charterhouse outside of Paris at the beginning of the seventeenth century. A few years later it came into the hands of the monks of the Grande Chartreuse, the chief Carthusian monastery, who simplified the elixir with the goal of selling it. Green Chartreuse, which is 55-percent alcohol and described as a "liqueur of health," was created in 1764. It was embraced immediately, but success was limited to the Dauphiné region. In 1838 the recipe was adapted to produce a sweeter, less potent liqueur, yellow Chartreuse, which is only 40-percent alcohol. To this day, the monks still create Chartreuse in secrecy—and they alone know the recipes for these sweet elixirs, which are made using 130 plants. It allows the monks of Chartreuse to survive and to continue praying in silence and solitude, in the spirit of the founder of the order, St. Bruno.

The *noix* (walnut) originally came from the East and was introduced to France by the Romans, who called it *jovis glans* (Jupiter's nut). Cultivation of the walnut in France developed mainly in the Périgord and Dauphiné regions. Noix de Grenoble won AOC status in 1938. This walnut, which comes in three varieties, franquette, mayette, and parisienne, is distinguished by and appreciated for its thin skin and the sweetness of its pale kernel; it is also said to possess healing properties: eating these walnuts is thought to reduce heart disease. Harvested at the beginning of September, fresh nuts are eaten soon after picking; dried varieties keep for a year.

Fresh walnuts can be eaten from September to November, and year-round if they are dried. The sweet flavor of the walnut creates a balance in appetizers, salads, and even meat or fish dishes; walnuts are also wonderful in cheeses and desserts.

*right*
*Gratin dauphinois* (scalloped potatoes) is a traditional gratin recipe using Bintje potatoes, creamy yellow-fleshed tubers that are also perfect for roasting and frying.

*facing page*
Green Chartreuse, a liqueur made from 130 plants and based on a secret recipe created by monks, can be added to cocktails and mixed with orange juice, pomegranate syrup, mint syrup, vodka, tequila, or whiskey.

# L Y O N

MÈRES AND BOUCHONS

LYON IS SADDLED WITH THE UNWARRANTED REPUTATION OF BEING AUSTERE and unwelcoming. Only people who have never wandered through the streets of Old Lyon, have never entered the aroma-filled, cozy bouchons, or never shopped at the Croix-Rousse market can still believe this myth. Lyon is, indisputably, one of the most beautiful cities in France, and it has one of the most glorious histories of any city in the country. Two thousand years ago it already numbered among the great metropolises of the Roman Empire, proudly bearing the title of "capital of the Gauls." Between its two hills, Fourvière and Croix-Rousse, and its two rivers, the Rhône and the Saône, the entire city harbors an architectural heritage of incomparable wealth—it has even been listed as a World Heritage Site.

Attractions in this city include the Gallo-Roman remains of ancient Lugdunum; Vieux Lyon, the old town whose Gothic and Renaissance fabric is the most extensive in the world after Venice; and, finally, the quarter known as the Presqu'île, a veritable repository of architecture and design of centuries past, where you pass straight from a Renaissance alleyway to an art deco building, from a Gothic church to a Belle Époque arcade, from Bartholdi to David Buren. Far from remaining fixed in contemplation of its past, Lyon is also leading the way in twenty-first-century urban planning, with bold projects such as the remodeling of the Opera by Jean Nouvel, or Renzo Piano Cité Internationale. In short, it is the only city that might have competed with Paris for the position of capital of France.

There is one area, however, in which it has retained supremacy: Lyon cuisine embodies the best of French gastronomy, which celebrates classicism and inventiveness. Lying at the crossroads between north and south, between the France of butter and the France of oil, it is surrounded by regions of extraordinary physical and climatic variety that provide it with an inexhaustible range of foods: dairy products, cheeses, and charcuterie from the Alps; pork products and mushrooms from Jura; fruit and wine from the Rhône River Valley; vegetables from the Ain River Valley; freshwater fish from the Dombes and the alpine lakes; poultry from Bresse; beef from Charolais; and, finally, from Beaujolais, more wines that, after the Rhône and the Saône, are said to form Lyon's third river.

Beignet-like fried dough called *bugnes* are eaten at Carnival.

*facing page*
Place des Terreaux and the Hôtel de Ville.

For two thousand years Lyon was a town that travelers passed through on their way from Italy to Flanders. As a result, Lyon was exposed to many influences, including Eastern Europe by way of the German Empire, on whose border it lay for a long time. The hybrid nature of Lyon cuisine has given rise to many local specialties with a hearty essence. Here are a few: *cardons à la moelle* (cardoons with marrow), *quenelles* (the Lyon version made with pike called *brochet*), *tablier de sapeur* (literally "fireman's apron," a breaded and fried tripe dish), *cervelle de canut* (literally "silkworker's brain," a cheese and herb combination), *ragôut d'abattis de volaille* (giblet stew), *bugne* (a kind of fritter), *paillasson de pommes de terre* (fried potato cake), *saucisson cuit à la pistache* (boiled sausage with pistachio), *andouillette*, and the list goes on. Everything has been invented or reinvented here: the cooked and the raw, the roasted and the boiled, the gratinéed and the poached, the spiced or the sweet and sour. Lyon dishes use everything, even the most unlikely ingredients, including donkey muzzle or pigs' ears, squash or cows' rumen.

Before being raised to dizzying heights by great chefs—Joël Robuchon, among others—Lyon's cuisine was created by women and characterized by a desire to please the palate as well as satisfy the appetite. Housekeepers, who in some cases had put their talents to use as cooks in homes, opened their own little restaurants, which attracted food lovers and gourmets. These *mères*, the most famous being Mère Fillioux and Mère Brazier, are the foundations of Lyon's gastronomic tradition.

Lyon has access to a bounty of produce and meat products from the surrounding area. Andouillette and tripe are just two popular local dishes.

These welcoming little bistros, known for their jovial and good-natured atmosphere, and as places where all social classes rub shoulders with one another, are the temples of Lyon's culinary tradition. They owe their name to the straw that used to serve as tavern signs. While coachmens' horses were being rubbed down, they would come and line their stomachs with a *mâchon*, a fortifying breakfast of tripe, sausage, cheese, and beaujolais. Though the coachmen are long gone, the bouchons continue to serve tasty meals to Lyon food lovers. Many restaurants improperly describe themselves as bouchons. Establishments endorsed by the Association de Défense des Bouchons Lyonnais, which has certified them as genuine, can be identified from a sign on the storefront that consists of a coat of arms upon which is written Authentique Bouchon Lyonnais.

*right*
Another Lyon specialty is *saucisson pistaché*, a cooked sausage made with pistachio nuts.

*far right*
Full of charm and old-world character, *bouchons* serve traditional local dishes. About twenty of these eateries in Lyon are certified "authentic."

242

# MONTÉLIMAR
## DELIGHTS OF THE SOUTH

THOSE AMONG THE GREAT MIGRATION OF VACATIONERS FROM NORTHERN EUROPE to the Mediterranean every summer will be familiar with the name of this quiet little village. Montélimar is the gateway to the south, where Provence opens its doors. Immediately the sky seems bluer, the landscapes appear in a more beautiful light, and the air is fragrant with thyme and lavender. And anyone who ventures to leave the great tide of cars flowing down the highway in the direction of the sun is met with the peacefulness of old villages with squares shaded by plane trees, trellised café terraces, and pétanque players.

But for how many of these vacationers does Montélimar remain a place they associate with one of the most infamous bottlenecks along the route to their final destinations? Unfortunately, they are numerous— and it is their loss. The town has something to offer, and it is worth the stop. Though its artistic heritage is not particularly exceptional, it does have a few fine houses; some vestiges of its ancient ramparts, the St. Martin gate; St. Croix Church, dating from the fifteenth and seventeenth centuries; and above all, a castle with a twelfth-century keep whose fortification systems are an interesting mix of five centuries' worth of military architecture. But its appeal lies mainly in the liveliness of its streets and markets, in the unpretentious grace of its architecture, and in that easygoing way of life that can only flourish in sunny climes.

It is hard to believe that a gourmet treat as delicate as nougat could have originated in any bleak and austere town. Probably introduced by the Greeks to Marseille, as its etymology —*nux gatum*—suggests, nougat is a cake of walnuts mixed with lavender honey. For a long time Marseille had the monopoly on nougat production; it was supplanted by Montélimar at the end of the sixteenth century, when almond trees were introduced to Provence. It was then that almonds replaced walnuts and nougat became associated with this place.

Nougat is a mixture of sugar, honey, egg yolk, vanilla, almonds, and pistachios. The honey and sugar are melted, and then cooked with beaten egg whites. Sugar is then incorporated, with vanilla, almonds, and pistachios added last. The ingredients are thoroughly combined before being poured into a mold lined with unleavened bread. It is then cut to give it its final shape. Every nougat maker has a secret finishing touch, and the confectioners of Montéli-mar have acquired an expertise that makes their nougat the best in the world.

*facing page*
The walls of the Château des Adhémar, which rises above the town.

*below*
The market in Richerenches specializes in a delicacy: black truffles.

The mildness of its climate makes Provençal Drôme and the adjoining regions particularly productive for fruit and vegetable cultivation. In orchards and fields protected from the wind by lines of poplar and cypress, apples, pears, peaches, plums, apricots, and cherries are harvested in abundance, as are zucchinis, cucumbers, tomatoes, peas, beans, and artichokes. Grapes served at the table, such as Chasselas and Muscat, or used for making wine, including Coteaux du Tricastin and Beaumes-de-Venise, are also abundant.

In the little village of Richerenches, not far from Montélimar, one of the most famous truffle markets in Provence is held from December to March. Truffles are a culinary treasure; unfortunately, their cultivation has yet to be mastered, keeping prices high. The black truffle (*le diamant noir*)—*Tuber melanosporum*—is the most highly prized, and the only truffle, produced in Drôme Provençal (it is not the same as the black truffle from China, which is not particularly interesting). At once strong and delicate, it can be used to flavor simple dishes, such as omelettes, scrambled eggs, or filleted steak, transforming them into masterpieces of haute cuisine.

# NANTUA

## THE LADY OF THE LAKE

IT IS OFTEN SAID OF HAUT-BUGEY THAT IT IS "BLACK," due to its narrow valleys and gloomy fir-tree forests. Luckily the spring brings color. Meadows are decked out with daffodils and narcissus, and the area's countless rivers sing. And when the steep hillsides and narrow valleys open up, when the blue waters of a lake reflect the blue of the sky, the Haut-Bugey, supposedly so grim, acquires a luminous beauty. Overlooking a vast lake that is 1.5 miles long and 2,133 feet wide, Nantua does not in the least convey the sense that it is a dark place. In this small town with its ancient history, the twelfth-century St. Michel Abbey-Church, the last vestige of an abbey founded in the eighth century, is certainly worth a visit. Its carved doorway—damaged during the Revolution—its nave with tapering basket-handle pillars, its Renaissance-style chapel of Saint Anne, and its Romano-Gothic choir make it one of the most beautiful religious edifices in the Ain. It houses several veritable masterpieces, including *The Martyrdom of St. Sebastian*, by Delacroix, and an organ made by Nicolas-Antoine Lété, one of the great organ builders of the nineteenth century. The charm of the town lies also in its old sections, where rue St.-Michel, rue de l'Hôtel-de-Ville, and rue Alphonse-Baudin are lined with houses and small shops dating from the fifteenth, six-

Fish quenelles made with crayfish and served with the delicious béchamel-based Nantua sauce.

*facing page*
A panoramic view of the lake and the town surrounded by mountains.

teenth, and seventeenth centuries, and in the path around the lake. Well-marked walking paths offer easy, though slightly hilly, strolls along the slopes and ridges of the valley, affording beautiful panoramic views of the town and the lake.

But it is to a delicious dish even more than its location and heritage that Nantua owes its fame. Crayfish once abounded in the local streams and lakes. Who conceived of the recipe for what is now called Nantua sauce? No one knows. In any case, for food lovers it is a favorite accompaniment with freshwater fish— pike, pike-perch, or féra (a type of salmon)—and especially quenelles. Made with a mixture of crayfish heads pounded with butter and passed through a sieve, it is then blended with béchamel to which crayfish tails, cayenne pepper, white wine, and Cognac are added. Transcendent, it brings a subtle yet strong flavor to the foods sauced with it.

A culinary specialty of Lyon, quenelles were for a long time a fairly simple dish made with milk, eggs, flour, and fat. It was in the nineteenth century that the recipe was embellished, making it fit for the grandest occasions. This new dish blended pike with *panade*, a binder, and the whole was coated with Nantua sauce. Here's the procedure: First the quenelle paste is prepared with flour and milk. The *panade* is heated to dry it out, then eventually cooled. The chopped pike is added to the panade, which is then rolled into little sausage shapes and poached. The quenelle doubles in size when cooked and is often served au gratin. Thanks to the lake and numerous rivers abounding in pike, where crayfish are caught, Nantua is the keeper of the great tradition of quenelles served in this incomparable sauce.

Whether red- or white-clawed, the European crayfish is a threatened species, because of polluted waterways and the introduction of the voracious Louisiana crayfish (or crawfish). These transplants, which occupy the same ecological niche, are triumphing over their European rivals; they also carry a bacteria that is killing off the native species. What makes this situation even more unfortunate is that the European crayfish is more flavorful than its bland-tasting American cousin.

# NYONS

BOTTLED SUNSHINE

"WHOEVER EATS OLIVES EVERY DAY, IN ALL SEASONS, will live to be as old as the beams of the most solidly built house." The south of France, which makes the most of its colors and fragrances, and also of what tastes good, has succeeded in bottling sunshine—in the form of olive oil.

Olive trees are common to the entire Mediterranean rim, a region that has not been spared from trou-

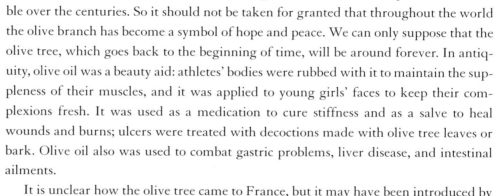

ble over the centuries. So it should not be taken for granted that throughout the world the olive branch has become a symbol of hope and peace. We can only suppose that the olive tree, which goes back to the beginning of time, will be around forever. In antiquity, olive oil was a beauty aid: athletes' bodies were rubbed with it to maintain the suppleness of their muscles, and it was applied to young girls' faces to keep their complexions fresh. It was used as a medication to cure stiffness and as a salve to heal wounds and burns; ulcers were treated with decoctions made with olive tree leaves or bark. Olive oil also was used to combat gastric problems, liver disease, and intestinal ailments.

It is unclear how the olive tree came to France, but it may have been introduced by the Greeks twenty-five centuries ago. Growing olive trees was abandoned at one point

Happy hordes participate in the annual Alicoque festival, when the new olive oil is sampled with toasted bread, garlic, and wine.

because it wasn't profitable, but there was a revival of interest in olive cultivation. Depending on the region, olive trees flower in April or June, offering the unusual spectacle of valleys blanketed with a snow-white covering. During the summer the trees drink in the sunshine and get water from the depths of the earth, which allows the pulp of the olive to develop; by October the olive reaches full size. It is very fragile at this point. Harvesting is done by hand or with a *peigne*, a kind of rake with which the branches are beaten, so the olives aren't damaged. The olives drop into a net, then are sorted before being pressed. Picholine olives are different from salonenques, or grossanes from the tanches—some olives are eaten when green and others are consumed when black and wrinkled; the color is an indicator of maturity. Olive oils are a lot like wines in some ways: the product's characteristics vary according to the terroir and methods of production.

Nyons is the capital of the tanche, a small, wrinkled black olive that grows on the surrounding hills, where devotees of olive oil gather on the first Sunday of February for the Alicoque Festival. During this all-day event, a crowd converges on Place des Arcades, where long tables covered with white tablecloths are set up so people can taste the new oil. At the appointed time, the grand master of the Confrérie des Chevaliers de l'Olivier grabs a crust of bread, rubs it with a clove of garlic, pours a little olive oil on it, and chases it all down with a generous glass of wine. A satisfied nod of the head signals the start of a good-natured frenzy that ends when everyone has had a chance to judge the subtleties of the new vintage.

The best oils are categorized as extra virgin olive oil or virgin olive oil. In 1993 the olive oil from Nyons was the first in France to attain the AOC designation of quality.

People sleep well in Buis-les-Baronnies—due to the pristine air quality, but also, it is said, because of lime-blossom drying in the storehouses. According to the locals, it is the best sleep in the world. On the first Wednesday of June, loaded with *bourras*, heavy squares of jute canvas in which the lime blossom is wrapped, the producers bring their pickings to sell to traders. Lime-blossom gathering is a family event, during which locals of the valley supplement their incomes. Lime-blossom competition is tough, with a lot of it being imported from China or Poland.

*facing page*
Through its collections, the Musee de l'Olivier (Olive Museum) explores the past and present cultivation of the rustic olive of Nyons.

248

# ROMANS

## MADE-TO-ORDER RAVIOLI

ROMANS IS A TOWN OF ECLECTIC TASTES. IT HAS ALWAYS APPEALED to those who like to dress and eat well. Initially wealth came from the cloth industry, but in the mid-nineteenth century this was superseded by the luxury leather tanning industry. Until recently, the most prestigious shoemakers had workshops on the banks of the Isère River. A history of shoemaking is housed at the Musée International de la Chaussure, an old eighteenth-century monastery. Displayed are approximately 10,000 boots, shoes, slippers, sandals, and pumps—presenting the art of shoemaking and every type of footwear created over 4,000 years.

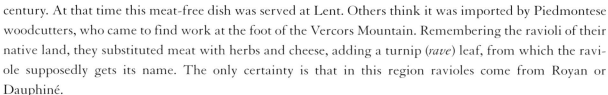

Food also plays an important role in this region of Dauphiné. Romans claims to be the capital of the raviole, an unusual food for a couple of reasons. For one, almost everything about its origins is unknown, and, perhaps more peculiarly, a cheese from a different region is used in it. Ravioles are a kind of small ravioli sold in sheets; the pastry is made with tender wheatgrain semolina and the stuffing is made with fresh cream cheese, parsley, egg, and Comté, a cheese from the Jura region. The raviole can be traced back to antiquity, although it is also said to date from the end of the fifteenth century. At that time this meat-free dish was served at Lent. Others think it was imported by Piedmontese woodcutters, who came to find work at the foot of the Vercors Mountain. Remembering the ravioli of their native land, they substituted meat with herbs and cheese, adding a turnip (*rave*) leaf, from which the raviole supposedly gets its name. The only certainty is that in this region ravioles come from Royan or Dauphiné.

A delicious local dish is cheese-filled *raviole*.

*facing page*
Pogne is a special brioche bread made in Romans and customarily eaten at Easter.

Until the nineteenth century *ravioleuses* (raviole makers) offered their services to bourgeois family households on fast and feast days. They went from house to house, farm to farm, making ravioles for money. They were the precursors of small artisanal businesses in the region. Every raviole maker has a secret method and recipe, but all agree on the cooking time. Once the ravioles are plunged into boiling water, you have to wait until they rise to the surface before removing them, but they should never be left in the pot for more than 90 seconds. They can be served fried in butter, with gratinées, with cream or tomato, and sprinkled with grated Comté. Today, adventurous chefs serve ravioles with foie gras, shellfish, mushrooms, and even chocolate.

In the past, pogne was made only during Easter. In the sixteenth century, people from Dauphiné used to attach this brioche to branches they carried to church on Palm Sunday. When the railroad reached Romans in 1864, demand increased and bakers began to make pogne well beyond Easter. Today bakers in and around Romans make it year-round. But paschal pogne is distinguished from ordinary pogne by its size; it is much bigger. This crown-shaped brioche with a golden crust is still made with flour, natural leaveners, eggs, butter, sugar, and orange-flower water.

This creamy, delicately flavored white cheese has graced the tables of food lovers since the fifteenth century. King Louis XI introduced it to the French court, and at that time it was made from goat cheese. Today this small, round cheese is made from 100-percent cow's milk. A soft-textured matured cheese, it is made in the village of Saint Marcellin, observing the rule of 22, which states that the milk is worked at 22 degrees Celcius, and that it is left for 22 days to mature to produce a cheese worthy of its name.

# ADDRESSES

## agen (aquitaine)

**Office du tourisme**
107, boulevard Carnot
47000 Agen
phone +33 05 53 47 36 09

**Hôtel Atlantic**
133, avenue Jean-Jaurès
47000 Agen
phone +33 05 53 96 16 56

**Royal Hôtel**
129, boulevard de la République
47000 Agen
phone +33 05 53 47 28

**Hôtel Régina**
139, boulevard Carnot
47000 Agen
phone +33 05 53 47 07 97

**Hôtel des Iles**
25, rue Baudin
47000 Agen
phone +33 05 53 47 11 33

**Château des Jacobins**
1ter, place des Jacobins
phone +33 05 53 47 03 31

**L'Atelier**
14, rue du Jeu-de-Paume
47000 Agen
phone +33 05 53 87 89 22

**Margoton**
52, rue Richard-Coeur-de-Lion
47000 Agen
phone +33 05 53 48 11 55
www.lemargoton.com

**La Maison sur la Place**
10, place Gambetta
47140 Penne d'Agenais
phone +33 05 53 01 29 18
www.lamaisonsurlaplace.com

**Confiserie Boisson**
20 rue Grande-Horloge
47000 Agen
phone +33 05 53 66 20 61

## aix-en-provence (provence)

**Office du tourisme**
2, place du Général-de-Gaulle
13100 Aix-en-Provence
phone +33 04 42161161
www.aixenprovencetourism.com

**Hôtel-restaurant Château l'Arc**
chemin Maurel
13710 Fuveau
phone +33 04 42 29 80 80
www.hotelchateaularc.fr

**Hôtel Le Pigonnet
restaurant Iᵉʳ Riviéra**
5, avenue du Pigonnet
13090 Aix-en-Provence
phone +33 04 42 59 02 90
www.hotelpigonnet.com

**Hôtel-restaurant de la Villa Gallici**
avenue de la Violette
13100 Aix-en-Provence
phone +33 04 42 23 29 23
www.villagallici.com

**La Mas d'Entremont**
315 route Nationale 7
Célony 13090 Aix-en-Provence
phone +33 04 42 17 42 42
www.masdentremont.com

**Maison Béchard**
12, cours Mirabeau
13100 Aix-en-Provence
phone +33 04 42 26 06 78

**L'Aixquis**
22, rue Victor-Leydet
13100 Aix-en-Provence
phone +33 04 42 27 76 16
www.aixquis.com

**Amphitryon**
2-4, rue Paul-Doumer
13100 Aix-en-Provence
phone +33 04 42 26 54 10

**La Bastide du Cours**
43-45 cours Mirabeau
13100 Aix-en-Provence
phone +33 04 42 26 10 06
www.bastideducours.com

**Le Petit Verdot**
7, rue d'Entrecasteaux
phone +33 04 42 27 30 12
13100 Aix-en-Provence
www.lepetitverdot.com

**Clos de la Violette**
10, avenue de la Violette
13100 Aix-en-Provence
phone +33 04 42 23 30 71
www.closdelaviolette.fr

**Les Deux Frères**
4, rue Reine-Astrid
13100 Aix-en-Provence
phone +33 04 42 27 90 32
www.les2freres.com

**Confiserie du Roy René**
10, rue Clemenceau
13100 Aix-en-Provence
phone +33 04 42 26 67 86
www.calisson.com

**Confiserie Léonard Parli**
35, Avenue Victor Hugo
13100 Aix-en-Provence
phone +33 04 42 26 05 71
www.leonard-parli.com

**Domaine du Pay Blanc**
1200, Chemin du Vallon des Mourgues
13090 Aix-en-Provence
phone +33 04 42 12 34 76
www.peyblanc.com

**Château des Gavelles**
165, Chemin de Maliverny
13540 Puyricard
phone +33 04 42 92 06 83
www.chateaudesgavelles.fr

**Château Simone**
13590 Meyreuil
phone +33 04 42 66 92 58
www.chateau-simone.fr

**SCEA Château Virant
Cheylan Père et fils**
13680 Lançon de Provence
phone +33 04 90 42 44 47

**Moulin à Huile Barles et fils**
avenue du Père Sylvain Giraud
13510 Eguilles
phone +33 04 42 92 55 14

## albi (midi-pyrénées)

**Office de tourisme**
Palais de la Berbie
Place Sainte-Cécile
81000 Albi
phone +33 05 63494880
www.albi-tourisme.fr

**Hôtel Mercure**
41 bis, rue Porta
81000 Albi
phone +33 05 63 47 66 66

**Hôtel-restaurant Le Vieil Alby**
25, rue Toulouse-Lautrec
81000 Albi
phone +33 05 63 54 14 69
http://perso.orange.fr/le-vieil-alby/

**Hôtel-restaurant Fusiès**
rue de la République
81230 Lacaune
phone +33 06 14 25 87 95
www.hotelfusies.fr

**Restaurant le Moulin de la Mothe**
rue de la Mothe
81000 Albi
phone +33 05 63 60 38 15

**L'Epicurien**
42, place Jean-Jaurès
81000 Albi
phone +33 05 63 53 10 70
www.restaurantlepicurien.com

**L'Esprit du Vin**
11, quai Choiseul
44 81000 Albi
phone +33 05 63 54 60

**Restaurant du Musée**
17, place de l'Archevêché
81000 Albi
phone +33 05 63 47 17 77
www.restaurantdumusee.com

**Les Planches**
16, quai Général de Gaulle
69250 Albigny sur Saône
phone +33 04 78 91 30 88

**Charcuterie de Millas**
81320 Moulin-Mage
phone +33 05 67 37 14 72
www.charcuterie-millas.fr

**Charcuterie Oberti**
rue Flandre Dunkerque
81230 Lacaune
phone +33 05 63 37 00 21
www.oberti.fr

**Maison de la Charcuterie**
3, rue Biarnès
81230 Lacaune
phone +33 05 63 37 46 31

**Pâtisserie Saint Honoré**
8 rue Saint Julien
81000 Albi
phone +33 05 63 38 22 25
www.patisserie-st-honore.com

**Pâtisserie Jean Paul Galy**
7, rue Saunal
81000 Albi
phone +33 05 63 54 13 37

## angers (pays de la loire)

**Office de Tourisme d'Angers Loire**
Métropole, 7, Place Kennedy, BP 15157
49100 Angers
phone +33 02 41 23 50 00
www.angers-tourisme.com

**Hôtel-restaurant de France**
8, place de la Gare
49100 Angers
phone +33 02 41 88 49 42
www.destination-anjou.com

**Hôtel-restaurant Château de Noirieux**
26, route du Moulin
49125 Briollay
phone +33 02 41 42 50 05
www.chateaudenoirieux.com

**Hôtel d'Anjou**
1, boulevard Foch
4900 Angers
phone +33 02 41 88 24 82

**Restaurant Le Bœuf Plessis**
10, rue Saint Jacques Foudon
49124 Le Plessis-Grammoire
phone +33 02 41 76 72 12

**Restaurant Ma Campagne**
14, promenade de Reculée
49100 Angers
phone +33 02 41 48 38 06

**Auberge d'Eventard**
rond point du Parc des Expositions
Le Bon Puits
49480 Saint Sylvain-d'Anjou
phone +33 02 41 43 74 25
www.auberge-eventard.com

**Provence Caffé**
9, place du Ralliement
phone +33 02 41 87 44 15
49000 Angers
www.provence-caffe.com

**Le Relais**
9, rue de la Gare
phone +33 02 41 88 42 51
49100 Angers
www.destination-anjou.com/relais

**La Salamandre**
1, boulevard du Mal-Foch
49000 Angers
phone +33 02 41 88 99 55
*www.restaurantlasalamandre.fr*

**Nicolas Joly**
Château de la Roche aux Moines
49170 Savennières
phone +33 02 41 72 22 32
*www.coulee-de-serrant.com*

**Musée Cointreau**
carrefour Molière
49690 Saint Barthélemy d'Anjou
phone +33 02 41 31 50 50
*www.remycointreau.com*

## apt (provence)

**Office de Tourisme du Pays d'Apt**
20 Avenue Philippe de Girard
84400 Apt
phone +33 04 90 74 03 18
*www.ot.apt.fr*

**Auberge du Luberon**
8, place du Faubourg du Ballet
84000 Apt en Provence
phone +33 04 90 74 12 50
*www.auberge-luberon-peuzin.com*

**Le Mas des Herbes Blanches**
Joucas 84220 Gordes
phone +33 04 90 05 79 79
*www.herbesblanches.com*

**Maison d'Hôtes**
Le Moulin de Mauragne, route de Marseille
84400 Apt
phone +33 04 90 74 31 37

**Restaurant Auberge des Seguins**
84480 Buoux
phone +33 04 90 74 19 89

**Bernard Mathys**
Le Chêne
84400 Apt
phone +33 04 90 04 84 64

**Bistro de France**
67, place de la Bouquerie
84400 Apt
phone +33 04 90 74 22 01

**Vidal**
Place du Marché
43260 Saint Julien Chapteuil
phone +33 04 71 08 70 50
*www.restaurant-vidal.com*

**Domaine des Andéols**
Les Andéols
84490 Saint Saturnin-les-Apts
phone +33 04 90 75 50 63
*www.domainedesandeols.com*

**Vins du Château de Mille
Conrad et Pierre Pinatel**
route de Bonnieux
84400 Apt
phone +33 04 90 74 11 94
*www.chateau-de-mille.fr*

**Confiserie Saint Denis**
les Janselmes
84400 Gargas
phone +33 04 90 74 07 35

**Denis Ceccon**
60, quai de la Liberté
84400 Apt
phone +33 04 90 74 21 90

**Marcel Richaud**
112, quai de la Liberté
84400 Apt
phone +33 04 90 74 43 50

**Le Mas des Abeilles**
Col le Pointu
84480 Bonnieux
phone +33 04 90 74 29 55

## arbois (franche–comté)

**Office de Tourisme**
10 rue de l'Hôtel-de-Ville
39600 Arbois
phone +33 03 84 66 55 50

**Hôtel-restaurant Jean-Paul Jeunet**
rue de l'Hôtel-de-Ville
39600 Arbois
phone +33 03 84 66 05 67

**Hôtel des Messageries**
2 rue de Courcelles
39600 Arbois
phone +33 03 84 66 15 45,
*www.hoteldesmessageries.com*

**Restaurant La Finette – Taverne d'Arbois**
22 avenue Louis-Pasteur
39600 Arbois
phone +33 03 84 66 06 78

**Restaurant La Balance – Mets et Vins**
47 rue de Courcelles
39600 Arbois
phone +33 03 84 37 45 00

**Le Caveau d'Arbois**
3 route de Besançon
39600 Arbois
phone +33 03 84 66 10 70
*www.caveau-arbois.com*

**Le Relais de Pont d'Héry**
Route de Champagnole
39110 Salins-les-Bains
phone +33 03 84 73 06 54
*www.relaispondhery.com*

**Le Relais**
place de l'Eglise
25610 Arc-et-Senans
phone +33 03 81 57 40 60

**Chocolats Hirsinger**
place de la Liberté
39600 Arbois
phone +33 03 84 66 06 97

**Caves Rolet**
11 rue de l'Hôtel-de-Ville
39600 Arbois
phone +33 03 84 66 08 89

**Caves Henri Maire**
place de la Liberté
39600 Arbois
phone +33 03 84 66 15 27

## arles (provence)

**Office de Tourisme d'Arles**
Boulevard des Lices
3200 Arles
phone +33 04 90 18 41 20
*www.tourisme.ville-arles.fr*

**Hôtel Jules César**
boulevard des Lices
13200 Arles
phone +33 04 90 52 52 52
*www.hotel-julescesar.fr*

**Grand Hôtel Nord Pinus**
place du Forum
13200 Arles
phone +33 04 90 93 44 44

**Hôtel-Restaurant Le Pont des Bannes**
route d'Arles
13460 Les Saintes Maries de la Mer
phone +33 04 90 97 81 09
*www.pontdesbannes.net*

**Hostellerie du Pont de Gau**
route d'Arles
13460 Les Saintes Maries de la Mer
phone +33 04 90 97 81 53
*www.pontdegau.camargue.fr*

**Restaurant La Charcuterie**
51, Rue des Arènes
13200 Arles
phone +33 04 90 96 56 96
*www.lacharcuterie.camargue.fr*

**Restaurant Le Criquet**
21, Rue Porte de l'Aude
13200 Arles
phone +33 04 90 96 80 51

**Lou Marques**
9, boulevard des Lices
13200 Arles
phone +33 04 90 52 52 52
*www.hotel-julescesar.fr*

**L'Atelier de Jean-Luc Rabanel**
7, rue des Carmes
13200 Arles
phone +33 04 90 91 07 69
*www.rabanel.com*

**La Chassagnette**
Route du Sambuc
13200 Arles
phone +33 04 90 97 26 96
*www.chassagnette.fr*

**Le Cilantro**
31, rue Porte-de-Laure
13200 Arles
phone +33 04 90 18 25 05

**Le Jardin de Manon**
14, avenue des Alyscamps
13200 Arles
phone +33 04 90 93 38 68

**La Farandole**
Maison Génin
11, rue des Porcelets
13200 Arles
phone +33 04 90 96 01 12
*www. lafarandole.arlacom.com*

**Riz de Canavère**
Chemin de Mérieux
Quartier d'Espeyran
30800 Saint-Gilles
phone +33 04 66 87 10 03

**Alain Imbert**
Chemin du Pavillon
13310 Saint Martin de Crau
phone +33 04 90 47 33 14

## aubrac (languedoc–roussillon)

**Office de Tourisme de la Terre de Peyre**
Maison du Prieuré
48130 Aumont-Aubrac
phone +33 04 66 42 88 70
*www.ot-aumont-aubrac.fr*

**Hôtellerie de Fontanges**
route de Conques et de Marcillac
12850 Onet-Le-Chateau
phone +33 05 65 77 76 00
*www.hostellerie-fontanges.com*

**Le Saloon. Guest-Ranch Landrevier**
12850 Sainte Radegonde
phone +33 05 65 42 47 46
*www.ranch-americain.com*

**Chambres d'hôtes Les Mazes
(Thérèse et Pierre Brousse)**
12130 Aurelle Verlac
phone +33 05 65 47 57 85
*www.hebergaubrac.com*

**Restaurant Michel et Sébastien Bras**
route de l'Aubrac
12210 Laguiole
phone +33 05 65 51 18 20

**Au Fil de l'Aubrac**
12460 Saint-Amans des Cots
phone +33 05 65 44 81 12

**Restaurant Chez Germaine**
place des Fêtes
12470 Saint-Chély d'Aubrac
phone +33 05 65 44 28 47

**Restaurant de la Dômerie**
village d'Aubrac
12470 Saint-Chély d'Aubrac
phone +33 05 65 44 28 42

**Hôtel-Restaurant Prouhèze**
2, route du Languedoc
48130 Aumont Aubrac
phone +33 04 66 42 80 07
*www.prouheze.com*

**Restaurant Cyril Attrazic
chez Camillou**
10, route du Languedoc
48000 Aumont-Aubrac
phone +33 04 66 42 86 14
*www.camillou.com*

**Bouloc**
12340 Gabriac
phone +33 05 65 44 92 89

**Conserverie de l'Aubrac
(Patrick et Brigitte Amilhat)**
12470 Saint-Chély d'Aubrac
phone +33 05 65 44 29 63

**Coutellerie de Laguiole**
Espace les Cayres
12210 Laguiole
phone +33 05 65 51 50 14
www.layole.com

**Le couteau de Laguiole**
8, rue de la Vergne
12210 Laguiole
phone +33 05 65 48 45 47

**La forge de Laguiole**
route de l'Aubrac
12210 Laguiole
phone +33 05 65 48 43 34

*avesne-sur-helpe (nord–pas–de–calais)*

**Office de Tourisme**
Ville d'Avesnes sur Helpe
13, place Leclerc, BP 208
59363 Avesnes-sur-Helpe
phone +33 03 27 56 57 58
www.avesnes-sur-helpe.com

**Hôtel Restaurant Le Château de la Motte**
59740 Liessies
phone +33 03 27 61 81 94
www.chateaudelamotte.fr

**Auberge du Brigand Moneuse**
route Nationale 49
59570 Saint Waast-la-Vallée
phone +33 03 66 88 66

**Auberge du Croisil**
route de Maroilles à Locquignol
phone +33 03 27 34 20 14

**Restaurant Le Framboisier**
1, rue François Ansieau
59132 Trélon
phone +33 03 27 59 73 34

**Auberge du Châtelet**
Les Haies à Charmes
59440 Avesnes-sur-Helpe
phone +33 03 27 61 06 70
www.aubergeduchatelet.com

**L'Auberge Fleurie**
67, rue du Général de Gaulle
59216 Sars-Poteries
phone +33 03 27 61 62 48
www.auberge-fleurie.net

**Le Relais de Beaufort**
59330 Beaufort
phone +33 03 27 63 50 36

**Fromages de Maroilles
Francis Lévêque**
1095, rue des Linières
59550 Prisches
phone +33 03 27 77 93 27

**La Pommeraie du Courtil
(Richard Lefèvre)**
66 Route Nationale
59216 Beugnies
phone +33 03 27 61 60 12

**Les Vergers de la Praye
(René Paindavoine)**
route de Valenciennes
59570 Houdain-les-Bavay
phone +33 03 27 63 11 60

**Chique de Bavay
(Christian Kamette)**
30, place du Général de Gaulle
59570 Bavay
phone +33 03 27 63 10 06

*avignon (provence)*

**Office du tourisme**
41, cours Jean-Jaurès
84000 Avignon
phone +33 04 32743270
www.ot-avignon.fr

**Hôtel-restaurant La Mirande**
4, place de la Mirande
84000 Avignon
phone +33 04 90 85 93 93
www.la-mirande.fr

**Hôtel Clarion Cloître Saint Louis**
20, rue du Portail Boquier
84000 Avignon
phone +33 04 92 47 24 72
www.cloitre-saint-louis.com

**Restaurant Christian Etienne**
10 rue de Mons
84000 Avignon
phone +33 04 90 86 16 50
www.christian-etienne.fr

**Chambres d'hôtes Lumani**
37, rue du Rempart Saint Lazare
84000 Avignon
phone +33 04 90 82 94 11
www.avignon-lumani.com

**Auberge de la Fontaine**
place de la Fontaine
84210 Venasque
phone +33 04 90 66 02 96
www.auberge-lafontaine.com

**Brunel**
46, rue de la Balance
84000 Avignon
phone +33 04 90 85 24 83

**L'Entrée des Artistes**
1, place des Carmes
84000 Avignon
phone +33 04 90 82 46 90

**La Fourchette**
17, rue Racine
84000 Avignon
phone +33 04 90 85 20 93

**Hiély-Lucullus**
5, rue de la République
84000 Avignon
phone +33 04 90 86 17 07

**Le Petit Bedon**
70, rue Joseph-Vernet
84000 Avignon
phone +33 04 90 82 33 98

**Inter Rhône**
6, rue des 3 Faucons
84000 Avignon
phone +33 04 90 27 24 00
www.vins-rhone.com

**Croquettes Aujoras**
route de St Saturnin
84310 Morières-les–Avignon
phone +33 04 90 32 21 40
www.biscuiterie-aujoras.fr

**Société Blachère**
route de Sorgues, quartier Cansaud
84230 Chateauneuf du Pape
phone +33 04 90 83 53 81

**Ferme sur le parc Lambertin Venasque**
84570 Malemort du Comtat
phone +33 04 90 69 93 02

*bar-le-duc (lorraine)*

**Office de Tourisme de Bar-le-Duc
et de sa région**
7, rue Jeanne d'Arc
55000 Bar-le-Duc
phone +33 03 29 79 11 13
www.tourisme-barleduc.com

**Hôtel-restaurant La Source**
2, rue Beurey
55000 Trémont-sur-Saulx
phone +33 03 29 75 45 22

**Auberge du Val d'Ornain**
côte Tanguin
55000 Varney
phone +33 03 29 45 29 23

**Hôtel du Château des Monthairons**
Le petit Monthairon
55320 Dieue-sur-Meuse
phone +33 03 29 87 78 55

**Hôtel Restaurant le Panoramique**
9, rue du Docteur Poulain
55600 Montmédy
phone +33 03 29 80 11 68

**Hôtel Restaurant des Côtes de Meuse**
1, avenue Général Le Lorrain
5210 Saint-Maurice-sous-les-Côtes
phone +33 03 29 89 35 61

**Bistrot Saint-Jean**
132, boulevard de La Rochelle
55000 Bar-le-Duc
phone +33 03 29 45 40 40

**Auberge du Moulin Haut**
Le Domaine du Moulin Haut
55260 Chaumont-sur-Aire
phone +33 03 29 70 66 46
www.moulinhaut.fr

**Gentilhommière**
29, rue Jean Jaurès
52100 Saint-Dizier
phone +33 03 25 56 32 97

**Confiture Dutriez**
35, rue de l'Etoile
55000 Bar-le-Duc
phone +33 03 29 79 06 81
www.groseille.com

**Saveurs des Ducs (Christian Desvoy)**
9, rue du Général de Gaulle
55000 Bar-le-Duc
phone +33 03 29 79 36 27
www.confreriegroseilles.com

**Madeleine Zins**
ZAE La Louvière
55200 Commercy
phone +33 03 29 91 40 86
www.madeleines-zins.fr

*bayonne (aquitaine)*

**Office de Tourisme**
Place des Basques, BP 819
64108 Bayonne
phone +33 05 820 42 64 64
www.bayonne-tourisme.com

**Le Grand Hôtel**
21, rue Thiers
64100 Bayonne
phone +33 05 59 59 62 00
www.bw-legrandhotel.com

**Restaurant Auberge du Cheval Blanc**
68, rue Bourgneuf
64100 Bayonne
phone +33 05 59 59 01 33

**Hôtel du Palais**
1, avenue de l'Impératrice
64200 Biarritz
phone +33 05 59 41 64 00
www.hotel-du-palais.com

**Chambres du Domaine Xixtaberri**
route d'Hasparren
64250 Cambo les Bains
phone +33 05 59 29 22 66
www.xixtaberri.com

**Le Bayonnais**
38, quai des Corsaires
64100 Bayonne
phone +33 05 59 25 61 19

**Le Chistera**
42, rue Port-Neuf
64100 Bayonne
phone +33 05 59 59 25 93
www.lechistera.com

**El Asador**
Place Montaut
64100 Bayonne
phone +33 05 59 59 08 57

**Au Peita**
7, avenue Capitaine-Resplandy
64100 Bayonne
phone +33 05 59 25 41 35

**Jambons de Bayonne (Pierre Ibaïalde)**
41, rue des Cordeliers
64100 Bayonne
phone +33 05 59 25 65 30
www.pierre-ibaialde.com

**Pierre Oteiza**
route d'Urepel
64430 Aldudes
phone +33 05 59 37 56 11
www.pierreoteiza.com

**Martine Parakian, Ibai Hegian**
quartier Haurtzain
64250 Cambo les Bains
phone +33 05 59 29 78 27
www.hegian.com

**Maialen Noblia**
Biperduna
64250 Cambo les Bains
phone +33 06 64 82 39 58
www.basque-food.fr

*beaufort (rhône–alpes)*

**Office de Tourisme**
route du Grand Mont
73270 Beaufort
phone +33 04 79 38 37 57
www.areches-beaufort.com

**Hôtel le Kililmandjaro**
route de l'Altiport
73120 Courchevel
phone +33 04 79 01 46 46
www.hotelkilimandjaro.com

**Hôtel Restaurant Tsanteleina**
BP 201
73155 Val d'Isère
phone +33 04 79 06 12 13
www.tsanteleina.com

**Hôtel-restaurant Evian Royal Palace**
Rive Sud du Lac de Genève
74501 Evian-les-Bains
phone +33 04 50 26 85 00
www.royalparcevioan.com

**Restaurant Le Prieuré**
68, Grande Rue
74200 Thonon les Bains
phone +33 04 50 71 31 89

**La Maison de Marc Veyrat**
13 vieille route des Pensières
74290 Veyrier-du-Lac
phone +33 04 50 60 24 00
www.marcveyrat.fr

**La Table du Berger**
Grande rue
73270 Beaufort
phone +33 04 79 38 37 91

**Ferme de Victorine**
Le Planay
73590 Notre-Dame-de-Bellecombe
phone +33 04 79 31 63 46
www.lafermedevictorine.com

**La Châtelle**
3, rue Paul Proust
73400 Ugine
phone +33 04 79 37 30 02
www.lachatelle.com

**Coopérative Laitière du Beaufortain**
73270 Beaufort sur Doron
phone +33 04 79 38 33 62
fax +33 04 79 38 33 40
www.cooperative-de-beaufort.com

**Coopérative Laitière
de Haute Tarentaise**
494, rue des Colombières
73700 Bourg St Maurice
phone +33 04 79 07 08 28
www.fromagebeaufort.com

**La Cave du Prieuré
(Barlet Raymond)**
Le Haut
73170 Jongieux
phone +33 04 79 44 02 22

**Domaine de l'Idylle
(Philippe et François Tiollier)**
Saint Laurent
73800 Cruet
phone +33 04 79 84 30 58

**Lou Pioton de Pouer**
40, chemin de la Curiale
74210 Faverges
phone +33 04 50 32 45 21
www.salaison.fr

**Guy Gros**
Le Villard du Planay
73350 Bozel
phone +33 04 79 55 00 22
www.guygros.com

**Alpina Savoie**
209, rue Aristide Bergès
73000 Chambéry
phone +33 04 79 68 54 00
www.alpina-savoie.com

**Chez le Père Rullier**
73700 Séez
phone +33 04 79 41 04 43

*beaujeu (rhône–alpes)*

**Office de Tourisme**
place de l'Hôtel-de-Ville
69430 Beaujeu
phone +33 04 74 69 22 88

**Hôtel Anne de Beaujeu**
28 rue de la République
69430 Beaujeu
phone +33 04 74 04 87 58

**Hôtel Château de Bagnols**
69620 Bagnols
phone +33 O4 74 71 40 00

**Le Savigny**
Le Bourg
69460 Blacé
phone +33 04 74 67 52 07

**Le Cep**
place de l'Église
69820 Fleurie
phone +33 04 74 04 10 77

**Château de Pizay**
hameau de Pizay
69220 Saint-Jean-d'Ardières
phone +33 04 74 66 51 41

**Auberge de Clochemerle**
rue Gabriel-Chevallier
69460 Vaux-en-Beaujolais
phone +33 04 74 03 20 16

**Le Mont-Brouilly**
Le Pont des Samsons
69430 Quincie en Beaujolais
phone +33 04 74 04 33 73
www.hotelbrouilly.com

**Le Villon**
Boulevard du Parc
69910 Villié-Morgon
phone +33 04 74 69 16 16

**Le Morgon**
69910 Villié-Morgon
phone +33 04 74 69 16 03

**Christian Mabeau**
261, route du Beaujolais
69460 Odenas
phone +33 04 74 03 41 79

**Huilerie Montegottero**
29 rue des Écharmeaux
69430 Beaujeu
phone +33 04 74 69 28 06

**Caveau des Beaujolais-Villages**
place de l'Hôtel-de-Ville
69430 Beaujeu
phone +33 04 74 04 81 18

**Caveau de Clochemerle**
69460 Vaux-en-Beaujolais
phone +33 04 74 03 26 58

*beaune (burgundy)*

**Office du Tourisme**
rue de l'Hôtel-Dieu
21200 Beaune
phone +33 03 80 26 21 30

**Hôtel Le Cep**
27, rue Maufoux
21200 Beaune
phone +33 03 80 22 35 48

**Hôtel de la Poste**
5, boulevard Georges-Clémenceau
21200 Beaune
phone +33 03 80 22 08 11

**La Closerie**
route d'Autun
21200 Beaune
phone +33 03 80 22 15 07

**Le Jardin des Remparts**
10, rue de l'Hôtel-Dieu
21200 Beaune
phone +33 03 80 24 79 41

**Le Benaton**
25, rue Faubourg-Bretonnière
21200 Beaune
phone +33 03 80 22 00 26
www.lebenaton.com

**Le Bistrot Bourguignon**
8, rue Monge
21200 Beaune
phone +33 03 80 22 23 24
www.lebistrotbourguignon.com

**Restaurant Le Conty**
5, rue Ziem
21200 Beaune
phone +33 03 80 22 63 94

**Restaurant La Bouzerotte**
Le Village
21200 Bouze-lès-Beaune
phone +33 03 80 26 01 37
www.perso.wanadoo.fr/la.bouzerotte

**L'Atheneaum de la Vigne et du Vin**
5, rue de l'Hôtel-Dieu
21200 Beaune
phone +33 03 80 22 35 48

*bordeaux (aquitaine)*

**Office de Tourisme**
12, cours du 30 Juillet
33000 Bordeaux
phone +33 05 56 00 66 00

**Le Burdigala**
115, rue Georges-Bonnac
33000 Bordeaux
phone +33 05 56 90 16 16

**Le Bayonne Etche-Ona**
4, rue de Martignac
33000 Bordeaux
phone +33 05 56 48 00 88

**Mercure Château-Chartrons**
81, cours Saint-Louis
33000 Bordeaux
phone +33 05 56 43 15 00

**Grand Hôtel Français**
12, rue du Temple
33000 Bordeaux
phone +33 05 56 48 10 35

**Le Tupina**
6, rue de la Porte-de-la-Monnaie
33000 Bordeaux
phone +33 05 56 91 56 37

**Le Vieux Bordeaux**
27, rue Buhan
33000 Bordeaux
phone +33 05 56 52 94 36

**Le Café Louis**
place de la Comédie
33000 Bordeaux
phone +33 05 56 44 07 00

**L'Aquitania**
avenue Jean-Gabriel-Domergue
33300 Bordeaux
phone +33 05 56 69 65 11
www.sofitel.com

**Baud et Millet**
19, rue Huguerie
33000 Bordeaux
phone +33 05 56 79 05 77

**Le Bistro du Sommelier**
163, rue Georges-Bonnac
33000 Bordeaux
phone +33 05 56 96 71 78
*www.bistrodusommelier.com*

**Le Café du Musée**
7, rue Ferrère
33026 Bordeaux
phone +33 05 56 44 71 61
*www.chezgreg.fr*

**Le Chapon Fin**
5, rue Montesquieu
33000 Bordeaux
phone +33 05 56 79 10 10
*www.chapon-fin.com*

**Caves Passavant**
44, allée de Tourny
33000 Bordeaux
phone +33 05 56 44 82 22

**Épicerie de la Tupina**
6, rue de la Porte-de-la-Monnaie
33000 Bordeaux
phone +33 05 56 91 56 37

**Pâtisserie Baillardran**
263, rue Judaïque
Galerie des Grands-Hommes
33000 Bordeaux
phone +33 05 56 51 02 09

*boulogne (nord–pas de calais)*

**Office de Tourisme
de Boulogne-sur-Mer**
Forum Jean Noël, BP 187
62203 Boulogne-sur-Mer
phone +33 03 21 10 88 10
*www.tourisme-boulognesurmer.com*

**Hôtel-restaurant Hamiot**
1, rue Faidherbe
62200 Boulogne-sur-Mer
phone +33 03 21 31 44 20
*www.hotelhamiot.com*

**Hôtel-restaurant La Matelote**
80, Boulevard Sainte-Beuve
62200 Boulogne-sur-Mer
phone +33 03 21 30 17 97
*www.la-matelote.com*

**Restaurant Poissonnerie
Aux Pêcheurs d'Etaples**
31, Grande Rue
62200 Boulogne-sur-Mer
phone +33 03 21 30 29 29

**Hôtel Westminster**
5, avenue du Verger
62520 Le Touquet
phone +33 03 21 05 48 48
*www.westminster.fr*

**Nausicaa. Centre National de la Mer**
Boulevard Sainte-Beuve B.P. 189
62203 Boulogne-sur-Mer
phone +33 03 21 30 98 98
*www.nausicaa.fr*

**Le Châtillon**
6, rue Charles-Tellier
62200 Boulogne sur Mer
phone +33 03 21 31 43 95
*www.chatillon-lecailler.com*

**La Coquillette**
10, rue de l'Enseignement-Mutuel
62200 Boulogne sur Mer
phone +33 03 21 83 37 51
*www.la-coquillette.com*

**Hostellerie de la Rivière**
17, rue de la Gare
62200 Boulogne sur Mer
phone +33 03 21 32 22 81
*www.hostelleriedelariviere.com*

**La Matelote**
80, boulevard Sainte-Beuve
62200 Boulogne sur Mer
phone +33 03 21 30 17 97
*www.la-matelote.com*

**Jen-Claude David**
20, rue d'Alsace
62200 Boulogne sur Mer
phone +33 03 21 87 38 31
*www.jcdavid.fr*

**Saurisserie Dutriaux**
29, Rue Félix Faure
59153 Grand-Fort-Philippe
phone +33 03 28 65 34 05

**Touquet Savour**
RN1, BP 60018
80160 Essertaux
phone +33 03 22 35 32 90
*www.touquetsavour.fr*

*bourg-en-bresse (rhône–alpes)*

**Office du tourisme**
6, avenue Alsace-Lorraine
01000 Bourg-en-Bresse
phone +33 04 74 22 49 40

**Hôtel de France**
19, place Bernard
01000 Bourg-en-Bresse
phone +33 04 74 23 30 24

**Le Prieuré**
49, boulevard de Brou
01000 Bourg-en-Bresse
phone +33 04 74 22 44 60

**Le Logis de Brou**
132, boulevard de Brou
01000 Bourg-en-Bresse
phone +33 04 74 22 11 55

**L'Auberge Bressane**
166, boulevard de Brou
01000 Bourg-en-Bresse
phone +33 04 74 22 22 68

**La Reyssouze**
20, rue Charles-Robin
01000 Bourg-en-Bresse
phone +33 04 74 23 11 50

**L'Amandine**
4, rue de la République
01000 Bourg en Bresse
phone +33 04 74 45 33 18

**L'Authentique Espace Buffet**
162, boulevard de Brou
01000 Bourg en Bresse
phone +33 04 74 22 15 28
*www.restaurant-lauthentique.com*

**Chapon d'Or**
4, rue Thomas-Riboud
01000 Bourg en Bresse
phone +33 04 74 23 02 66

**La Reyssouze**
20, rue Charles-Robin
01000 Bourg en Bresse
phone +33 04 74 23 11 50

**Volailler boucher Bozon**
18 avenue de Mâcon
01000 Bourg-en-Bresse
phone +33 04 74 22 49 40

**Au Chapon Bressan**
L'Huppe, BP 8
01340 Montrevel-en-Bresse
phone +33 04 74 25 43 54

*brive–la–gaillarde (limousin)*

**Office du Tourisme de Brive et son Pays**
place du 14 Juillet
19100 Brive-la-Gaillarde
phone +33 05 55 24 08 80
*www.brive-tourisme.com*

**Hôtel-restaurant La Truffe Noire**
22, boulevard Anatole France
19100 Brive-la-Gaillarde
phone +33 05 55 92 45 00
*www.la-truffe-noire.com*

**Le Cheval Blanc**
19, place du Marché
87500 Saint Yrieix la Perche
phone +33 05 55 75 01 46
*www.restaurant-lechevalblanc.com*

**Restaurant La Potinière**
6, boulevard de Puyblanc
19100 Brive-la-Gaillarde
phone +33 05 55 24 06 22

**Les Arums**
15, avenue Alsace-Lorraine
19100 Brive-la-Gaillarde
phone +33 05 55 24 26 55
*www.lesarums.fr*

**Chez Francis**
61, avenue de Paris
19100 Brive-la-Gaillarde
phone +33 05 55 74 41 72
*www.chezfrancis.fr*

**Restaurant Toupine**
27, avenue Pasteur
19450 Brive-la-Gaillarde
phone +33 05 55 23 71 58

**La Truffe Noire**
22, boulevard Anatole-France
19100 Brive-la-Gaillarde
phone +33 05 55 92 45 00
*www.la-truffe-noire.com*

**La Ferme de Boud'eau**
Le Boudaud
87110 Le Vigen
phone +33 05 55 00 41 03

**Charcuterie artisanale
(Pierre Giraud)**
place de l'église
19410 Vigeois
phone +33 05 55 98 92 56
*www.giraudpierre.com*

**Producteur de châtaignes
(Jean-Marie Cousty)**
Mépiaud
19230 Troche
phone +33 05 55 73 35 29

**Cave viticole**
Le Bourg Branceilles
phone +33 05 55 84 09 01

**Domaine La Croix du Battut
(Jean Gaubert)**
19120 Queyssac-les-Vignes
phone +33 05 55 91 13 13
*www.domainelacroixdubattut.com*

**Moutarde violette Denoix**
9, boulevard du Maréchal Lyautey
19108 Brive-la-Gaillarde
phone +33 05 55 74 34 27
*www.denoix.fr*

*caen (normandy)*

**Office de Tourisme**
place Saint Pierre
14000 Caen
phone +33 02 31 27 14 14
*www.tourisme.caen.fr*

**Hôtel Best Western Le Dauphin**
29, rue Gemare
14000 Caen
phone +33 02 31 86 35 14

**Ferme-auberge des Massinots**
14190 Saint Germain-le-Vasson
phone +33 02 31 90 54 22

**Restaurant l'Alcide**
1, place Courtonne
14000 Caen
phone +33 02 31 44 18 06

**Restaurant Le Pressoir**
3, avenue Henry Cheron
14000 Caen
phone +33 0820 20 19 20

**Restaurant La Petite Auberge**
17, rue des Équipes-d'Urgence
phone +33 02 31 86 43 30

**Le Bouchon du Vaugueux**
12, rue Graindorge
phone +33 02 31 44 26 26
14000 Caen

**Le Dauphin**
29, rue Gemare
14000 Caen
phone +33 02 31 86 22 26
www.le-dauphin-normandie.com

**L'Embroche**
17, rue Porte-au-Berger
14000 Caen
phone +33 02 31 93 71 31

**Maître Corbeau**
8, rue Buquet
14000 Caen
phone +33 02 31 93 93 00
www.maitre-corbeau.com

**Le Quatre Epices**
25, rue Porte-au-Berger
14000 Caen
phone +33 02 31 93 40 41

**Calvados Roger Groult**
route des Calvados
14290 Saint-Cyr-du-Ronceray
phone +33 02 31 63 71 53
www.calvados-roger-groult.com

**Calvados Maison Boulard**
route de Manerbe
14130 Coquainvilliers
phone +33 02 31 48 24 00
www.calvados-boulard.com

**Boucherie Alain et Claudine Marie**
8, rue Larcher
14400 Bayeux
phone +33 02 31 92 02 16

**Boucherie Saint Sauveur**
4, rue Pémagnie
14000 Caen
phone +33 02 31 85 43 24

cahors (midi–pyrénées)

**Maison du Tourisme**
place François Mitterrand
46000 Cahors
phone +33 05 65 53 20 65
www.mairie-cahors.fr
www.quercy.net

**Hôtel Terminus**
**Restaurant Le Balandre**
5, avenue Charles de Freycinet
46000 Cahors
phone +33 05 65 53 32 00
www.balandre.com

**Hôtel de France**
252, avenue Jean Jaurès
46000 Cahors
phone +33 05 65 35 16 76
www.hoteldefrance-cahors.fr

**Restaurant L'O à la Bouche**
134, rue St Urcisse
46000 Cahors
phone +33 05 65 35 65 69

**Restaurant Au fil des douceurs**
90, quai de la Verrerie
46000 Cahors
phone +33 05 65 22 13 04

**Le Balandre**
5, avenue Charles-de-Freycinet
46000 Cahors
phone +33 05 65 53 32 00
www.balandre.com

**La Garenne**
D 820 Cahors-Nord
46000 Cahors
phone +33 05 65 35 40 67

**La Ferme du Mas de Thomas**
**(Jean-François et Maryline Lafon)**
46160 Saint Sulpice
phone +33 05 65 40 02 55

**Ferme du Rouquet**
**(Famille Cazal)**
46 130 Loubressac
phone +33 05 65 33 61 04

**GAEC des Aulnes**
24200 Borrèze
phone +33 05 53 28 89 11

**Château Lagrézette**
46140 Caillac
phone +33 05 65 20 07 42
www.chateau-lagrezette.tm.fr

**Château Latuc**
**(Jean-François & Geneviève Meyan)**
46700 Mauroux
phone +33 05 65 36 58 63
www.latuc.com

**Domaine de Maison Neuve**
**(Delmouly et fils)**
46800 Le Boulvé
phone +33 05 65 31 95 76
www.domainemaisonneuve.com

**Truffes Pébeyre**
66, Rue Frédéric Suisse
46000 Cahors
phone +33 05 65 22 24 80
www.pebeyre.fr

**Syndicat des trufficulteurs**
**de la Région de Lalbenque**
La Borie Rouge
46230 Lalbenque
phone +33 05 65 24 75 27

cambrai (nord–pas–de–calais)

**Office de Tourisme**
Maison Espagnole
48, rue de Noyon
59400 Cambrai
phone +33 03 27 78 36 15
www.tourisme-cambrai.fr

**Hôtels-Restaurant Béatus**
718, avenue de Paris
59400 Cambrai
phone +33 03 27 81 45 70
www.cambraihotel.fr

**Hôtel-Restaurant Le Mouton Blanc**
33, rue d'Alsace-Lorraine
59400 Cambrai
phone +33 03 27 81 30 16

**Hôtels-Restaurant du Château**
**de la Motte Fénelon**
square du Château, BP 174
59403 Cambrai
phone +33 03 27 83 61 38
www.cambrai-chateau-motte-fenelon.com

**Restaurant L'Escargot**
10, rue du Général de Gaulle
59400 Cambrai
phone +33 03 27 81 24 54

**Le clos saint jacques**
9, rue Saint-Jacques
59400 Cambrai
phone +33 03 27 74 37 61
www.leclosstjacques.com

**Beatus**
Avenue de Paris
59400 Cambrai
phone +33 03 27 81 45 70
www.hotel.beatus.fr

**Château de la Motte Fénelon**
Square du Château
59400 Cambrai
phone +33 03 27 83 61 38
www.cambrai-chateau-motte-fenelon.com

**Confiserie Afchain**
Z.I de Cantimpré
59400 Cambrai
phone +33 03 27 81 25 49
www.betises-de-cambrai.fr

**À la Renommée**
21, rue des Rôtisseurs
59400 Cambrai
phone +33 03 27 81 50 22
www.alarenommee.com

**Confrérie de l'Andouillette**
1622, Route Nationale
59400 Fontaine-Notre-Dame
phone +33 03 27 81 55 62

camembert (normandy)

**Office de Tourisme**
Maison du Camembert
61120 Camembert
phone +33 02 33 39 43 35
www.camembert-france.com

**Chambres d'hôtes Jardins du Prieuré**
**Saint-Michel**
61120 Crouttes
phone +33 02 33 39 15 15
www.prieure-saint-michel.com

**Restaurant La Camembertière**
hôtellerie Faroult, route d'Argentan
61120 Les Champeaux en Auge
phone +33 02 33 39 31 87

**Restaurant La Maison du Vert**
Ticheville
61120 Vimoutiers
phone +33 02 33 36 95 84
www.maisonduvert.com

**Auberge de l'Aigle d'or**
68, rue Vaucelles
14130 Pont-l'Évêque
phone +33 02 31 65 05 25
www.laigledor.com

**Auberge de la Levrette**
48, rue de Lisieux
14140 Saint-Julien-le-Faucon
phone +33 02 31 63 81 20

**Au Caneton**
32, rue Grande
14290 Orbec
phone +33 02 31 32 73 32

**L'Orbecquoise**
60, Rue Grande
14290 Orbec
phone +33 02 31 62 44 99

**Domaine de Saint Loup**
Saint Loup de Fribois
14340 Cambremer
phone +33 02 31 63 04 04

**Ferme de la Héronniere**
**(François Durand)**
61120 Camembert
phone +33 02 33 39 08 08

**Fromagerie Graindorge**
42, rue du Général Leclerc
14140 Livarot
phone +33 02 31 48 20 10
www.graindorge.fr

**Fromagerie du Plessis**
Noards
27560 Lieurey
phone +33 02 32 20 27 27

**Jérôme Srruytte**
Ferme du Bourg Saint-Philbert-des-Champs
14130 Pont-l'Évêque
phone +33 02 31 04 72 43

cassis (provence)

**Office de Tourisme et des Congrès**
quai des Moulins
13260 Cassis
phone +33 0892 259 892
www.ot-cassis.fr

**Hôtel Royal Cottage**
6, avenue du 11 Novembre
13260 Cassis
phone +33 04 42 01 33 34
www.royal-cottage.com

**Hôtel Les Jardins de Cassis**
rue Auguste Favier
13260 Cassis
phone +33 04 42 01 84 85
www.hotel-lesjardinsde-cassis.com

**Golf Hôtel**
plage de Rènecros
83150 Bandol
phone +33 04 94 29 45 83
www.golfhotel.fr

**Restaurant La Presqu'île**
quartier Port Miou, direction les Calanques
13260 Cassis
phone +33 04 42 01 03 77
www.restaurant-la-presquile.com

**Restaurant le Clocher**
1, rue de la Paroisse
83150 Bandol
phone +33 04 94 32 47 65

**Le Clos des Arômes**
10, rue Paul Mouton
13260 Cassis
phone +33 04 42 01 71 84
www.le-clos-des-aromes.com

**Restaurant Nino**
1, quai Barthélemy
13260 Cassis
phone +33 04 42 01 74 32
www.nino-cassis.com

**Fleurs de Thym**
5, rue Lamartine
13260 Cassis
phone +33 04 42 01 23 03

**Auberge Le Revestel**
13600 La Ciotat
phone +33 04 42 83 11 06
www.revestel.com

**Le Château de Fontblanche**
route de Carnoux
13260 Cassis
phone +33 04 42 01 00 11

**Mas du Boudard**
**(Pierre Marchand)**
7, route de Bellefille
13260 Cassis
phone +33 04 42 01 72 66

**Château de Pibarnon**
410, chemin de la Croix-des-Signaux
83741 La Cadière d'Azur
phone +33 04 94 90 12 73
www.pibarnon.com

**Domaine de Bunan**
Moulin des Costes, Château La Rouvière
83740 La Cadière d'Azur
phone +33 04 94 98 58 98
www.bunan.com

**Maison des Vins du Bandol**
Les Domaines du Bandol
122, allées Vivien
83150 Bandol
phone +33 04 94 29 45 03
http://maisondesvins.free.fr

*castelnaudary (languedoc–roussillon)*

**Office de tourisme**
place de Verdun
11400 Castelnaudary
phone +33 04 68 23 05 73

**Hôtel du Canal**
2 ter avenue Arnaut-Vidal
11400 Castelnaudary
phone +33 04 68 94 05 05

**Hôtel de France**
2 avenue Frédéric Mistral
11400 Castelnaudary
phone +33 04 68 23 10 18

**Hôtel du Centre et du Lauragais**
31 cours de la République
11400 Castelnaudary
phone +33 04 68 23 25 95

**Le Clos Fleuri Saint-Siméon**
134 avenue Monseigneur-de-Langle
11400 Castelnaudary
phone +33 04-68-94-01-20

**Hôtel Restaurant Fourcade**
14 rue des Carmes
11400 Castelnaudary
phone +33 04 68 23 02 08

**Le Tirou**
90, avenue Mgr-Delangle
11400 Castelnaudary
phone +33 04 68 94 15 95
www.le-tirou.com

**Hostellerie du Château de la Pomarède**
11400 La Pomarède
phone +33 04 68 60 49 69

**Auberge du Poids Public**
31540 Saint-Félix-Lauragais
phone +33 05 62 18 85 00
www.auberge-du-poidspublic.com

**Hostellerie de la Montagne Noire**
Place des Promenades
phone +33 05 63 50 31 12
81110 Dourgne
www.montagnenoire.net

**La Maison du Cassoulet**
24 cours de la République
11400 Castelnaudary
phone +33 04 68 23 27 23

**Belloc**
48 rue du Onze-Novembre
11400 Castelnaudary
phone +33 04 68 23 02 20

**Gabriel Parédès**
42 place de Verdun
11400 Castelnaudary
phone +33 04 68 23 11 34

*cavaillon (provence)*

**Office de Tourisme Intercommunal**
**Cavaillon-Luberon**
place Francois Tourel, B.P. 176
84305 Cavaillon
phone +33 04 90 71 32 01
www.cavaillon-luberon.com

**Hôtel du Parc**
183, place François Tourel
84300 Cavaillon
phone +33 04 90 71 57 78
www.hotelduparccavaillon.com

**Hôtel Best Western le Comtadin**
65, boulevard Albin Durand
84200 Carpentras
phone +33 04 90 67 75 00

**Hôtel Château de Mazan**
place Napoléon
84380 Mazan
phone +33 04 90 69 62 61
www.chateaudemazan.com

**Restaurant Prévôt**
353, avenue de Verdun
84300 Cavaillon
phone +33 04 90 71 32 43
www.restaurant-prevot.com

**Restaurant L'Atelier de Pierre**
30, place de l'Horloge
84200 Carpentras
phone +33 04 90 60 75 00

**Les Jardins du Portail Rouge**
59, quartier Grand Grès
84300 Cavaillon
phone +33 04 90 78 06 60

**Côté Jardin**
49, rue Lamartine
84300 Cavaillon
phone +33 04 90 71 33 58

**Les Gérardies**
140, cours Gambetta
84300 Cavaillon
phone +33 04 90 71 35 55
www.lesgerardies.com

**La Ferme Lou Pous**
428, route de Saumane
84800 Isle sur la Sorgue
phone +33 04 90 38 23 30

**Syndicat de défense des raisins de table**
**du Mont-Ventoux**
89, place du 8 Mai
84380 Mazan
phone +33 04 90 69 51 26
www.aoc-muscat-du-ventoux.com

*chablis (burgundy)*

**Office du tourisme**
1, quai du Biez
89800 Chablis
phone +33 03 86 42 80 80

**Hostellerie des Clos**
rue Jules-Rathier
89800 Chablis
phone +33 03 86 42 10 63

**Au Relais de la Belle Étoile**
4, rue des Moulins
89800 Chablis
phone +33 03 86 18 96 08

**Hôtel de la Poste**
24, rue Auxerroise
89800 Chablis
phone +33 03 86 42 11 94

**Au Lys de Chablis**
38, route d'Auxerre
89800 Chablis
phone +33 03 86 42 49 20

**Le Bistrot des Grands Crus**
rue Jules-Rathier
89800 Chablis
phone +33 03 86 42 19 41

**Laroche Wine Bar**
18, rue des Moulins
89800 Chablis
phone +33 03 86 42 47 30

**Le Moulin de la Coudre**
89290 Venoy
phone +33 03 86 40 23 79
www.moulindelacoudre.com

**Le Saint Père**
2, avenue G. Pompidou
89700 Tonnerre
phone +33 03 86 55 12 84

**Le Bourgogne**
15, rue de Preuilly
89000 Auxerre
phone +33 03 86 51 57 50

**La Maison de l'Andouillette Artisanale**
3 bis, place du Général-de-Gaulle
89800 Chablis
phone +33 03 86 42 12 82

**Marc Colin**
3 place du Général-de-Gaulle
89800 Chablis
phone +33 03 86 42 10 62

*chantilly (picardy)*

**Office de tourisme de Chantilly**
60, Avenue du Maréchal Joffre
60500 Chantilly
phone +33 03 44 67 37 37
www.chantilly-tourisme.com

**Hôtel Dolce Chantilly**
route d'Apremont Vineuil Saint Firmin
60500 Chantilly
phone +33 03 44 58 47 85
www.chantilly.dolce.com

**Château Mont Royal**
Route de Plailly
60250 La Chapelle en Serval
phone +33 03 44 54 50 50
www.chateau-mont-royal.com

**Restaurant La Ferme de Condé**
42, avenue du Maréchal Joffre
60500 Chantilly
phone +33 03 44 57 32 31
www.lafermedeconde.fr.st

**Restaurant Relais d'Aumale**
37, place des Fêtes
60560 Montgresin
phone +33 03 44 54 61 31
www.relais-aumale.fr

**La Belle Bio**
22, rue du Connétable
60500 Chantilly
phone +33 03 44 57 02 25
www.labellebio.com

**Carmontelle**
route d'Apremont
60500 Chantilly
phone +33 03 44 58 47 57
www.chantilly.dolce.com

**La Renardière**
2, rue des Frères Segard
60270 Gouvieux
phone +33 03 44 57 08 23

**Fromagerie Ganot**
4, rue Cécile Dumez
77640 Jouarre
phone +33 01 60 22 06 09
www.fermes-brie.fr

**Société Fromagère de la Brie**
19, avenue Du Grand Morin
77169 Saint Siméon
phone +33 01 64 34 44 61

**Fromagerie Renard-Gillard**
Biencourt-Sur-Orge
55260 Montier-sur-Saulx
phone +33 03 29 75 91 82

**Compagnie Fermière B. et E. Rotschild**
Domaine des 30 Arpents
77220 Favières
phone +33 01 64 07 02 12

*clermont-ferrand (auvergne)*

**Office de tourisme**
Place de la Victoire
63000 Clermont-Ferrand
phone +33 04 73 98 65 00
www.ot-clermont-ferrand.fr

**Hôtel restaurant des Puys Arvernes**
16, place Delille
63000 Clermont-Ferrand
phone +33 04 73 91 92 06

**Restaurant Emmanuel Hodencq**
place Saint-Pierre
63000 Clermont-Ferrand
phone +33 04 73 31 23 23
www.hodencq.com

**Restaurant l'Imprévu**
4, rue Ribeyre Jaffeux
63000 Clermont Ferrand
phone +33 04 73 31 36 72

**Hôtel restaurant Aletti Palace**
3, place Joseph Aletti
03200 Vichy
phone +33 04 89 61 90 01

**Restaurant Jacques Decoret**
7, avenue de Gramont
03200 Vichy
phone +33 04 70 97 65 06
www.jacquesdecoret.com

**Noël Cruzilles**
226, avenue Jean Mermoz BP 05
63015 Clermont Cedex 02
phone +33 04 73 91 24 46
www.cruzilles.fr

**Maison Vieillard**
avenue Ernest Cristal, BP 20
63064 Clermont-Ferrand
phone +33 04 73 28 64 30
www.vieillard.fr

**Jean-Claude Leclerc**
12, rue Saint-Adjutor
63000 Clermont-Ferrand
phone +33 04 73 36 46 30

**L'Alambic**
6, rue Sainte-Claire
63000 Clermont-Ferrand
phone +33 04 73 36 17 45
www.alambic-restaurant.com

**Amphitryon Capucine**
50, rue de Fontgiève
63000 Clermont-Ferrand
phone +33 04 73 31 38 39

**Bernard Andrieux**
route de la Baraque
63830 Durtol
phone +33 04 73 19 25 00

**Boulangerie Christian Nury**
1, place de l'Eglise
63530 Volvic
phone +33 04 73 33 53 48

**Boulangerie Le Pistore**
place de l'Eglise
63230 Pontgibaud
phone +33 04 73 88 70 37

**Au Bon Pain de Seigle**
**(Christine et Patrick Fayard)**
17, rue de la République
42440 Noirétable
phone +33 04 77 24 71 33

**Société Nouvelle des Pastilles De Vichy**
94, allée des Ailes
03200 Vichy
phone +33 04 70 30 94 70

**La Maison du Bon Fromage**
Marché Saint Pierre
63000 Clermont-Ferrand
phone +33 04 73 36 16 13

**Fromagerie Vauzeilles**
2, rue Chaux Blanche
63800 Cournon d'Auvergne
phone +33 04 73 69 10 01

**Fromagerie le Montcyneire**
28, rue de la Berbiziale
63500 Issoire
phone +33 04 73 89 19 26

*cognac (poitou–charentes)*

**Office du tourisme**
16, rue du 14 Juillet
16100 Cognac
phone +33 05 45 82 10 71

**Les Pigeons Blancs**
110, rue Jules-Brisson
16100 Cognac
phone +33 05 45 82 16 36

**L'Héritage**
25, rue d'Angoulême
16100 Cognac
phone +33 05 45 82 01 26

**Le François 1er**
3, place François 1er
16100 Cognac
phone +33 05 45 32 07 18

**Le Valois**
35, rue du 14 Juillet
16100 Cognac
phone +33 05 45 36 83 00

**La Résidence**
25, avenue Victor-Hugo
16100 Cognac
phone +33 05 45 36 62 40

**Château de l'Yeuse**
65, rue de Bellevue
16100 Châteaubernard-Cognac
phone +33 05 45 36 82 60
www.yeuse.fr

**La Courtine**
Allée Fichon
16100 Cognac
phone +33 05 45 82 34 78
www.restaurant-la-courtine.fr

**La Ribaudière**
16200 Bourg-Charente
phone +33 05 45 81 30 54
www.laribaudiere.com

**Du Château**
Place du Château
16200 Jarnac
phone +33 05 45 81 07 17
www.restaurant-du-chateau.com

**Le Domaine du Breuil**
104, rue Bernard-Daugas
16100 Cognac
phone +33 05 45 35 32 06

**La Cognathèque**
8, place Jean-Monnet
16100 Cognac
phone +33 05 45 82 43 31

**Maison Martell**
place Édouard-Martell
16100 Cognac
phone +33 05 45 36 33 33

**Maison Hennessy**
rue de la Bichonne
16100 Cognac
phone +33 05 45 35 72 68

*collioure (languedoc–roussillon)*

**Office de Tourisme**
place du 18 Juin
66190 Collioure
phone +33 04 68 82 15 47
www.collioure.com

**Hôtel Relais des 3 Mas**
**restaurant La Balette**
route de Port Vendres
66190 Collioure
phone +33 04 68 82 05 07
www.relaisdestroismas.com

**Hôtel L'arapède**
**restaurant La Farigole**
route de Port Vendres
66190 Collioure
phone +33 04 68 98 09 59
www.arapede.com

**Hôtel-restaurant Les Templiers**
12, quai de l'Amirauté
66190 Collioure
phone +33 04 68 98 31 10

**Restaurant L'Amphitryon**
17, rue Jean Bart
66190 Collioure
phone +33 04 68 82 36 00

**La Frégate**
24, quai de l'Amirauté
66190 Collioure
phone +33 04 68 82 06 05

**Le Neptune**
Route de Port-Vendres
66190 Collioure
phone +33 04 68 82 02 27

**La Balette**
Route de Port-Vendres
66190 Collioure
phone +33 04 68 82 05 07
www.relaisdestroismas.com

**L'Arapède**
Route de Port-Vendres
66190 Collioure
phone +33 04 68 98 09 59
www.arapede.com

**Ets Roque**
17, route d'Argelès-sur-Mer
66190 Collioure
phone +33 04 68 82 04 99

**Ets Desclaux**
3, route d'Argelès-sur-Mer
66190 Collioure
phone +33 04 68 82 05 25

**Cave Veuve Banyuls**
4, route de Port Vendres
66190 Collioure
phone +33 04 68 82 05 22

**Le Cellier des Dominicains**
route de Port Vendres, Place Orphila
66190 Collioure
phone +33 04 68 82 05 63
www.dominicain.com

**Le Croquant à L'Ancienne**
8, rue Berthelot
66190 Collioure
phone +33 04 68 98 08 90

**Office de Tourisme**
place Bossuet
32100 Condom
phone +33 05 62 28 00 80

**Le Logis des Cordeliers**
2 bis, rue de la Paix
32100 Condom
phone +33 05 62 28 03 68

**Les Trois Lys**
38, rue Gambetta
32100 Condom
phone +33 05 62 28 33 33

**Le Moulin du Petit Gascon**
route d'Eauze
32100 Condom
phone +33 05 62 28 28 42

**Le Relais de la Ténarèze**
20, avenue d'Aquitaine
32100 Condom
phone +33 05 62 28 02 54

**La Ferme de Flaran**
Route de Condom
32310 Valence-sur-Baise
phone +33 05 62 28 58 22
www.fermedeflaran.com

**Le Relais de la Hire**
11, rue Porte neuve
47600 Francescas
phone +33 05 53 65 41 59
www.la-hire.com

**Le Florida**
32410 Caster-Verduzan
phone +33 05 62 68 13 22

**Musée de l'Armagnac (boutique)**
2, rue Jules Ferry
32100 Condom
phone +33 05 62 28 00 80

**La Maison de l'Armagnac**
Château de Bordeneuve
32440 Castelnau-d'Auzan
phone +33 05 62 29 26 49

**Société Armagnacaise de Distribution**
7 avenue d'Aquitaine
32100 Condom
phone +33 05 62 68 29 00

**Philippe Aurian**
27, rue de la République
32100 Condom
phone +33 05 62 28 13 29

**Agence du Tourisme de la Corse**
17, boulevard Roi-Jérôme, BP 19
20181 Ajaccio cedex 01
phone +33 04 95 51 00 00
www.visit-corsica.com

**Restaurant A Funtana**
7, rue Notre Dame
20000 Ajaccio
phone +33 04 95 21 78 04

**Hôtel-restaurant Eden Roc**
route des Iles Sanguinaires
20000 Ajaccio
phone +33 04 95 51 56 00
www.edenroc-corsica.fr

**Hôtel-restaurant Maquis**
BP 94
20166 Porticcio
phone +33 04 95 25 05 55
www.lemaquis.com

**Restaurant Le Floride**
route de l'Amirauté, Port Charles Ornano
20000 Ajaccio
phone +33 04 95 22 67 48

**Clos d'Alzeto**
20151 Sari d'Orcino
phone +33 04 95 52 24 67
www.closdalzeto.com

**Clos Capitoro**
**(Jacques Bianchetti Pisciatella)**
20166 Porticcio
phone +33 04 95 25 19 61
www.clos-capitoro.com

**Domaine Peraldi**
**(Comte Guy Tyrel de Poix)**
Chemin de Stiletto
20167 Mezzavia
phone +33 04 95 22 37 30

**Domaine Antoine Arena**
20253 Patrimonio
phone +33 04 95 37 08 27

**Domaine Gentile**
Olzo
20217 Saint Florent
phone +33 04 95 37 01 54
www.domaine-gentile.com

**Ferme-auberge "U Taravu"**
**(Nadia Andreucci)**
20173 Zevacu
phone +33 04 95 24 46 06

**L'Estaminet**
5-7, rue Roi-de-Rome
20000 Ajaccio
phone +33 04 95 50 10 42

**U Pampasgiolu**
15, rue de la Porta
20000 Ajaccio
phone +33 04 95 50 71 52

**A Casarella**
6, rue Sainte-Croix
20200 Bastia
phone +33 04 95 32 02 32
www.acasarella.fr

**Caveau du Marin**
Quai des Martyrs-de-la-Libération
20200 Bastia
phone +33 04 95 31 62 31

**Marina di Cavu**
Calalonga
20169 Bonifacio
phone +33 04 95 73 14 13
www.marinadicavu.com

**Stella d'Oro**
7, rue Doria
20169 Bonifacio
phone +33 04 95 73 03 63
www.bonifacio.com/stella.oro/

**Paul Leoni**
quartier Pucasa
20173 Zevacu
phone +33 04 95 24 42 49

**Jo Giannesini**
20128 Grosseto-Prufna
phone +33 04 95 25 71 44

**Jean-Paul Vincensini et fils**
20244 San Lurenzu
phone +33 04 95 47 15 45
www.vincensini.fr

**Jean-David Sommovigo**
20230 San Nicolao
phone +33 04 95 38 56 98
www.castaneiculteur.over-blog.com

**Office de tourisme**
Rond Point du 11 Novembre, BP 201
04001 Digne-les-Bains
phone +33 04 92 36 62 62
www.ot-dignelesbains.fr

**Hôtel-restaurant du Grand Paris**
19, boulevard Thiers
04000 Digne-les-Bains
phone +33 04 92 31 11 15
www.hotel-grand-paris.com

**Hôtel Villa Gaia**
24, route de Nice
04000 Digne les Bains
phone +33 04 92 31 21 60
www.hotelvillagaia.fr

**Grand Hôtel du Cours**
allée de Verdun
04200 Sisteron
phone +33 04 92 61 04 51
www.hotel-lecours.com

**Chambres d'hôtes
"Le Vieil Aiglun"**
04510 Aiglun
phone +33 04 92 34 67 00
www.vieil-aiglun.com

**Le Coin Fleuri**
9, boulevard Victor Hugo
04000 Digne-les-Bains
phone +33 04 92 31 04 51

**Au Goût du Jour**
face au Château N 85
04160 Château-Arnoux-Saint-Auban
phone +33 04 92 64 48 48

**La Magnanerie**
Les Fillières
04200 Aubignosc
phone +33 04 92 62 60 11
www.la-magnanerie.net

**Restaurant L'Oustaou de la Foun**
Route Nationale 85
04160 Château Arnoux
phone +33 04 92 62 65 30

**Les Becs Fins**
16, rue Saunerie
04200 Sisteron
phone +33 04 92 61 12 04
www.becsfins.free.fr

**Alpes Provence Agneaux**
10, allée des Romarins, BP 5
04200 Sisteron
phone +33 04 92 61 33 50
www.alpesprovenceagneaux.fr

**Association César**
route de la Durance
04100 Manosque
phone +33 04 92 72 56 81

**Le Grand Rubren**
1, rue de Savoie
04400 Barcelonnette
phone +33 04 92 81 44 07
www.legrandrubren.fr

**Office du tourisme**
place Darcy
21000 Dijon
phone +33 03 80 44 11 44

**Hôtel restaurant Sofitel La Cloche**
14, place Darcy
21000 Dijon
phone +33 03 80 30 12 32

**Hostellerie de Chapeau Rouge**
5, rue Michelet
21000 Dijon
phone +33 03 80 50 88 88

**Le Wilson**
place Wilson
21000 Dijon
phone +33 03 80 66 82 50

**Hôtel du Palais**
23, rue du Palais
21000 Dijon
phone +33 03 80 67 16 26

**Le Pré aux Clercs**
13, place de la Libération
21000 Dijon
phone +33 03 80 38 05 05

**Restaurant Stéphane Derbord**
10, place Wilson
21000 Dijon
phone +33 03 80 67 74 64

**Le Bistrot des Halles**
10, rue Bannelier
phone +33 03 80 49 94 15
21000 Dijon

**Le Cézanne**
38-36, rue de l'Amiral-Roussin
21000 Dijon
phone +33 03 80 58 91 92
www.bourgogne-resto.com

**Le Chabrot**
36, rue Monge
21000 Dijon
phone +33 03 80 30 69 61

**L'Epicerie et Cie**
5, place Emile Zola
21000 Dijon
phone +33 03 80 30 70 69

**Rôtisserie le Central**
3, place Grangier
21000 Dijon
phone +33 03 80 30 44 00
www.accor.com

**Moutarde Maille**
32, rue de la Liberté
21000 Dijon
phone +33 03 80 30 41 02

**Bourgogne Street**
61, rue de la Liberté
21000 Dijon
phone +33 03 80 30 26 28

*fécamp (normandy)*

**Office du tourisme**
113, rue Alexandre-Le-Grand
76400 Fécamp
phone +33 02 35 28 51 01

**Le Grand Pavois**
15, quai de la Vicomté
76400 Fécamp
phone +33 02 35 10 01 01

**Ferme de la Chapelle**
Côte de la Vierge par la route du Phare
76400 Fécamp
phone +33 02 35 10 12 12

**Auberge de la Rouge**
route du Havre
70400 Saint-Léonard
phone +33 02 35 28 07 59

**Hôtel Vent d'Ouest**
3, avenue Gambetta
76400 Fécamp
phone +33 02 35 28 04 04

**Hôtel de la Mer**
89, boulevard Albert 1er
76400 Fécamp
phone +33 02 35 28 01 57

**Café de la Boucane**
12, Grand Quai
76400 Fécamp
phone +33 02 35 10 50 50

**La Marée**
77, quai Bérigny
76400 Fécamp
phone +33 02 35 29 39 15
www.fecamp-restaurant-la-maree.com

**Les Terre-Neuvas**
63, boulevard Albert-1er
76400 Fécamp
phone +33 02 35 29 22 92
www.lesterreneuvas.com

**Palais de la Bénédictine**
110, rue Alexandre-Le-Grand
76400 Fécamp
phone +33 02 35 10 26 10

*fleurance (midi–pyrénées)*

**Office du tourisme du Jura dolois**
112, bis rue de la République
32500 Fleurance
phone +33 05 62 64 00 00

**Le Relais**
32, avenue du Général-de-Gaulle
32500 Fleurance
phone +33 05 62 06 05 08

**Le Fleurance**
route d'Agen
32500 Fleurance
phone +33 05 62 06 14 85

**Château de Fourcès au village**
32250 Fourcès
phone +33 05 62 29 49 53

**Le Bastard**
rue Lagrange
32700 Lectoure
phone +33 05 62 68 82 44

**La Lumiane**
Grande Rue
32310 Saint-Puy
phone +33 05 62 28 95 95
www.lalumiane.com

**Le Papillon**
N 21
32810 Montaut-les-Créneaux
phone +33 05 62 65 51 29
www.restaurant-lepapillon.com

**Le Florida**
32410 Castera-Verduzan
phone +33 05 62 68 13 22

**La Table d'Oste**
7, rue Lamartine
32000 Auch
phone +33 05 62 05 55 62
www.table-oste-restaurant.com

**La Ferme de Flaran**
route de Condom
32310 Valence-sur-Baïse
phone +33 05 62 28 58 22

**Gersica**
Zone Industrielle
32500 Fleurance
phone +33 05 62 64 24 24

*foix ( midi–pyrénées)*

**Office de Tourisme du Pays de Foix**
29, rue Delcassé
09000 Foix
phone +33 05 61 65 12 12
www.ot-foix.fr

**Hôtel-restaurant Lons**
6 place Georges Dutilh
09000 Foix
phone +33 05 34 09 28 00
www.hotel-lons-foix.com

**L'Hostellerie de la Poste**
16, avenue Victor Pilhes
09400 Tarascon-sur-Ariège
phone +33 05 61 05 60 41
www.hostellerieposte.com

**Hôtel-Restaurant Eychenne**
8, avenue Paul-Laffont
09200 Saint-Girons
phone +33 05 61 04 04 50
www.ariege.com/hotel-eychenne

**Chambres d'hôtes au
Château de Montcru**
09240 Allières
phone +33 05 61 03 86 49

**Ferme-auberge de Caussou**
09000 Cos
phone +33 05 61 65 34 42
www.ariege.com/ferme-de-caussou

**Le Médiéval**
42, rue des Chapeliers
09000 Foix
phone +33 05 34 09 01 72

**Le Phoebus**
3, cours Irénée-Cros
09000 Foix
phone +33 05 61 65 10 42
www.ariege.com/le-phoebus

**Le Sainte-Marthe**
21, rue Noël-Peyrevidal
09000 Foix
phone +33 05 61 02 87 87
www.le-saintemarthe.fr

**Le Moulin Gourmand**
09800 Engomer
phone +33 05 61 96 83 38

**Croustades Martine Crespo**
21, rue des Marchands
09000 Foix
phone +33 05 34 09 34 27
www.croustade.com

**Hypocras**
SARL Seguelas
09400 Tarascon-sur-Ariège
phone +33 05 61 05 60 38
www.hypocras.com

*grenoble (rhône–alpes)*

**Office de Tourisme**
14, rue de la République
38 000 Grenoble
phone +33 04 76 42 41 41
www.grenoble-isere-tourisme.com

**Park Hôtel Grenoble**
10, place Paul Mistral
38027 Grenoble Cedex
phone +33 04 76 85 81 23
www.park-hotel-grenoble.fr

**Hôtel Restaurant Les 3 Roses**
32, avenue du Grésivaudan
38700 Corenc
phone +33 04 76 90 35 09
www.lestroisroses.activehotels.com

**Auberge Napoléon**
7, rue Montorge
38000 Grenoble
phone +33 04 76 87 53 64
www.auberge-napoleon.fr

**Restaurant La Panse**
7, rue de la Paix
38000 Grenoble
phone +33 04 76 54 09 54

**Bistrot Lyonnais - La Glycine**
168, cours Berriat
38000 Grenoble
phone +33 04 76 21 95 33

**L'Escalier**
6, place de Lavalette
38000 Grenoble
phone +33 04 76 54 66 16

**Le Fantin Latour**
1, rue du général Beylié
38000 Grenoble
phone +33 04 76 01 00 97
www.fantin-latour.net

**La Girole**
15, rue du Dr-Mazet
38000 Grenoble
phone +33 04 76 43 09 70

**Noix de Grenoble
(Jean-Louis Blanchon)**
route de Parnans, quartier du Saladot
26750 Montmiral
phone +33 06 62 42 50 91
www.grignote.com

**Gaec des Signaux
(Joël, Danielle Cony et Marie-Pierre
Ferrouillat)**
Les Signaux
38470 Têche
phone +33 04 76 36 83 78
www.noix-des-signaux.com

**Ferme de la Chatonnière
(Jacques Boucher)**
38470 Cognin-les-Gorges
phone +33 04 76 38 18 76
www.la-chato.com

**Musée de la Grande Chartreuse**
La Correrie
38380 St Pierre de Chartreuse
phone +33 04 76 88 60 45
www.musee-grande-chartreuse.fr

**Caves de la Chartreuse**
10, Boulevard Edgar Kofler
38500 Voiron
phone +33 04 76 05 81 77
www.chartreuse.fr

**Hôtel-Restaurant Le Relais du Cor d'Argent**
39, rue Nationale
18410 Argent-sur-Sauldre
phone +33 02 48 73 63 49

**Hôtel Restaurant Tatin**
5 avenue de Vierzon
41600 Lamotte-Beuvron
phone +33 02 54 88 00 03
www.hotel-tatin.fr

**Grand Hôtel du Lion d'Or**
69, rue Clemenceau
41200 Romorantin-Lanthenay
phone +33 02 54 94 15 15
www.hotel-liondor.fr

**Hostellerie de la Cloche**
39, avenue République
41600 Lamotte Beuvron
phone +33 02 54 88 02 20

**Restaurant Le Raboliot**
4, place Saint-Martin
41600 Nouan-le-Fuzelier
phone +33 02 54 94 40 00

**Restaurant Le Dahu**
14, rue Henri Chapron
41600 Nouan-le-Fuzelier
phone +33 02 54 88 72 88

**Tarte tatin
(Jean-Luc Bouchet)**
9, avenue Emile Morin
41600 Lamotte-Beuvron
phone +33 02 54 88 05 98

**Tarte tatin
(Jacques Sailer)**
60, avenue de la République
41600 Lamotte-Beuvron
phone +33 02 54 88 06 83

**Sablés de Nançay Maison Fleurier**
3, place de l'Eglise
18330 Nançay
phone +33 02 48 51 81 19

## le guilvinec (brittany)

**Office de Tourisme**
62, rue de la Marine, BP 14
29730 Le Guilvinec
phone +33 02 98 58 29 29
www.leguilvinec.com

**Hôtel-restaurant Villa Tri Men**
16, route du Phare
29120 Sainte Marine
phone +33 02 98 76 24 42
www.trimen.fr

**Hôtel Gradlon**
30, rue de Brest
29000 Quimper
phone +33 02 98 95 04 39
www.hotel-gradlon.fr

**Hôtel-Restaurant Le Poisson d'Avril**
19, rue Men Meur
29730 Le Guilvinec
phone +33 02 98 58 23 83

**Hôtel restaurant La Pointe de Mousterlin**
29170 Mousterlin Fouesnant
phone +33 02 98 56 04 12
www.mousterlinhotel.com

**L'Auberge des Glazicks**
7, rue de la plage
29550 Plomodiern
phone +33 02 98 81 52 32
www.auberge-des-glazick.com

**Restaurant L'Ambroisie**
49, rue Elie Fréron
29000 Quimper
phone +33 02 98 95 00 02
www.ambroisie-quimper.com

**Sterenn**
route d'Eckmühl
29760 Penmarch
phone +33 02 98 58 60 36
www.le-sterenn.com

**La Mer**
184, rue F. Peron
29760 Penmarch
phone +33 02 98 58 62 22
www.hotelstgue.com

**De Bretagne**
24, place de la République
29120 Pont-l'Abbé
phone +33 02 98 87 17 22

**Conserveries de langoustines
(Jean-Francois Furic)**
rue des Marais, Port de Saint Guenolé
29760 Penmarc'h
phone +33 02 98 58 52 62

**Conserverie Gonidec**
ZA Keramporiel, 2 rue Henri Fabre
29900 Concarneau
phone +33 02 98 97 07 09
www.gonidec.com

**Boulangerie-Pâtisserie
Thierry et Sylvie Lucas**
20, rue des Plomarc'h
29100 Douarnenez
phone +33 02 98 92 37 24

**Boulangerie-Pâtisserie Jean Le Guellec**
21, quai de l'Yser
29100 Douarnenez
phone +33 02 98 74 18 45

**Pâtisserie du Marché**
85, rue ar Veret
29100 Douarnenez
phone +33 02 98 74 23 94)

**Cidrerie Manoir du Kinkiz**
75 Chemin du Quinquis
Ergué-Armel 29000 Quimper
phone +33 02 98 90 20 57

**Les Vergers de Kermao**
Kermao 29950 Gouesnac'h
phone +33 02 98 54 60 64

**Cidrerie de Menez Brug**
56, Hent Carbon
Beg-Meil 29170 Fouesnant
phone +33 02 98 94 94 50

## le mans (pays de la loire)

**Office de Tourisme**
Hôtel des Ursulines
rue de l'Etoile
72000 Le Mans
phone +33 02 43 28 17 22
www.lemanstourisme.com

**Hôtel Concorde**
16, avenue du Général Leclerc
72000 Le Mans
phone +33 02 43 24 12 30

**Auberge de la Foresterie**
route de Laval
72000 Le Mans
phone +33 02 43 51 25 12

**Auberge des 7 plats**
79, Grande-Rue
72000 Le Mans
phone +33 02 43 24 57 77

**Restaurant La Vie en Rose**
55, Grande Rue
72000 Le Mans
phone +33 02 43 23 27 37

**Restaurant Le Beaulieu**
24, rue des Ponts-Neufs
72000 Le Mans
phone +33 02 43 87 78 37

**Le 21 Arts et Saveurs**
21, rue de Bolton
72000 Le Mans
phone +33 02 43 28 53 47
www.warain-reigner.fr

**Auberge des Sept Plats**
79, Grande-Rue
72000 Le Mans
phone +33 02 43 24 57 77

**Le Bistro du Mans**
12, rue Hippolyte-Lecornué
72000 Le Mans
phone +33 02 43 87 51 00
www.lebistrotdumans.com

**La Ciboulette**
14, rue de la Vieille-Porte
72000 Le Mans
phone +33 02 43 24 65 67

**La Grande Epicerie**
19 , rue Bolton
72000 Le Mans
phone +33 02 43 24 02 15

**Chocolatier Béline**
5, place Saint Nicolas
72000 Le Mans
phone +33 02 43 28 00 43

**Rillettes Daniel Després**
5, rue de Paris
72160 Connéré
phone +33 02 43 89 00 56

**Caves Joël Gigou**
4, rue des Caves
72340 La Chartre sur le Loir
phone +33 02 43 44 42 15

**Vins du Domaine de Bellivière
(Eric Nicolas)**
72340 Lhomme
phone +33 02 43 44 59 97

## le puy-en-velay (auvergne)

**Office de Tourisme**
2, Place du Clauzel
43000 Le Puy-en-Velay
phone +33 04 71 09 38 41
www.ot-lepuyenvelay.fr

**Restaurant François Gagnaire**
4, avenue Clément Charbonnier
43000 Le Puy-en-Velay
phone +33 04 71 02 75 55
www.francois-gagnaire-restaurant.com

**Eric et Ludivine Tournayre**
12, rue Chênebouterie
43000 Le Puy-en-Velay
phone +33 04 71 09 58 94
www.restaurant-tournayre.com

**Hôtel-restaurant Régis et Jacques Marcon**
Le Clos des Cimes, Larsiallas
43290 Saint-Bonnet-Le-Froid
phone +33 04 71 59 93 72
www.regismarcon.fr

**Chambres d'hôtes au Château de Durianne**
43700 Le Monteil
phone +33 04 71 02 90 36
www.chateaudedurianne.com

**Lapierre**
6, rue des Capucins
43000 Le Puy-en-Velay
phone +33 04 71 09 08 44
www.archeologis.free.fr/

**L'Olympe**
8, rue du Collège
43000 Le Puy-en-Velay
phone +33 04 71 05 90 59

**Groupement des Producteurs
de Lentilles Vertes du Puy**
16, Boulevard Bertrand - BP 63
43002 Le Puy en Velay
phone +33 04 71 02 60 44

**Boutique de la Lentille Verte du Puy**
rue des Tables
43000 Le Puy-en-Velay

**Cilverpuy**
BP 63
43002 Le Puy-en-Velay
phone +33 04 71 02 60 44
www.lalentillevertedupuy.com

**Distillerie de la Verveine du Velay Pagès**
BP 12, Route Nationale 88, Sortie ZI Blavozy
43001 Saint-Germain Laprade
phone +33 04 71 03 04 11
www.verveine.com

**Gaec des Prunelles**
le Bourg St-Etienne-du-Vigan
phone +33 04 71 00 83 20

**Michel Pagès**
Chazelles
43220 St-Vidal
phone +33 04 71 08 03 12

**Gisèle Gaillard**
Conil 43510 Saint-Jean-Lachalm
phone +33 04 71 57 58 06

*lille (nord–pas–de–calais)*

**Office de Tourisme**
Palais Rihour
place Rihour, B.P. 205
59002 Lille
phone +33 08 91 56 2004
*www.lilletourism.com*

**Hôtel Hermitage Gantois**
224, rue de Paris
59000 Lille
phone +33 03 20 85 30 30
*www.hotelhermitagegantois.com*

**Hôtel Alliance**
17-22 quai de Wault
59000 Lille
phone +33 03 20 30 62 62
*www.alliance-lille.com*

**La Châtellerie du Schoebeque**
32 rue Foch
59670 Cassel
phone +33 03 28 42 42 67
*www.schoebeque.com*

**Restaurant À l'Huitrière**
3, rue des Chats Bossus
59000 Lille
phone +33 03 20 55 43 41
*www.huitriere.fr*

**Restaurant Le Sébastopol**
1, place Sébastopol
59000 Lille
phone +33 03 20 57 05 05
*www.restaurant-sebastopol.fr*

**Brasserie 'T Rijsel**
25, rue de Gand
59000 Lille
phone +33 03 20 15 01 59

**Brasserie Alcide**
5, rue des Débris-Saint-Etienne
59000 Lille
phone +33 03 20 12 06 95
*www.restaurantalcide.com*

**Brasserie André**
71, rue de Béthune
59000 Lille
phone +33 03 20 54 75 51

**Aux Trois Brasseurs**
22, place de la Gare
59000 Lille
phone +33 03 20 06 46 25

**Aux Moules**
34, rue de Béthune
59000 Lille
phone +33 03 20 57 12 46
*www.auxmoules.com*

**Au roi du po'tje vleesch**
59270 Godewaersvelde
phone +33 03 28 42 52 56

**Terrines westcappelloises**
1476, route du Rattekot
59380 West Cappel
phone +33 03 28 68 36 46

**Au Chapon d'Or**
7, rue Esquermoise
59000 Lille
phone +33 03 28 38 06 10

**Restaurant Au Tord Boyaux**
11, place Nouvelle Aventure
59000 Lille
phone +33 03 20 57 73 67

**Le 86**
86, rue de Gand
59000 Lille
phone +33 03 20 78 19 86

**À côté aux Arts**
5, place du Concert
59000 Lille
phone +33 03 28 52 34 66

**Alcide**
5, rue des Débris-Saint-Etienne
59000 Lille
phone +33 03 20 12 06 95
*www.restaurantalcide.fr*

**Le Bistrot Tourangeau**
61, boulevard Louis-XIV
59800 Lille
phone +33 03 20 52 74 64

**Le Champlain**
13, rue Nicolas-Leblanc
59000 Lille
phone +33 03 20 54 01 38
*www.lechamplain.fr*

**Chez la Vieille**
60, rue de Gand
59000 Lille
phone +33 03 28 36 40 06

**À la petite ferme**
9, rue Fily
59151 Arleux
phone +33 03 27 89 50 77

**Monsieur Marquet**
501, rue André Joseph Leglaly
59151 Arleux
phone +33 03 27 89 54 43

*limoux (languedoc–roussillon)*

**Service Tourisme**
Promenade du Tivoli, BP 88
11304 Limoux Cedex
phone +33 04 68 31 11 82
*www.limoux.fr*

**Hôtel Moderne et Pigeon**
1, place Général Leclerc
11300 Limoux
phone +33 04 68 31 00 25
*ww.grandhotelmodernepigeon.fr*

**Restaurant La Maison
de la Blanquette**
46 bis, promenade du Tivoli
11300 Limoux
phone +33 04 68 31 28 37

**Restaurant La Forge**
22, avenue Abbé Tarroux
34600 Bédarieux
phone +33 04 67 95 13 13

**Auberge de Combes**
34240 Combes
phone +33 04 67 95 66 55

**Auberge de l'Abbaye**
34600 Villemagne l'Argentière
phone +33 04 67 95 34 84

**Château des Ducs de Joyeuse**
11190 Couiza
phone +33 04 68 74 23 50
*www.chateau-des-ducs.com*

**Château de Cavanac**
11570 Cavanac
phone +33 04 68 79 61 04
*www.chateau-de-cavanac.fr*

**Domaine d'Auriac**
Route de Saint-Hilaire
11000 Carcassonne
phone +33 04 68 25 72 22
*www.domaine-d-auriac.com*

**Association des producteurs
de navet de Pardailhan**
Le Crouzal
34360 Pardailhan
phone +33 04 67 97 65 44

**Sica du Caroux**
route Nationale 608
34600 Bédarieux
phone +33 04 67 95 00 74

**Caves du Sieur D'arques**
avenue du Mauzac
11300 Limoux
phone +33 04 68 74 63 00
*www.sieurdarques.com*

**Maison Guinot**
Chemin de Ronde
11300 Limoux
phone +33 04 68 31 01 33
*www.blanquette.fr*

*lyon (rhône–alpes)*

**Office du Tourisme et des Congrès
du Grand Lyon**
place Bellecour, BP 2254
69214 Lyon Cédex 02
phone +33 04 72 77 69 69

**Hôtel restaurant La Tour Rose**
22, rue du Bœuf
69001 Lyon
phone +33 04 78 37 25 90

**Hôtel restaurant La Villa Florentine**
25-27, montée Saint-Barthélémy
69001 Lyon
phone +33 04 72 56 56 56

**Le Garet**
7, rue du Garet
69001 Lyon
phone +33 04 78 28 16 94

**Chez Paul**
11, rue du Major Martin
69001 Lyon
phone +33 04 78 28 35 83

**Café-comptoir Abel**
25, rue Guynemer
69002 Lyon
phone +33 04 78 37 46 18

**Le Jura**
25, Rue Tupin
69002 Lyon
phone +33 04 78 42 20 57

**Chez Georges, le Petit Bouchon**
8, rue du Garet
69002 Lyon
phone +33  04 78 28 30 46

**Les Adrets**
30, rue du Boeuf
69005 Lyon
phone +33 04 78 38 24 30

**L'Alexandrin**
83, rue Moncey
69003 Lyon
phone +33 04 72 61 15 69
*www.lalexandrin.com*

**L'Arc en Ciel**
129, rue Servient
69003 Lyon
phone +33 04 78 63 55 00
*www.lyonradissonsas.com*

**Bar de la Marée**
36, rue Casimir-Perrier
69002 Lyon
phone +33 04 78 42 25 22

**Bouchon Authentique Lyonnais –
Chez Hugon**
12, rue Pizay
69001 Lyon
phone +33 04 78 28 10 94

**Brasserie de l'Est**
14, place Jules-Ferry
69006 Lyon
phone +33 04 37 24 25 26
*www.bocuse.com*

**Brasserie de l'Ouest**
1, quai du Commerce
69009 Lyon
phone +33 04 37 64 64 64
*www.bocuse.com*

**La Mère Jean**
5 rue des Marronniers
69002 Lyon
phone +33 04 78 37 81 27

**La Mère Brazier**
12 rue Royale
69001 Lyon
phone +33 04 78 28 15 49

## manosque (provence)

**Office de Tourisme**
place du Docteur Joubert
04100 Manosque
phone +33 04 92 72 16 00
*www.manosque-tourisme.com*

**Chambres La Bastide de l'Adrech**
avenue des Serrets
04100 Manosque
phone +33 04 92 71 14 18
*www.bastide-adrech.com*

**Hôtel La Bastide Saint Georges**
route de Banon
04300 Forcalquier
phone +33 04 92 75 72 80
*www.bastidesaintgeorges.com*

**Hôtel Le Mas du Pont Roman**
chemin de Châteauneuf
04300 Mane
phone +33 04 92 75 49 46
*www.ifrance.com/pontroman*

**Chambres et table d'hôte
Le Relais d'Elle**
route de la Brillanne
04300 Niozelle
phone +33 04 92 75 06 87
*www.relaisdelle.com*

**Le Petit Lauragais**
6, place du Terreau
04100 Manosque
phone +33 04 92 72 13 00

**Producteur d'amandes Marc Schultz**
Mas de Trotte-Vache
04210 Valensole
phone +33 04 92 74 84 02
*www.plateau-valensole.fr*

**Producteur d'amandes Alain Blanc**
Domaine de Play, Le Village
04500 Roumoules
phone +33 04 92 77 85 11

**Association de Promotion des Fruits
des Alpes de Haute Durance**
11 allée des Gentes
04200 Sisteron
phone +33 04 92 33 18 39

**Fromagerie de Banon**
route de Carniol
04150 Banon
phone +33 04 92 73 25 03

**Les Capitelles**
Chemin Maragonelle
04210 Valensole
phone +33 04 92 74 95 89

**Conserverie Artisanale Richaud & Fils**
Zone Artisanale
04210 Valensole
phone +33 04 92 74 82 60
*www.etsrichaud.com*

**Confiseur François Doucet**
BP 107 Zone Artisanale
04700 Oraison
phone +33 04 92 78 61 15
*www.francois-doucet.com*

**Distilleries et Domaines de Provence**
avenue Saint Promasse
04300 Forcalquier
phone +33 04 92 75 15 41
*www.distilleries-provence.com*

## marseille (provence)

**Office du Tourisme et des Congrès**
4, La Canebière
13000 Marseille
phone +33 04 91 13 89 00
*www.marseille-tourisme.com*

**New Hotel Bompard**
2, rue des Flots Bleus
13007 Marseille
phone +33 04 91 99 22 22
*www.new-hotel.com/bompard*

**Le Petit Nice Relais & Châteaux**
Anse de Maldormé, Corniche J.F. Kennedy
13007 Marseille
phone +33 04 91 59 25 92
*www.passedat.fr*

**Restaurant Le Miramar**
12, quai du Port
13002 Marseille
phone +33 04 91 91 10 40
*www.bouillabaisse.com*

**Restaurant Les Arcenaulx**
25, cours Estienne d'Orves
13000 Marseille
phone +33 04 91 59 80 49

**Restaurant Une Table au Sud**
2, quai du Port
13002 Marseille
phone +33 04 91 90 63 53
*www.unetableausud.com*

**Restaurant Chez Fonfon**
140, rue du Vallon-des-Auffes
13007 Marseille
phone +33 04 91 52 14 38

**504**
34, place aux Huiles
13000 Marseille
phone +33 04 91 33 57 74

**Les Arcenaulx**
25, cours d'Estienne-d'Orves
13001 Marseille
phone +33 04 91 59 80 30
*www.les-arcenaulx.com*

**Le Bistrot à Vins**
17, rue Sainte
13001 Marseille
phone +33 04 91 54 02 20

**Bouchon Marseillais**
41, rue Adolphe-Thiers
13000 Marseille
phone +33 04 91 42 47 33

**Café des Epices**
4, rue Lacydon
13000 Marseille
phone +33 04 91 91 22 69

**Le Four des Navettes**
136, rue Sainte
13007 Marseille
phone +33 04 91 33 32 12
*www.fourdesnavettes.com*

**Fromagerie Georges Bataille**
25 place Notre-Dame du Mont
Marseille
phone +33 04 91 47 06 23

**Boucherie Perrin, Chez Jean-Luc**
80 Boulevard de Saint Loup
13010 Marseille
phone +33 04 91 35 02 01
*www.boucher-marseille.com*

## meaux (île de france)

**Office de Tourisme**
1 Place Doumer
77100 MEAUX
phone +33 01 64 33 02 26
*www.ville-meaux.fr*

**Hôtellerie-restaurant du Bas-Bréau**
2 rue Grande
77630 Barbizon
phone +33 01 60 66 40 05
*www.bas-breau.com*

**Hôtel-restaurant du Manoir de Gressy**
77410 Gressy
phone +33 01 60 26 68 00
*www.manoirdegressy.com*

**Hôtel-restaurant Le Château des Bondons**
47, rue des Bondons
77260 La Ferté-sous-Jouarre
phone +33 01 60 22 00 98

**Auberge du Cheval Blanc**
55, rue Victor Clairet
77910 Varreddes
phone +33 01 64 33 18 03
*www.auberge-cheval-blanc.fr*

**La Grignotière**
36, rue de la Sablonnière
77100 Meaux
phone +33 01 64 34 21 48

**Les assaisonnements Briards**
Z.A. des Bordes Rouges
5, Rue Louise Michel
77100 Nanteuil-les-Meaux
phone +33 01 64 35 00 82
*www.moutarde-de-meaux.com*

**Maison Gaufillier**
5, place du Maréchal Leclerc
77160 Provins
phone +33 01 64 00 03 71

**La Ronde des Abeilles**
3, rue des Beaux Arts
77160 Provins
phone +33 01 60 67 65 97

**Sucre d'Orge des Religieuses de Moret,
Ets Jean Rousseau**
5, rue du Puits du Four
77250 Moret-sur-Loing
phone +33 01 60 70 35 63

## menton (provence)

**Office de Tourisme**
8, Avenue Boyer, B.P. 239
06506 menton
phone +33 04 92 41 76 76
*www.menton.fr*
*www.villedementon.com*

**Grand-Hôtel des Ambassadeurs**
3, rue Partouneaux
06500 Menton
phone +33 04 92 28 75 75
*www.ambassadeurs-menton.com*

**Hôtel Chambord**
6, avenue Boyer
06500 Menton
phone +33 04 93 35 94 19
*www.hotel-chambord.com*

**Hôtel Aiglon**
7, avenue de la Madone
06500 Menton
phone +33 04 93 57 55 55
*www.hotelaiglon.net*

**Restaurant A Braïjade Meridiounale**
66, rue Longue
06500 Menton
phone +33 04 93 35 65 65
*www.abraijade.com*

**Restaurant Au Pistou**
9, quai Gordon Bennett
06500 Menton
phone +33 04 93 57 45 89

**Auberge Pierrot-Pierrette**
place de l'église, Monti
06500 Menton
phone +33 04 93 35 79 76

**Restaurant La Marina**
17, promenade de la Mer
06500 Menton
phone +33 04 93 57 15 27
*www.restaurant-menton.com*

**Le Louvre**
3, rue Partouneaux
06500 Menton
phone +33 04 93 28 75 75

**Mirazur**
30, avenue Aristide-Briand
06500 Menton
phone +33 04 92 41 86 86

**La Cantinella**
8, rue Trenca
06500 Menton
phone +33 04 93 41 34 20

**L'Arche des Confitures
de la Maison Herbin**
2, rue du Vieux-Collège
06500 Menton
phone +33 04 93 57 20 29
*www.confitures-herbin.com*

**Le Tuyé de Papy Gaby**
25650 Gilley
phone +33 O3 81 68 80 03

## moulins (auvergne)

**Office de tourisme**
11, rue François Péron, BP 641
03006 Moulins
phone +33 04 70 44 14
www.pays-bourbon.com

**Hôtel-restaurant le Clos de Bourgogne**
83, rue de Bourgogne
03000 Moulins
phone +33 04 70 44 03 00
www.closdebourgogne.fr

**Hôtel-restaurant du Château Saint Jean**
rue du Roc de la Brosse, Parc Saint Jean
03100 Montluçon
phone +33 04 70 02 71 71
www.chateaustjean.net

**Grand Hôtel Montespan Talleyrand**
2-3-4, place des Thermes
03160 Bourbon l'Archambault
phone +33 04 70 67 00 24
www.hotel-montespan.com

**Restaurant des Cours**
**(Martine et Patrick Bourhy)**
36, Cours Jean Jaurès
03000 Moulins
phone +33 04 70 44 25 66
www.restaurant-des-cours.com

**Restaurant Le Chêne Vert**
**(Jean-Guy Siret)**
35, boulevard Ledru Rollin
03500 Saint-Pourcain sur Sioule
phone +33 04 70 45 40 65
www.hotel-chenevert.com

**Le Clos de Bourgogne**
83, rue de Bourgogne
03000 Moulins
phone +33 04 70 44 03 00
www.closdebourgogne.fr

**Auberge du Daguet**
Face à l'église
60350 Vieux Moulin
phone +33 03 44 85 60 72

**Les Palets d'or**
11, rue de Paris
03007 Moulins
phone +33 04 70 44 02 71
www.les-palets-or.fr

**Union des Vignerons de Saint-Pourçain**
3, quai de la Ronde
03500 Saint-Pourçain
phone +33 04 70 45 42 82

**Domaine Gardien, Chassignolles**
03210 Besson
phone +33 04 70 42 80 11
www.domainegardien.com

**Jean et François Ray**
Venteuil
03500 Saulcet
phone +33 04 70 45 35 46

## munster (alsace)

**Office du tourisme de la Vallée de Munster**
1 rue du Couvent, BP 21,
68140 Munster
phone +33 03 89 77 31 80

**La Cigogne**
4 place du Marché
68140 Munster
phone +33 03 89 77 32 27

**À la Verte Vallée**
10 rue Alfred-Hartmann
68140 Munster
phone +33 03 89 77 15 15

**Au Val Saint-Grégoire**
5 rue Saint-Grégoire
68140 Munster
phone +33 03 89 77 36 22

**Grand Hôtel**
1 rue de la Gare
68140 Munster
phone +33 03 89 77 30 37

**À l'Agneau d'Or**
2, rue Saint-Grégoire
68140 Munster
phone +33 03 89 77 34 08
www.martinfache.com

**Verte Vallée**
10, rue A. Hartmann
68140 Munster
phone +33 03 89 77 15 15
www.vertevallee.com

**Panorama**
3, route Linge
68140 Hohrodberg
phone +33 03 89 77 36 53
www.hotel-panorama-alsace.com

**Ferme Daniel Roess**
4, Oberer Geisberg
68140 Soultzeren
phone +33 03 89 77 13 72

**Ferme Bertrand Heinrich**
17, chemin du Hohneck
68140 Stosswihr
phone +33 03 89 77 58 03

## nancy (lorraine)

**Office du tourisme**
place Stanislas, BP 810
phone +33 03 85352241
www.ot-nancy.fr

**Grand Hôtel de la Reine**
2, place Stanislas
54000 Nancy
phone +33 03 83 73 49 00
www.concorde-hotels.fr

**Hôtel de Guise**
18, rue de Guise
54000 Nancy
phone +33 03 83 32 24 68

**Brasserie L'Excelsior**
50, rue Henri-Poincaré
54000 Nancy
phone +33 03 83 35 24 57
www.brasserie-excelsior.com

**Restaurant Chez Bagot**
**Le Chardon Bleu**
45, Grand Rue
54000 Nancy
phone +33 03 83 37 42 43

**Restaurant Le Gastrolâtre**
**(Patrick Tanésy)**
1, place Vaudémont
54000 Nancy
phone +33 03 83 35 51 94

**Restaurant La Mignardise**
28, rue Stanislas
54000 Nancy
phone +33 03 83 32 20 22
www.lamignardise.com

**Restaurant Chez Lize**
52, rue Henri Déglin
54000 Nancy
phone +33 03 83 30 36 26

**Les Agaves Côté Sud**
2, rue des Carmes
54000 Nancy
phone +33 03 83 32 14 14

**Le Cap Marine**
60, rue Stanislas
54000 Nancy
phone +33 03 83 37 05 03
www.restaurant-capmarine.com

**Le Capucin Gourmand**
31, rue Gambetta
54000 Nancy
phone +33 03 83 35 26 98
www.lecapu.com

**Le Stanislas**
2, place Stanislas
54000 Nancy
phone +33 03 83 35 03 01
www.hoteldelareine.com

**Distillateur de mirabelle**
**Pierre Maucourt**
Vezon 57420 Verny
phone +33 03 87 52 80 72

**Maison de la Mirabelle**
16, rue du Capitaine Durand
54290 Rozelieures
phone +33 03 83 72 32 26
www.maisondelamirabelle.com

**Pâtisserie Adam**
3, place Saint Epvre
54000 Nancy
phone +33 03 83 32 04 69

**Maison des Sœurs Macarons**
21, rue Gambetta
54000 Nancy
phone +33 03 83 32 24 25

## nantes (pays de la loire)

**Office de tourisme Nantes-Métropole**
7, rue de Valmy, B.P. 64106
44041 Nantes 01
phone +33 0 892 464 044
www.nantes-tourisme.com

**Hôtel La Pérouse**
3, allée Duquesne
44000 Nantes
phone +33 02 40 89 75 00
www.hotel-laperouse.fr

**Hôtel Cœur de Loire**
3 rue Anatole Le Braz
44000 Nantes
phone +33 02 40 74 35 61
www.coeurdeloirehotel.com

**Chambres d'hôtes au château de la Sébinière**
44330 Le Pallet
phone +33 02 40 80 49 25
www.chateausebiniere.com

**Restaurant Lou Pescadou**
8, allée Baco
44000 Nantes
phone +33 02 40 35 29 50

**Restaurant Les Temps Changent**
1, place Aristide Briand
44000 Nantes
phone +33 02 51 72 18 01

**Restaurant La Cigale**
4, place Graslin
44000 Nantes
phone +33 02 51 84 94 94
www.lacigale.com

**Restaurant La Cantine du Général**
36, boulevard de Launay
44300 Nantes
phone +33 02 40 73 19 18

**Restaurant La Châtaigneraie**
156, route de Carquefou
44240 Sucé sur Erdre
phone +33 02 40 77 90 95
www.delphin.fr

**L'Abélia**
125, boulevard des Poilus
44300 Nantes
phone +33 02 40 35 40 00
www.restaurantlabelia.com

**Les Capucines**
11, bis rue de la Bastille
44000 Nantes
phone +33 02 40 20 41 58
www.restaurant-capucines.com

**La Courtine**
15, rue de Strasbourg
44000 Nantes
phone +33 02 40 48 13 30
www.la-courtine.com

**L'Engoulevent**
4, rue des Trois-Croissants
44000 Nantes
phone +33 02 40 20 33 86

**Domaine Louis Métaireau**
La Févrie
44690 Maisdon sur Sèvre
phone +33 02 40 54 81 92
www.muscadet-grandmouton.com

**Domaine Landron**
Les Brandières
44690 La Haye-Fouassière
phone +33 02 40 54 83 27
www.domaines-landron.com

**Les Frères Couillaud**
**GAEC de la Grande Ragotière**
La Regrippière 44330 Vallet
phone +33 02 40 33 60 56
www.freres-couillaud.com

*nantua (rhône–alpes)*

**Office de Tourisme du Pays**
**de Nantua et du Haut-Bugey**
13 place de la Déportation
01130 Nantua
phone +33 04 74 75 00 05

**L'Embarcadère**
13 avenue du Lac
01130 Nantua
phone +33 04 74 75 22 88

**Auberge du Lac Genin**
Lac Genin
01130 Charix
phone +33 04 74 75 52 50

**Restaurant La Soupière a des Oreilles**
01260 Le Petit-Abergement
phone +33 04 79 87 65 81

**L'Embarcadère**
13, avenue du Lac
01130 Nantua
phone +33 04 74 75 22 88
www.hotelembarcadere.com

**Bernard Charpy**
1, rue de la Croix-Chalon
01460 Brion
phone +33 04 74 76 24 15

**Auberge du Lac Genin**
01130 Charix
phone +33 04 74 75 52 50
www.lacgenin.com

**Nolo frères**
18, rue du Docteur-Mercier
01130 Nantua
phone +33 04 74 75 00 43

**Bugey Gastronomie**
01130 Saint-Germain-deJoux
phone +33 04 50 59 84 25

*nîmes (languedoc–roussillon)*

**Office de Tourisme**
6, rue Auguste
30020 Nîmes
phone +33 04 66583800
fax +33 04 66583801
www.ot-nimes.fr

**Royal Hôtel**
place d'Assas
34000 Nîmes
phone +33 04 66 58 28 27
www.royalhotel-nimes.com

**New Hotel La Baume**
21, rue Nationale
34000 Nîmes
phone +33 04 66 76 28 42
www.new-hotel.com

**Hôtel du Général d'Entraigues**
8, rue de la Calade
30700 Uzès
phone +33 04 66 22 32 68
www.hoteldentraigues.com

**Hôtel La Taverne**
rue Xavier Cigalon
30700 Uzès
phone +33 04 66 22 13 10
www.lataverne-uzes.com

**Hôtel-restaurant de la Bégude Saint Pierre**
**Famille Griffoul**
30210 Vers-Pont du Gard
phone +33 04 66 63 63 63
www.hotel-saintpierre.fr

**Restaurant Chez Jacotte**
15, impasse Fresque
34000 Nîmes
phone +33 04 66 21 64 59

**Le Bouchon et l'Assiette**
5, bis rue de Sauve
30900 Nîmes
phone +33 04 66 62 02 93
www.bouchon-assiette.com

**Le Cheval Blanc**
11, square de la Couronne
30000 Nîmes
phone +33 04 66 76 19 59

**L'Enclos de la Fontaine**
Quai de la Fontaine
30900 Nîmes
phone +33 04 66 21 90 30
www.hotel-imperator.com

**Le Lisita**
2, bis boulevard des Arènes
30000 Nîmes
phone +33 04 66 67 29 15

**Brandade Raymond Geoffroy**
34, rue Nationale
34000 Nîmes
phone +33 04 66 27 11 98

**Musée du Bonbon Haribo**
Pont des Charettes
30700 Uzès
phone +33 04 66 22 74 39
www.haribo.com

*niort (poitou–charentes)*

**Office de tourisme**
16, rue du Petit Saint-Jean, B.P. 277
79008 Niort
phone +33 05 49 24 18 79
www.niortourisme.com

**Grand Hôtel Niort**
32 avenue de Paris
79000 Niort
phone +33 05 49 24 22 21
www.grandhotelniort.com

**Château du Domaine du Griffier**
10, route Sud Niort
79360 Granzay Gript
phone +33 05 49 32 62 62
www.domainedugriffier.com

**Hôtel restaurant Le Central**
4, rue de l'Autremont
79510 Coulon
phone +33 05 49 35 90 20
www.hotel-lecentral-coulon.com

**Restaurant Le Mélane**
1, place du Temple
79000 Niort
phone +33 05 49 79 25 61
www.lemelane.com ù

**La Belle Etoile**
115, quai Maurice-Métayer
79000 Niort
phone +33 05 49 73 31 29
www.la-belle-etoile.fr

**Restaurant Mélane**
1, place du Temple
79000 Niort
phone +33 05 49 04 00 40

**L'Angélique de Niort - Ets Thonnard**
avenue de Sevreau
79000 Niort
phone +33 05 49 73 47 42
www.angelique-niort.com

**Angeli Cado**
6 bis , rue Sainte-Marthe
79000 Niort
phone +33 05 49 24 10 23

**GAEC des Châtaigniers La Petite**
**Morinière**
79400 Nanteuil
phone +33 05 49 05 71 65

**Fromagerie Lavergne**
Bellevue 79500 Chail
phone +33 05 49 29 0 82

**La Ferme de Loujeanne Fayolle**
79230 Brulain
phone +33 05 49 26 42 46

*noirmoutier (pays de la loire)*

**Office de tourisme**
route du Pont, B.P. 125
85630 Barbatre
phone +33 02 51 39 80 71
www.ile-noirmoutier.com

**Hôtel-restaurant Château de Sable**
**Punta Lara**
chemin de la Noure
85680 La Guérinière
phone +33 02 51 39 11 58
www.hotelpuntalara.com

**Hôtel Général d'Elbée**
place d'Armes
85330 Noirmoutier
phone +33 02 51 39 10 29
www.generaldelbee.com

**Hôtel-restaurant Château de Pélavé**
9, allée de Chaillot
85330 Noirmoutier
phone +33 02 51 39 01 94
www.chateau-du-pelave.fr

**Hôtel-restaurant Les Prateaux**
8, allée du Tambourin
85330 Noirmoutier
phone +33 02 51 39 12 52
www.lesprateaux.com

**Restaurant Le Grand Four**
1, rue de la Cure
85330 Noirmoutier
phone +33 02 51 39 61 97
www.legrandfour.com

**La Bisquine**
30-A, rue du Port-l'Herbaudière
85330 Noirmoutier en l'Ile
phone +33 02 51 35 78 72

**Fleur de Sel**
Rue des Saulniers
85330 Noirmoutier en l'Ile
phone +33 02 51 39 09 07
www.fleurdesel.fr

**Le Grand Four**
1, rue de la Cure
85330 Noirmoutier en l'Ile
phone +33 02 51 39 61 97
www.legrandfour.com

**Le Petit Bouchot**
3, rue Saint-Louis
85330 Noirmoutier en l'Ile
phone +33 02 51 39 32 56

**Coopérative agricole Le Petit Chéssé**
85330 Noirmoutier
phone +33 02 51 35 76 76
www.coop-noirmoutier.com

**Sel Michel Gallois**
46, rue Pierre Monnier
85330 Noirmoutier
phone +33 02 51 39 52 72

**Sel Martine Ruffio**
28, rue du Port
85740 L'Epine
phone +33 02 51 35 97 40

**Aquasel**
10, rue des Marouettes, BP 535
85330 Noirmoutier
phone +33 02 51 39 08 30
www.aquasel.fr

*nyons (rhône–alpes)*

**Office du tourisme**
Pavillon du Tourisme
Place de la Libération, B.P. 3
26111 Nyons
phone +33 04 75 26 10 35
www.paysdenyons.com

**Hôtel La Bastide des Monges**
route d'Orange
26110 Nyons
phone +33 04 75 26 99 69
www.bastidedesmonges.com

**Hôtel La Picholine**
promenade de la Perrière
26110 Nyons
phone +33 04 75 26 06 21

**Resto des Arts**
13, rue des Déportés
26110 Nyons
phone +33 04 75 26 31 49
http://lerestodesarts.free.fr

**Restaurant La Table de Nicole**
quartier des Petites Condamines
26230 Valaurie
phone +33 04 75 98 52 03
www.latabledenicole.com

**Le Petit Caveau**
9, rue Victor Hugo
26110 Nyons
phone +33 04 75 26 20 21

**La Picholine**
Promenade de la Perrière
26110 Nyons
phone +33 04 75 26 06 21
www.picholine26.com

**La Charrette Bleue**
"La Bonte"
26110 Nyons
phone +33 04 75 27 72 33

**Moulin à huile Autran-Dozol**
Le Pont Roman
26110 Nyons
phone +33 04 75 26 02 52
www.moulin-dozol.com

**Moulin Ramade**
7, Impasse du Moulin
26110 Nyons
phone +33 04 75 26 08 18
www.moulinramade.com

**Musée de l'Olivier**
place Olivier de Serres
26110 Nyons
phone +33 04 75 26 12 12

*oléron (poitou–charentes)*

**Maison du Tourisme de l'île d'Oléron
et du Bassin de Marennes**
route du Viaduc
17560 Bourcefranc
phone +33 05 46 85 65 23
www.ile-oleron-marennes.com

**Hôtel-Restaurant l'Ecailler**
65, rue du Port
17310 La Cotinière, Ile d'Oléron
phone +33 05 46 47 10 31
www.ecailler-oleron.com

**Hôtel Restaurant la Chaudrée**
7, Place Pasteur
17840 La Brée-les-Bains, Ile d'Oléron
phone +33 05 46 47 81 85

**Restaurant La Claire**
Chenal de la Cayenne
17320 Marennes
phone +33 05 46 36 78 92
www.cite-huitre.com

**Relais des Salines**
Port des Salines
17370 Grand Village Plage, Ile d'Oléron
phone +33 05 46 75 82 42

**Les Alizés**
4, rue Dubois-Aubry
17310 Saint-Pierre d'Oléron
phone +33 05 46 47 20 20

**Le Petit Coivre**
10, avenue de Bel-Air
17310 Saint-Pierre d'Oléron
phone +33 05 46 47 44 23

**Huitres Stéphane Guilbaud**
prise des Aubains
17920 Breuillet
phone +33 05 46 85 24 84
www.huitres-guilbaud.com

**Huitres Olivier Jauneau**
rue de la Corderie
17390 La Tremblade
phone +33 05 46 36 00 33
www.huitres-jauneau.net

**Huitres Jean-Michel Seguin**
route de la Pointe Blanche
17480 Le Château d'Oléron
phone +33 05 46 47 77 98
www.huitres-seguin.com

**Charente-escargots**
32, rue de la Maigrerie
17240 Lorignac
phone +33 05 46 49 03 86

**Confrérie de la Cagouille**
4, rue du 8 Mai 1945
17540 Saint Sauveur d'Aunis
phone +33 05 46 01 98 07
www.cagouille.com

*orléans (centre)*

**Office de tourisme**
2, place de l'Etape, BP 95632
45000 Orléans
phone +33 02 38 24 05 05
www.tourisme-orleans.com

**Hôtel Mercure**
44, quai Barentin
45000 Orléans
phone +33 02 38 62 17 39
www.mercure.com

**Restaurant La Dariole**
25, rue Etienne Dolet
45000 Orléans
phone +33 02 38 77 26 67

**Restaurant La Petite Marmite**
178, rue de Bourgogne
45000 Orléans
phone +33 02 38 54 23 83
www.lapetitemarmite.net

**Restaurant Les Antiquaires**
2 rue au Lin
45000 Orléans
phone +33 02 38 53 63 48
www.restaurantlesantiquaires.com

**L'Epicurien**
54, rue des Turcies
45000 Orléans
phone +33 02 38 68 01 10

**Eugène**
24, rue Sainte-Anne
45000 Orléans
phone +33 02 38 53 82 64

**Next Door**
6, rue au Lin
45000 Orléans
phone +33 02 38 62 40 00
www.nextdoor45.com

**Terrasses du Parc**
Avenue du Parc Floral
45000 Orléans
phone +33 02 38 25 92 24
www.laterrasse45.com

**Vinaigrier Martin-Pouret**
236, faubourg Bannier
45400 Fleury Orléans
phone +33 02 38 88 78 49
www.martin-pouret.com

**Chocolaterie Royale**
53, rue Royale
45000 Orléans
phone +33 02 38 53 93 43

**Hôtel d'Arc**
37ter rue de la République
45000 Orléans
phone +33 02 38 53 10 94
www.hoteldarc.fr

*paris (île de france)*

**Office de Tourisme et des Congres**
25 rue des Pyramides
75001 Paris
phone +33 0 892 68 30 00
www.parisinfo.com

**Hôtel Ampère**
102, avenue de Villiers
75017 Paris
phone +33 01 44 29 17 17
www.villadelles.com/ampere/fr

**Hôtel Bel-Ami**
7, rue St-Benoît
75006 Paris
phone +33 01 42 61 53 53
www.hotel-bel-ami.com

**Hôtel de Sers**
41, avenue Pierre 1er de Serbie
75008 Paris
phone +33 01 53 23 75 75
www.hoteldesers.com

**Hôtel Daniel**
8, rue Fréderic Bastiat
75008 Paris
phone +33 01 42 56 17 00

**Benoît**
20, rue Saint-Martin
75004 Paris
phone +33 01 42 72 25 76
www.alain-ducasse.com

**Fleurs de Thym**
19, rue François-Miron
75004 Paris 04
phone +33 01 48 87 01 02

**Le Dôme du Marais**
53, bis rue Francs-Bourgeois
75004 Paris
phone +33 01 42 74 54 17

**Lapérouse**
51, quai des Grands Augustins
75006 Paris
phone +33 01 43 26 68 04

**Relais Louis XIII**
8, rue des Grands Augustins
75006 Paris
phone +33 01 43 26 75 96
www.relaislouis13.com

**Jacques Cagna**
14 rue des Grands-Augustins
75006 Paris
phone +33 01 43 26 49 39
www.jacques-cagna.com

**404**
69, rue des Gravilliers
75003 Paris
phone +33 01 42 74 57 81

**1728**
8, rue d'Anjou
75008 Paris
phone +33 01 40 17 04 77
www.restaurant-1728.com

**6 New York**
6, avenue de New York
75016 Paris
phone +33 01 40 70 03 30

**Boulangerie Poilâne**
8, rue du Cherche-Midi
75006 Paris
phone +33 01 45 44 99 80
www.poilane.fr

**Ladurée**
16, rue Royale
75008 Paris
phone +33 01 42 60 21 79

**Ladurée**
75, avenue des Champs Elysées
75008 Paris
phone +33 01 40 75 08 75

**Ladurée**
21 rue Bonaparte
75006 Paris
phone +33 01 44 07 64 87
www.laduree.fr

**Syndicat d'initiative du Vieux Montmartre**
21, place du Tertre
75018 Paris
phone +33 01 42 62 21 21
www.parisinfo.com

**Le Clos du Pas Saint Maurice**
92150 Suresnes
phone +33 01 41 18 15 51
*www.ville-suresnes.fr*

**Fauchon**
24-26 place de la Madeleine
Paris 8ème
phone +33 01 70 39 38 00

*pau (aquitaine)*

**Office de Tourisme et des Congres**
Place Royale (Hôtel de Ville)
64000 Pau
phone +33 05 59 27 27 08
*www.pau-pyrenees.com*

**Hôtel de Gramont**
3, place de Gramont
84000 Pau
phone +33 05 59 27 84 04
*www.hotelgramont.com*

**Hôtel Restaurant les Bains de Secours**
route des Bains de Secours
64260 Sévignacq-Meyracq
phone +33 05 59 05 62 11
*www.hotel-les-bains-secours.com*

**Restaurant Au Fin Gourmet**
24, avenue Gaston Lacoste
64000 Pau
phone +33 05 59 27 47 71
*www.restaurant-aufingourmet.com*

**Restaurant Chez Pierre**
16, rue Louis Barthou
64000 Pau
phone +33 05 59 27 76 86
*www.restaurant-chez-pierre.com*

**Le Berry**
4, rue Gachet
64000 Pau
phone +33 05 59 27 42 95

**Le Jeu de Paume**
1, avenue Edouard VII
64000 Pau
phone +33 05 59 11 84 00
*www.hôtel-parc.beaumont.com*

**Le Majestic**
9, place Royale
64000 Pau
phone +33 05 59 27 56 83

**Le Clos Husté, Cours Père et Fils**
Chemin Cours Husté
64290 Gan
phone +33 05 59 21 75 52

**Domaine Lapeyre en Jurançon**
La Chapelle de Rousse
64110 Jurançon
phone +33 05 59 21 50 80
*www.jurancon-lapeyre.fr*

**Pâtisserie Artigarrède**
1, place de la Cathédrale
64400 Oloron Sainte Marie
phone +33 05 59 39 01 38

**Pâtisserie Artigarrède**
3, rue Gassion
64000 Pau
phone +33 05 59 27 47 40

*perpignan (languedoc–roussillon)*

**Office de tourisme**
Palais des Congrès
Place Armand Lanoux, B.P.215
66002 Perpignan
phone +33 04 68 66 30 30
*www.perpignantourisme.com*

**Hôtel-restaurant Villa Duflot**
rond-point Albert Donnezan
(Serrat d'en Vaquer)
66000 Perpignan
phone +33 04 68 56 67 67
*www.villa-duflot.com*

**Le Mas Trilles**
Le Pont de Reynès
66400 Céret
phone +33 04 68 87 38 37
*www.le-mas-trilles.com*

**Grand Hôtel de la Reine Amélie**
32, boulevard de la petite Provence
66110 Amélie les Bains
phone +33 04 68 39 04 38
*www.reineamelie.com*

**Restaurant La Casa Sansa**
4, Rue Fabrique Couverte
66000 Perpignan
phone +33 04 68 34 21 84

**Restaurant Le Clos des Lys**
660, Chemin de la Fauceille
66100 Perpignan
phone +33 04 68 56 79 00
*www.closdeslys.com*

**Ail i Oli**
Allée des Chênes
66000 Perpignan
phone +33 04 68 55 58 75

**Les Antiquaires**
Place Desprès
66000 Perpignan
phone +33 04 68 34 06 58

**Le Chapon Fin**
18, boulevard Jean-Bourrat
66000 Perpignan
phone +33 04 68 35 14 14
*www.parkhotel-fr.com*

**La Galinette**
23, rue Jean-Payra
66000 Perpignan
phone +33 04 68 35 00 90

**Coopérative Céret Primeurs**
avenue de la Gare
66400 Céret
phone +33 04 68 87 00 69

**Confiserie du Tech**
Z.A Mas Guerido
66630 Cabestany
phone +33 04 68 50 69 63
*www.confiseriedutech.com*

**Anne Alart-Delahays**
Mas Alart
66280 Saleilles
phone +33 04 68 50 22 07

**Pâtisserie Pi Roué**
6, avenue du Vallespir
66112 Amélie les Bains
phone +33 04 68 39 05 46

**Pâtisserie Perez Aubert**
12, rue des Thermes
66112 Amélie les Bains
phone +33 04 68 39 00 16

*pithiviers (centre)*

**Office du tourisme**
1, mail Ouest, Maison Les Remparts
45300 Pithiviers
phone +33 02 38 30 50 02
*www.ville-pithiviers.fr*

**Hôtel-restaurant la Clé des Champs**
les 4 Croix, route de Joigny
45320 Courtenay
phone +33 02 38 97 42 68

**Hôtel-restaurant de la Gloire**
74, avenue du Général de Gaulle
45200 Montargis
phone +33 02 38 85 04 69

**Hôtel-restaurant du Domaine des Roches**
2, rue de la Plaine
45250 Briare-le-Canal
phone +33 02 38 05 09 00
*www.domainedesroches.fr*

**Aux Saveurs Lointaines**
1, place du Martroi
45300 Pithiviers
phone +33 02 38 30 18 18

**Auberge de la Rive du Bois**
45340 Chambion-la-forêtt
phone +33 02 38 32 28 44
*www.auberge-rivedubois.com*

**Lancelot**
12 rue des Déportés
45170 Chilleurs-aux-Bois
phone +33 02 38 32 91 15
*www.restaurant-le-lancelot.com*

**Miel**
**Dominique et Jacques Goût**
La Cassine, route de Chuelles
45220 Château-Renard
phone +33 02 38 95 35 56
*www.museevivant.com*

**Les ruchers Dosnon**
6, route de Paris
89300 Saint-Aubin
phone +33 03 86 62 43 01

**Safran**
**Michel et Anne-Marie Fouquin**
113, La Champagne
45490 Corbeilles en Gâtinais
phone +33 02 38 92 23 67

**Safran du Gâtinais**
5, Place de l'Église
45390 Echilleuses
phone +33 02 38 34 31 79
*www.safrandugatinais.fr*

**Confiserie Mazet**
43 rue du Général Leclerc
45200 Montargis
phone +33 02 38 98 63 55
*www.mazetconfiseur.com*

**Confrérie du Pithiviers
(Bernard Boré)**
22, lieudit La Chapellerie
45300 Courcy-aux-Loges
phone +33 06 24 84 75 21

*plougastel-daoulas (brittany)*

**Office de Tourisme Brest Métropole Océane**
place de la Liberté, BP 91012
29210 Brest 1
phone +33 02 98 44 24 96
*www.brest-metropole-tourisme.fr*

**Hôtel Holiday Inn Garden Court**
41 rue Branda
29200 Brest
phone +33 02 98 80 84 00

**Restaurant Nouveau Rossini
(Maurice Mével)**
22, rue du Commandant Drogou
29200 Brest
phone +33 02 98 47 90 00

**Restaurant Le Ruffé**
1 bis, rue Yves Collet
29200 Brest
phone +33 02 98 46 07 70

**Le Chevalier de l'Auberlac'h**
rue Mathurin Thomas
29470 Plougastel-Daoulas
phone +33 02 98 40 54 56

**Le Ruffé**
1, bis rue Yves Collet
29200 Brest
phone +33 02 98 46 07 70

**Le Nouveau Rossini**
22, rue du Commandant Drogou
29200 Brest
phone +33 02 98 47 90 00

**Lozachmeur**
400, route de Quimperlé
29300 Baye
phone +33 02 98 96 80 20

**Liqueurs Jacques Fisselier**
56, rue du Verger, BP 77123
35571 Chantepie
phone +33 02 99 41 00 00
*www.jacques-fisselier.com*

**Fraises Pierre Rolland**
Ty Neol
29470 Loperhet
phone +33 02 98 07 09 23

**Fraises Régis Pichon**
10, chemin Kernie
29470 Plougastel Daoulas
phone +33 02 98 40 62 26

## poitiers (poitou–charentes)

**Office du tourisme**
45, Place Charles de Gaulle, B.P. 377
86009 Poitiers
phone +33 05 49 41 21 24
www.ot-poitiers.fr

**Grand Hôtel**
28, rue Carnot
86000 Poitiers
phone +33 05 49 60 90 60
www.grandhotelpoitiers.fr

**Hôtel-restaurant du Château du Clos de la Ribaudière**
86360 Chasseneuil du Poitou
phone +33 05 49 52 86 66
www.ribaudiere.com

**Restaurant Alain Boutin**
65, Rue Carnot
86000 Poitiers
phone +33 05 49 88 25 53
www.alainboutin.com

**Restaurant Maxime**
4, rue Saint Nicolas
86000 Poitiers
phone +33 05 49 41 09 55

**Les Bons Enfants**
11, bis rue Cloche-Perse
86000 Poitiers
phone +33 05 49 41 49 82

**Maxime**
4, rue Saint-Nicolas
86000 Poitiers
phone +33 05 49 41 09 55
www.maitrescuisiniersdefrance.com

**Nardo's Bouchon**
27, place Charles-de-Gaulle
86000 Poitiers
phone +33 05 49 52 80 03

**Broyé du Poitou Goulibeur**
10, rue Victor Grignard, Pôle République
86000 Poitiers
phone +33 05 49 41 34 75
www.goulibeur.com

**Laiterie Coopérative d'Echiré**
76 place de l'Eglise
79410 Echiré
phone +33 05 49 25 70 01
www.echire.com

**Melons Jean-Pierre Decourt**
La Grand Cour
86140 Lencloître
phone +33 05 49 90 73 42

**Melons Laurent Tranchant**
7 route de la Boutinière
86140 Saint Genest d'Ambière
phone +33 05 49 90 86 41

**Melon Le Chapeau (Christian Rondeleux)**
Maulay
86200 Loudun
phone +33 05 49 98 30 80
www.melon-lechapeau-86.com

**Pâtisserie Lescure Bougon**
rue Fontaine Bernière
79800 La Mothe Saint Heray
phone +33 05 49051544

**Maison Jousseaume**
Logis de Goin
16440 Roullet
phone +33 05 45 66 33 41

## pont-aven (brittany)

**Office du tourisme**
5, place de l'Hôtel de Ville, B.P. 36
29930 Pont-Aven
phone +33 02 98 06 04 70
www.pontaven.com

**Hôtel La Chaumière Roz Aven**
11 quai Théodore Botrel
29930 Pont-Aven
phone +33 02 98 06 13 06
www.hotelpontaven.online.fr

**Hostellerie Moulin de Rosmadec**
venelle de Rosmadec
29930 Pont-Aven
phone +33 02 98 06 00 22

**Hôtel Kermoor**
Plage des Sables Blancs
29900 Concarneau
phone +33 02 98 97 02 96
www.hotel-kermor.com

**Restaurant La Taupinière**
route de Concarneau, Croissant Saint-André
29930 Pont-Aven
phone +33 02 98 06 03 12
www.la-taupiniere.com

**Restaurant Le Buccin**
1, rue Duguay Trouin
29900 Concarneau
phone +33 02 98 50 54 22
www.le-buccin.com

**Le Talisman**
4, rue Paul-Sérusier
29930 Pont Aven
phone +33 02 98 06 02 58

**Les Ajoncs d'Or**
1, place de l'Hôtel de ville
29930 Pont-Aven
phone +33 02 98 06 02 06
www.ajoncsdor-pontaven.com

**Le Bistrot de l'Écailler**
Port de Kerdruc
29920 Nevez
phone +33 02 98 06 78 60

**Auberge Les Grandes Roches**
Rue des Grandes Roches
29910 Trégunc
phone +33 02 98 97 62 97
www.hotel-lesgrandesroches.com

**Huîtrière de Bélon**
Château de Bélon
29340 Riec sur Bélon
phone +33 02 98 06 90 58

**Boutique Traou-Mad**
10 Place Gauguin
29930 Pont-Aven
phone +33 02 98 06 01 94
www.traoumad.com

**Les Délices de Pont-Aven**
1, quai Théodore Botrel
29330 Pont-Aven
phone +33 02 98 06 05 87
www.galettes-penven.com

## pontarlier (franche–comté)

**Maison du Tourisme**
14 bis rue de la Gare
25300 Pontarlier
phone +33 03 81 46 48 33

**Hôtel Saint-Pierre**
3, place Saint-Pierre
25300 Pontarlier
phone +33 03 8146 50 80
www.hotel-st-pierre-pontarlier.com

**Grand Hôtel de la Poste**
55, rue de la République
25300 Pontarlier
phone +33 03 81 39 18 12 -

**Hôtel Le Bon Accueil**
Grande Rue
25160 Malbuisson
phone +33 03 81 69 30 58

**Hôtel Le Lac**
31, Grande Rue
25160 Malbuisson
phone +33 03 81 69 34 80
www.lelac-hotel.com

**L'Alchimie**
1, avenue de l'Armée de l'Est
25300 Pontarlier
phone +33 03 81 46 65 89
www.lalchimie.fr

**Le Doubs Passage**
11, Grande rue
25300 Doubs
phone +33 03 81 39 72 71

**Jean-Michel Tannières**
17, Grande Rue
25160 Malbuisson
phone +33 03 81 69 30 89
www.restaurant-tannieres.com

**Cremerie Comté Marcel Petite**
25300 Pontarlier
7, rue Sainte-Anne
phone +33 03 81 39 09 50

**Distillerie Pierre Guy**
49, rue des Lavaux
25300 Pontarlier
phone +33 03 81 39 04 70
www.pontarlier-anis.com

## reims (champagne–ardenne)

**Office de Tourisme**
2, rue Guillaume de Machault
51100 Reims
phone +33 03 26 77 45 00
www.reims-tourisme.com

**Grand Hôtel des Templiers**
22, rue des Templiers
51100 Reims
phone +33 03 26 88 55 08
http://hotel.templiers.perso.wanadoo.fr

**Hôtel Restaurant Les Crayères**
64, boulevard Henry Vasnier, BP 1019
51685 Reims
phone +33 03 26 82 80 80
www.gerardboyer.com

**Restaurant Café du Palais**
14, place Myron Herrick
51100 Reims
phone +33 03 26 47 52 54
www.cafedupalais.fr

**Brasserie le Boulingrin**
48, rue de Mars
51100 Reims
phone +33 03 26 40 96 22
www.boulingrin.fr

**Au Cul de Poule**
46, boulevard Carteret
51100 Reims
phone +33 03 26 47 60 22

**Da Nello Ristorante**
39, rue Cérès
51100 Reims
phone +33 03 26 47 33 25

**Le Matsuri**
9, rue de la Châtivesle
51100 Reims
phone +33 03 26 86 10 10
www.matsuri.fr

**Le Millénaire**
4, rue Bertin
51000 Reims
phone +33 03 26 08 26 62
www.lemillenaire.com

**Au Petit Comptoir**
17, rue de Mars
51100 Reims
phone +33 03 26 40 58 58
www.au-petit-comptoir.com

**Foch**
37, boulevard Foch
51100 Reims
phone +33 03 26 47 48 22
www.lefoch.com

**Champagne Veuve Clicquot Ponsardin**
Caves les Crayères
13r Albert Thomas
51100 Reims
phone +33 03 26 89 54 40
www.veuve-clicquot.com

**Mumm**
29 rue du Champ de Mars
51100 Reims
phone +33 03 26 49 59 69
www.mumm.com

**Champagne Louis Roederer**
21 boulevard Lundy
51100 Reims
phone +33 03 26 40 42 11
www.champagne-roederer.com

**Aux Gourmets des Halles, Bruno Herbin**
3, rue de Mars
51100 Reims
phone +33 03 26 06 92 83
www.bruno-herbin-mof.com

**Charcuterie du Forum**
8, place du Forum
51100Reims
phone +33 03 26 47 40 47

**Boucherie Digrazia**
68, rue de Vesle
51100 Reims
phone +33 03 26 47 21 60

**Moutarde de Reims Charbonneaux-Brabant**
5, rue de Valmy, BP 341
51062 Reims
phone +33 03 26 49 58 70
www.vinaigre.com

**Biscuits Fossier Boutique**
25, cours Jean-Baptiste Langlet
51100 Reims
phone +33 03 26 47 59 84
www.fossier.fr

*riquewihr (alsace)*

**Office de tourisme du Pays de Ribeauvillé et Riquewihr**
B.P. 28
68340 Riquewihr
phone +33 0 820 360 922; 03 89 49 08 40

**Hôtel À l'Oriel**
3, rue des Écuries-Seigneuriales
68340 Riquewihr
phone +33 03 89 49 03 13

**Hôtel Le Riquewihr**
3, route de Ribeauvillé
68340 Riquewihr
phone +33 03 89 47 99 76

**Hôtel-restaurant Au Dolder**
52, rue du Général-de-Gaulle
68340 Riquewihr
phone +33 03 89 47 92 56

**Restaurant Au Moulin**
3, rue du Général-de-Gaulle
68340 Riquewihr
phone +33 03 89 86 05 52

**Hôtel-restaurant Le Saint-Nicolas**
2, rue Saint-Nicolas
68340 Riquewihr
phone +33 03 89 49 01 51

**Restaurant Au Cep de Vigne**
13, rue du Général-de-Gaulle
68340 Riquewihr
phone +33 03 89 47 92 34

**Brendel Stub**
48, rue du Gén-de-Gaulle
68340 Riquewihr
phone +33 03 89 86 54 54
www.jlbrendel.com

**Le Sarment d'Or**
4, rue du Cerf
68340 Riquewihr
phone +33 03 89 86 02 86
www.riquewihr-sarment-dor.com

**La Table du Gourmet**
5, rue de la 1re-Armée
68340 Riquewihr
phone +33 03 89 49 09 09
www.jlbrendel.com

**Vins Hugel & Fils**
3, rue de la Première-Armée
68340 Riquewihr
phone +33 03 89 47 92 15

**Distillerie G. Miclo**
68650 Lapoutroie
phone +33 03 89 47 50 16

*romans-sur-isère (rhône–alpes)*

**Office du tourisme**
Le Neuilly, Place Jean Jaurès, B.P. 13
26101 Romans-sur-Isère
phone +33 04 75 02 28 72
www.ville-romans.com

**Auberge du Moulin de la Pipe**
26400 Omblèze
phone +33 04 75 76 42 05
www.moulindelapipe.com

**Auberge Le Collet**
26420 St Agnan-en-Vercors
phone +33 04 75 48 13 18
www.aubergelecollet.com

**Hôtel-restaurant du Col de la Machine**
26190 St Jean en Royans
phone +33 04 75 48 26 36
www.hotel-coldelamachine.com

**Mandrin**
70, rue Saint-Nicolas
26100 Romans-sur-Isère
phone +33 04 75 02 93 55

**Les Cèdres**
26600 Granges-les-Beaumont
phone +33 04 75 71 50 67
www.restaurantlescedres.fr

**La Malle Poste**
26750 Saint-Paul-les-Romains
phone +33 04 75 45 35 43

**La Raviole Gourmande**
53, rue Jacquemart
26100 Romans sur Isère
phone +33 04 75 02 62 11
www.laraviolegourmande.com

**Fromagerie l'Etoile du Vercors**
38680 Saint-Just-de-Claix
phone +33 04 76 64 40 64

**Ravioles à l'ancienne**
avenue du Vercors
26190 St Jean en Royans
phone +33 08 20 00 01 82

**La Raviole du Dauphin**
ZA La Gloriette Chatte
38160 Saint-Marcellin
phone +33 04 76 64 02 64
www.ravioledauphin.fr

**Ravioles Mère Maury**
38 rue Félix Faure
26100 Romans sur Isère
phone +33 04 75 70 03 59
www.raviolesmeremaury.com

**Le Relais de la Pogne**
avenue Dauphiné-Provende
26300 Alixan
phone +33 04 75 47 08 67
www.relaisdelapogne.fr

**Pâtissier-chocolatier Luc Guillet**
76, Place J. Jaurès
26100 Romans
phone +33 04 75 02 26 80
www.guillet.com

*roquefort-sur-soulzon (midi–pyrénées)*

**Office de Tourisme du Pays de Roquefort**
avenue de Lauras
12250 Roquefort-sur-Soulzon
phone +33 05 65 58 56 00
www.roquefort.com

**Hôtel Restaurant du Château de Creissels**
12100 Creissels
phone +33 05 65 60 16 59
www.chateau-de-creissels.com

**Hôtel du Lion d'Or**
12140 Entraygues-sur-Truyère
phone +33 05 65 44 50 01
www.hotel-lion-or.com

**Auberge La Cardabelle**
12230 Sainte-Eulalie-de-Cernon
phone +33 05 65 62 74 64
www.auberge-la-cardabelle.com

**Auberge du Père Roussel**
Les Mourguettes
12230 La Couvertoirade
phone +33 05 65 62 28 25

**Le Moderne**
54, avenue A. Pezet
12400 Saint-Afrique
phone +33 05 65 49 20 44
www.lemoderne.com

**Les Raspes**
12490 Saint-Romme-de-Tarn
phone +33 05 65 58 11 44

**La Braconne**
7, place du maréchal Foch
12100 Millau
phone +33 05 65 60 30 93

**Fromages Le Vieux Berger (Yves Combes)**
avenue du Combalou
12250 Roquefort sur Soulzon
phone +33 05 65 59 91 48
www.le-vieux-berger.com

**Fromages Gabriel Coulet**
3, avenue de Lauras
12250 Roquefort sur Soulzon
phone +33 05 65 59 90 21
www.gabriel-coulet.fr

**Caves Roquefort Papillon**
rue de la Fontaine
12250 Roquefort sur Soulzon
phone +33 05 65 58 50 08
www.roquefort-papillon.com

**Vins de Marcillac**
Domaine du Cros, Philippe Teulier
12390 Goutrens
phone +33 05 65 72 71 77
www.domaine-du-cros.com

**Domaine Laurens**
7, avenue de la Tour
12330 Clairvaux d'Aveyron
phone +33 05 63 72 69 37
www.domaine-laurens.com

*roscoff (brittany)*

**Office de Tourisme**
46, rue Gambetta, B.P. 58
29680 roscoff
phone +33 02 98 61 12 13
www.roscoff-tourisme.com

**Hôtel-restaurant Le Brittany**
BP 47
29681 Roscoff
phone +33 02 98 69 70 78
www.hotel-brittany.com

**Grand Hôtel-restaurant Talabardon**
place de l'Eglise BP 71
29681 Roscoff
phone +33 02 98 61 24 95 — phone +33 03 80 22 83 84
www.talabardon.fr

**Hôtel-restaurant Le Temps de Vivre**
19, place Lacaze Duthiers
29680 Roscoff
phone +33 02 98 19 33 19 / 98 61 27 28
www.letempsdevivre.net

**Restaurant Le Jardin de L'Aber**
1, route de Plourin
29810 Brélès
phone +33 02 98 04 40 86
www.jardindelaber.com

**Restaurant La Ferme de Keringar**
Lochrist, Le Conquet
phone +33 02 98 89 09 59
www.keringar.com

**Crêperie Ti Saozon**
30, rue Gambetta
phone +33 02 98 69 70 89
29680 Roscoff

**Le Yachtman**
Boulevard Sainte-Barbe
29680 Roscoff
phone +33 02 98 69 70 78
www.hotel-brittany.com

**Pommes de terre Noël et Bénédicte Menon**
Pors Melloc'h
29253 Ile de Batz
phone +33 02 98 61 74 03

**Jean Prigent**
le Bourg 29253 Ile de Batz
phone +33 02 98 61 76 91

*rouen (normandy)*

**Office du tourisme et des Congrès
de Rouen**
25, Place de la Cathédrale, B.P. 666
76000 Rouen
phone +33 02 32 08 32 40)
www.rouentourisme.com

**Hôtel Le Vieux Carré**
34 rue Ganterie
76000 Rouen
phone +33 02 35 71 67 70
www.le-vieux-carre.com

**Hôtel du Vieux Marché**
33, rue du Vieux Palais
76000 Rouen
phone +33 02 35 71 00 88
www.hotelduvieuxmarche.com

**Restaurant L'Ecaille**
26, rampe Cauchoise
76000 Rouen
phone +33 02 35 70 95 52
www.lecaille.fr

**Restaurant La Couronne**
31 Place du Vieux Marché
76000 Rouen
phone +33 02 35 71 40 90
www.lacouronne.com.fr

**Le Rouennais**
5, rue de la Pie
76000 Rouen
phone +33 02 35 07 55 44

**Le Quatre Saisons**
place Bernard Tissot
76000 Rouen
phone +33 02 35 71 96 00
www.hotel-dieppe.fr

**Bandol**
27, rue Verte
76000 Rouen
phone +33 02 35 71 46 43

**Le Bistrot d'Arthur**
27, rue Cauchoise
76000 Rouen
phone +33 02 35 70 34 09

**Bistrot des Hallettes**
43, place du Vieux Marché
76000 Rouen
phone +33 02 35 71 05 06

**Le Bistrot du Chef... en Gare**
26, rue Verte
76000 Rouen
phone +33 02 35 71 41 15

**L'Ecaille**
26, Rampe-Cauchoise
76000 Rouen
phone +33 02 35 70 95 52
www.lecaille.fr

**Fromages Ferme des Fontaines**
427 route de Gaillefontaine
76270 Nesle-Hodeng
phone +33 02.32.97.06.46

**Fromages Francis Ouin**
76440 Sainte Geneviève en Bray
phone +33 02 35 90 45 72

**Confrérie des compagnons
du fromage de Neufchâtel**
Mairie BP 88
76270 Neufchâtel-en-Bray
phone +33 02 32 97 53 01
www.neufchatel-aoc.org

**La Chocolatière**
18, rue Guillaume le Conquérant
76 000 Rouen
phone +33 02 35 71 00 79

**Au délice de Lise**
60, rue Cauchoise
76000 Rouen
phone +33 02 35 71 26 61
www.audelicedelise.com

*saint-brieuc (brittany)*

**Office de tourisme de la Baie de Saint Brieuc**
Bureau central
7, rue Saint-Guéno, BP 4435
22044 Saint-Brieuc
phone +33 0 825 00 22 22
www.baiedesaintbrieuc.com

**Hôtel Beauséjour**
21, route de la Corniche
22430 Erquy
phone +33 02 96 72 30 39
www.beausejour-erquy.com

**Hôtel Le Repaire de Kerroc'h**
29, quai Morand
22500 Paimpol
phone +33 02 96 20 50 13

**Hôtel L'Orégano**
7 bis, rue du Quai
22500 Paimpol
phone +33 02 96 22 05 49

**Restaurant Youpala**
5, rue Palasne-de-Champeaux
22000 Saint-Brieuc
phone +33 02 96 94 50 74
www.youpala.com

**Restaurant La Cuisine du Marché**
4, rue des Trois Frères Merlin
22000 Saint-Brieuc
phone +33 02 96 61 70 94
http://teamftw.free.fr/la-cuisine-du-marche

**Restaurant Aux Pesked**
59, rue du Légué
22000 Saint Brieuc
phone +33 02 96 33 34 65
www.auxpesked.com

**Restaurant À la table de Margot**
place de l'église
22520 Binic
phone +33 02 96 73 35 56

**Amadeus**
22, rue du Gouët
22000 Saint-Brieuc
phone +33 02 96 33 92 44

**Au Petit Bouchon Briochin**
10, rue Jules Ferry
22000 Saint-Brieuc
phone +33 02 96 94 05 34

**Manoir le Quatre Saisons**
61, Chemin des Courses
22000 Saint-Brieuc
phone +33 02 96 33 20 38
www.manoirquatresaisons.fr

*saint-tropez (provence)*

**Office de tourisme**
40, rue Gambetta
83990 Saint-Tropez
phone +33 0892 68 48 28
www.saint-tropez.st

**Hôtel Byblos**
avenue Paul Signac
83990 Saint-Tropez
phone +33 04 94 56 68 00
www.byblos.com

**Hôtel Restaurant La Bastide de St Tropez**
route des Carles
83990 Saint-Tropez
phone +33 04 94 55 82 55
www.bastide-sainttropez.com

**Hôtel le Mas des Oliviers**
quartier de la Croisette
83120 Sainte-Maxime
phone +33 04 94 96 13 31
www.hotellemasdesoliviers.com

**Chambres d'hôtes La Petite Nice**
9 rue Pierre Curie
83670 Barjols
phone +33 04 94 77 26 75
www.lapetitenice.com

**Le Café des Arts**
place des Lices
83990 Saint-Tropez
phone +33 04 94 97 02 25

**Restaurant Nioulargo**
boulevard Patch
83350 Ramatuelle
phone +33 04 98 12 63 12
www.nioulargo.fr

**Résidence de la Pinède**
Plage de la Bouillabaisse
83990 Saint-Tropez
phone +33 04 94 55 91 00
www.residencepinede.com

**La Tarte Tropézienne**
place des Lices
83990 Saint-Tropez
phone +33 04 94 97 04 69
www.tarte-tropezienne.com

*salers (auvergne)*

**Office de Tourisme du Pays de Salers**
Place Tyssandier d'Escous
15140 Salers
phone +33 04 71 40 70 68
www.pays-de-salers.com

**Hôtel-restaurant Le Bailliage**
rue Notre-Dame
15140 Salers
phone +33 04 71 40 70 68
www.salers-hotel-bailliage.com

**Hôtel Le Gerfaut**
route du Puy Mary
15140 Salers
phone +33 04 71 40 75 75
www.salers-hotel-gerfaut.com

**Restaurant Les Templiers
(Annie et Henri Bouyge)**
Centre Ville
15140 Salers
phone +33 04 71 40 71 35

**Chambres et table d'hôtes d'hôte
du Château de la Fromental**
15140 Fontanges
phone +33 04 71 40 77 20

**La ferme du Meynial
(Jean François Martin)**
Noille
15380 Anglards de Salers
phone +33 04 71 40 00 52

**Chateau de Chanterelle**
15380 Saint-Vincent de Salers
phone +33 04 71 40 01 89
www.chateaudechanterelle.com

**Le Bailliage**
Rue Notre-Dame
15140 Salers
phone +33 04 71 40 71 95
www.salers-hotel-bailliage.com

**Fromages Gilles et Chantal Benech**
Ferme d'Anglards-le-Pommier
15310 St-Cernin
phone +33 04 71 47 67 72
www.anglardspommier.com

**Fromagers Cantaliens**
14 boulevard Pavatou, BP 37
15018 Aurillac
phone +33 04 71 48 03 04

**Distillerie de la Salers**
rue du Stade
19300 Montaignac Saint-Hippolyte
phone +33 05 55 27 61 01
www.salers-gentiane.com

**Château de Courcelles**
02220 Courcelles-sur-Vesle
phone +33 03 23 74 13 53
*www.chateau-de-courcelles.fr*

**Le Petit Cochon**
56 rue Georges-Deviolaine
02880 Cuffies
phone +33 03 23 53 05 01

**Vive la Campagne**
64 avenue de Paris
02200 Soissons
phone +33 03 23 73 26 29

*strasbourg (alsace)*

**Office de Tourisme de Strasbourg
et de sa région**
17 place de la Cathédrale
67000 Strasbourg
phone +33 03 88 52 28 22

**Restaurant Le Crocodile
(Émile Jung)**
10 rue de l'Outre
67000 Strasbourg
phone +33 03 88 32 13 02

**Restaurant Le Buerehiesel
(Antoine Westermann)**
4 parc de l'Orangerie
67000 Strasbourg
phone +33 03 88 45 56 65

**Restaurant La Maison Kammerzel**
16 place de la Cathédrale
67000 Strasbourg
phone +33 03 88 32 42 14

**Chez Yvonne**
10 rue du Sanglier
67000 Strasbourg
phone +33 03 88 32 84 15

**L'Ami Schutz**
1 rue des Pont-Couverts
67000 Stasbourg
phone +33 03 88 32 76 98

**Muenstertuewel**
8 place du Marché-au-Cochon-de-Lait
67000 Strasbourg
phone +33 03 88 3217 63

**Hôtel Le Dragon**
2 rue de l'Écarlate
67000 Strasbourg
phone +33 03 88 35 79 80

**L'Europe**
38 rue du Fossé-des-Tanneurs
67000 Strasbourg
phone +33 03 88 32 17 88

**Maison Rouge**
4 rue des Francs-Bourgeois
67000 Strasbourg
phone +33 03 88 32 08 60

**L'Alsace à Table**
8, rue des Francs-Bourgeois
67000 Strasbourg
phone +33 03 88 32 50 62
*www.alsace-a-table.fr*

**Ami Fritz**
8, rue des Dentelles
67000 Strasbourg
phone +33 03 88 32 80 53
*www.ami-fritz.com*

**Art Café Restaurant**
1, place Jean-Hans-Arp
67000 Strasbourg
phone +33 03 88 22 18 88

**L'Atable 77**
77, Grand'Rue
67000 Strasbourg
phone +33 03 88 32 23 37
*www.latable77.com*

**La Cambuse**
1, rue des Dentelles
67000 Strasbourg
phone +33 03 88 22 10 22

**La Casserole**
24, rue des Juifs
67000 Strasbourg
phone +33 03 88 36 49 68

**Produits regionaux Kirn**
19 rue du 22 Novembre
67000 Strasbourg
phone +33 03 88 32 16 10

**Produits regionaux Klein**
26-28 boulevard d'Enghien
67000 Strasbourg
phone +33 03 88 61 16 10

**Produits regionaux Gross**
24 place des Halles
67000 Strasbourg
phone +33 03 88 22 22 77

*tarbes (midi–pyrénées)*

**Office du tourisme**
cours Gambetta
65000 Tarbes
phone +33 05 62 51 30 31

**Rex Hôtel**
10, cours Gambetta
65000 Tarbes
phone +33 05 62 54 44 44

**Le Henri-IV**
7, avenue Bertrand-Barère
65000 Tarbes
phone +33 05 62 34 01 68

**Hôtel de l'Avenue**
80, avenue Bertrand-Barère
65000 Tarbes
phone +33 05 62 93 06 36

**Le Petit Gourmand**
62, avenue Bertrand-Barère
65000 Tarbes
phone +33 05 62 34 01 68

**L'Ambroisie**
48, rue de l'Abbé-Torné
65000 Tarbes
phone +33 05 62 93 09 34

**Le Bistro Lafontaine**
2, rue Jean-Pellet
65000 Tarbes
phone +33 05 62 93 37 95

**Le Fil à la Patte**
30, rue Georges-Lassalle
65000 Tarbes
phone +33 05 62 93 39 23

**Le Petit Gourmand**
62, avenue Bertrand-Barère
65000 Tarbes
phone +33 05 62 34 26 86

**Coopérative du Haricot**
Z.I. de Bastillac
65000 Tarbes
phone +33 05 62 34 76 76

**Gailhou-Durdof**
9, avenue Bertrand-Barère
65000 Tarbes
phone +33 05 62 93 82 65

**Hoornaert**
3, rue Jean-Pellet
65000 Tarbes
phone +33 05 62 44 39 65

*toul-le-vrai (lorraine)*

**Office du tourisme**
Parvis de la Cathédrale, B.P. 90084
54204 Toul
phone +33 03 83 64 11 69
*www.ot-toul.fr*

**Restaurant Le Commerce**
10, place de la République
54200 Toul
phone +33 03 83 43 00 41

**Restaurant des Roches**
29, rue des Roches
57000 Metz
phone +33 03 87 74 06 51

**Le Dauphin**
Z I Croix de Metz
54200 Toul
phone +33 03 83 43 13 46

**Auberge du Pressoir**
54200 Lucey
phone +33 03 83 63 81 91
*www.aubergedupressoir.com*

**L'Union**
1 impasse Aristide Briand
54230 Neuves-Maisons
phone +33 03 83 47 30 46

**Vins du Domaine Laroppe**
253 , rue de la République
54200 Bruley-en-France
phone +33 03 83 43 11 04
*www.laroppe.com*

**Vins André et Roland Lelièvre**
3, rue de la Gare
54200 Lucey
phone +33 03 83 63 81 36
*www.vins-lelievre.com*

**Vins du Pays de la Meuse,
Laurent Degenève**
7 rue des Lavoirs
55210 Creuë
phone +33 03 29 89 30 67

**Cave Coopérative**
43, place de la Mairie
54113 Mont-le-Vignoble
phone +33 03 83 62 59 93

**Macarons de Boulay**
13, rue de Saint-Avold
57220 Boulay
phone +33 03 87 79 11 22
*www.macaronsdeboulay.com*

**Pâtisserie le Royal**
39 avenue de Nancy
57000 Metz
phone +33 03 87 66 59 52

*toulouse (midi–pyrénées)*

**Office du tourisme**
square Charles-de-Gaulle
31000 Toulouse
phone +33 05 61 11 02 22

**Grand Hôtel de l'Opéra**
1 place du Capitole
31000 Toulouse
phone +33 05 61 21 82 66

**Hôtel Garonne**
22 descente de la Halle-aux-Poissons
31000 Toulouse
phone +33 05 34 31 94 80

**Hôtel des Beaux-Arts**
1 place du Pont-Neuf
31000 Toulouse
phone +33 05 34 45 42 42

**Le 19**
19, descente de la Halle-aux-Poissons
31000 Toulouse
phone +33 05 34 31 94 84

**Les Jardins de l'Opéra**
1, place du Capitole
31000 Toulouse
phone +33 05 61 23 07 76

**Grand Café de l'Opéra**
1, place du Capitole
31000 Toulouse
phone +33 05 61 21 37 03

**Le Colombier**
14, rue Bayard
31000 Toulouse
phone +33 05 61 62 40 05

**L'Amuse Bouche**
28, rue Palaprat
31000 Toulouse
phone +33 05 61 99 64 70

**Bistrot du Chevillard**
4, boulevard Mal-Leclerc
31000 Toulouse
phone +33 05 61 21 32 02

**Brasserie du Stade Toulousain**
114, rue des Troënes
31022 Toulouse
phone +33 05 34 42 24 20
www.stadetoulousain.fr

**Café Evangelina**
33, boulevard du Mal-Leclerc
31000 Toulouse
phone +33 05 61 21 30 00
www.evangelina.fr

**Caffé Cotti**
108, boulevard Silvio-Trentin
31000 Toulouse
phone +33 05 34 41 63 89

**La Cantine du Curé**
2, rue des Couteliers
31000 Toulouse
phone +33 05 61 25 83 42
www.lacantineducuré.com

**Chez Emile**
13, place Saint-Georges
31000 Toulouse
phone +33 05 61 21 05 56

**Samaran**
18, place Victor-Hugo
31000 Toulouse
phone +33 05 61 21 26 91

**Confiserie Olivier**
20, rue Lafayette
31000 Toulouse
phone +33 05 61 23 21 87

## tours (centre)

**Office du tourisme**
78-82, rue Bernard Palissy, B.P. 4201
37000 Tours
phone +33 02 47 70 37 37
www.ligeris.com

**Hôtel-restaurant Domaine de Beauvois**
Le Pont Clouet
37230 Luynes
phone +33 02 47 55 50 11
www.beauvois.com

**Hôtel-restaurant Château d'Artigny**
route de Monts
37250 Montbazon
phone +33 02 47 34 30 30
www.artigny.com

**Restaurant Jean Bardet**
57, Rue Groison
37100 Tours
phone +33 02 47 41 41 11
www.jeanbardet.com

**Restaurant Charles Barrier**
101, Avenue de la Tranchée
37100 Tours
phone +33 02 47 54 20 39

**L'Atelier Gourmand**
3,7 rue Etienne-Marcel
37000 Tours
phone +33 02 47 38 59 87
www.lateliergourmand.fr

**Bistrot de la Tranchée**
103, avenue de la Tranchée
37100 Tours
phone +33 02 47 41 09 08

**Maison Hardouin**
l'Étang Vignon
37210 Vouvray
phone +33 02 47 40 40 40
www.hardouin.fr

**Maison Galland**
Ferme des Bournaichères
37600 Betz le Château
phone +33 02 47 92 30 85
www.les-bournaicheres.fr

**Fromages Le Vazereau**
Elevage des Baronneries
83 route du Côteau
37500 La Roche-Clermault
phone +33 02 47 93 18 89
www.levazereau.fr

**Fromages Mr et Mme Bacquart**
Elevage de la Babinière
37120 Braslou
phone +33 02 47 95 66 07

**Château Gaudrelle**
SCEA Monmousseau
87, route de la Monnaie
37210 Vouvray
phone +33 02 47 52 67 50

**Domaine Georges Brunet**
12, rue de la Croix Mariotte
37210 Vouvray
phone +33 02 47 52 60 36
www.vouvray-brunet.com

**Coopérative La Dame Noire**
la Psaudière
37350 La Celle-Guenand
phone +33 02 47 94 95 99

**Aux Volailles Rabelaisiennes**
9 rue de Paume
37170 Chinon
phone +33 02 47 93 07 85

## troyes (champagne–ardenne)

**Office de tourisme**
16, boulevard Carnot
10000 Troyes
phone +33 03 25 82 62 70

**Hôtel Le Champ des Oiseaux**
20, rue Linard-Gonthier
10000 Troyes
phone +33 03 25 80 58 50

**Hôtel de la Poste**
35, rue Émile-Zola
10000 Troyes
phone +33 03 25 73 05 05

**Relais Saint-Jean**
51, rue Paillot-de-Montabert
10000 Troyes
phone +33 03 25 73 89 90

**Le Bourgogne**
40, avenue du Général-de-Gaulle
10000 Troyes
phone +33 03 25 73 02 67

**Le Bistroquet**
place Langevin
10000 Troyes
phone +33 03 25 73 65 65

**Le Cellier Saint-Pierre**
1, place Saint-Pierre
10000 Troyes
phone +33 03 25 80 59 25

**Aux Crieurs de Vin**
4, place Jean-Jaurès
10000 Troyes
phone +33 03 25 40 01 01

**Les Gourmets**
3, rue Raymond-Poincaré
10000 Troyes
phone +33 03 25 73 80 78
www.hotel-de-la-poste.com

**Charcuterie Gilbert Lemelle**
Z.I. des Écrevolles
10000 Troyes
phone +33 03 25 70 42 50

## valençay (centre)

**Office de tourisme**
2, Avenue de la Résistance
36600 Valençay
phone +33 02 54 00 04 42
www.pays-de-valencay.fr

**Hôtel les Dryades**
8, Rue du Golf
36160 Pouligny-Notre-Dame
phone +33 02 54 06 60 67
www.les-dryades.fr

**Le Relais Du Moulin**
94, Rue Nationale
36600 Valencay
phone +33 02 54 00 38 00
www.hotel-lerelaisdumoulin.com

**Restaurant Auberge Saint-Fiacre**
5, Rue de la Fontaine
36600 Veuil
phone +33 02 54 40 32 78
www.aubergesaintfiacre.com

**Relais Saint-Jean**
34, rue Nationale
36110 Levroux
phone +33 02 54 35 81 56
www.relais-saint-jean.com

**Les Deux Pierrots**
41320 Saint-Julien-sur-Cher
phone +33 02 54 96 40 07

**Grand Hôtel du Lion d'Or**
69, rue Clemenceau
41200 Romorantin-Lanthenay
phone +33 02 54 94 15 15
www.hotel-liondor.fr

**Fromages Solange et Catherine Louet**
La Morelière
36600 Pellevoisin
phone +33 02 54 39 03 14

**Domaine de Preuguéronde
(Francis Chauvette)**
36230 Gournay
phone +33 02 54 30 83 10

**SCEA Domaine de la Garenne**
"La Garenne"
36600 Valençay
phone +33 02 54 00 27 60

**Domaine Preys Jacky & Fils**
Le Bois Pontois
41130 Meusnes
phone +33 02 54 71 00 34

## verdun (lorraine)

**Maison du tourisme**
place de la Nation, B.P. 60232
55106 Verdun
phone +33 03 29 86 14 18
www.verdun-tourisme.com

**Hostellerie du Coq Hardi**
8, avenue de la Victoire
55100 Verdun
phone +33 03 29 83 36 36
www.coq-hardi.com

**Relais de la Voie Sacrée**
1, Voie Sacrée
55200 Issoncourt
phone +33 03 29 70 70 46
www.voiesacree.com

**Hôtel du Commerce**
9r Aristide Briand
55700 Stenay
phone +33 03 29 80 30 62
www.hotel-commerce-stenay.com

**Lodge du Domaine
de Sommedieue**
1 rue du Parc
55320 Sommedieue
phone +33 03 29 85 78 70

**Chambres d'hôtes au château
de Labessière**
9, rue du Four
55320 Ancemont
phone +33 03 29 85 70 21

**L'Atelier Restaurant**
33, rue des Gros-Degrés
phone +33 03 29 84 45 29
55100 Verdun
www.atelierrestaurant.fr

**L'Hostellerie Bourguignonne**
2, avenue du Pdt-Borgeot
71350 Verdun sur le Doubs
phone +33 03 85 91 51 45
www.hostelleriebourguignonne.com

**Musée Européen de la Bière**
rue de la Citadelle
55700 Stenay
phone +33 03 29 80 68 78
www.musee-de-la-biere.com

**La Dragée de Verdun**
50, rue du Fort de Vaux, BP 104
55100 Verdun
phone +33 03 29 84 30 00
*www.dragees-braquier.com*

*vittel (lorraine)*

**Maison du tourisme**
Place de la Marne, B.P.11
88801 Vittel
phone +33 03 29 08 08 88
*www.vitteltourisme.com*

**Hôtel L'Angleterre - Restaurant Le Dickens**
162, rue de Charmey
88800 Vittel
phone +33 03 29 08 08 42

**L'Orée du Bois**
D 18, Entrée Hippodrome
88800 Norroy
phone +33 03 29 08 88 88

**Restaurant Le Rétro**
180, rue Jeanne d'Arc
88800 Vittel
phone +33 03 29 08 05 28
*www.le-retro.com*

**Hôtel Le Manoir – Restaurant les Ducs de Lorraine**
5, avenue de Provence
88000 Epinal
phone +33 03 29 29 55 55
*www.manoir-hotel.com*

**Hôtel Cosmos**
88140 Contrexéville
phone +33 03 29 07 61 61
*www.cosmos-hotel.com*

**Hôtel-restaurant des Lacs**
route des Lac de la Folie
88140 Contrexéville
phone +33 03 29 08 28 28
*www.hoteldeslacscontrexeville-vittel.com*

**D'Angleterre**
rue Charmey
88800 Vittel
phone +33 03 29 08 08 42
*www.abc-gesthotel.com*

**César**
125, avenue de Châtillon
88800 Vittel
phone +33 03 29 08 61 73

**La Marmite Beaujolaise**
34, rue de l'Hôtel de ville
88140 Bulgneville
phone +33 03 29 09 16 58

**Frezelle**
88170 Rouvres-La Chétive
phone +33 03 29 94 51 51

**Ferme Moine**
1090 la Manche-Rasey
88220 Xertigny
phone +33 03 29 30 83 78
*www.crillon-moine.fr*

# SUGGESTED READING

## ART AND CULTURE

Blunt, F. Anthony. *Art and Architecture in France, 1500–1700*. New Haven: Yale University Press, 1999.

Child, Julia, and Alex Prud'Homme. *My Life in France*. New York: Knopf, 2006.

de Borchgrave, Isabelle, and Jean-André Charial. *The Flavors of Provence*. New York: Rizzoli, 2004.

Friedrich, Jacqueline. *The Wine and Food Guide To the Loire, France's Royal River*. New York: Owl Books, 1998.

Horne, Alistair. *Seven Ages of Paris*. New York: Vintage, 2004.

King, Ross. *The Judgment of Paris: The Revolutionary Decade that Gave the World Impressionism*. New York: Walker and Company, 2006.

Mayle, Peter. *French Lessons: Adventures with Knife, Fork, and Corkscrew*. New York: Vintage, 2002.

Murat, Laure. *The Splendor of France: Châteaux, Mansions, and Country Houses*. New York: Rizzoli, 1991.

## LITERATURE

de Balzac, Honoré. *The Wrong Side of Paris*. New York: Modern Library, 2003.

Dumas, Alexandre. *The Three Musketeers*. New York: Oxford University Press, 1991.

Flaubert, Gustave. *Madame Bovary*. rev. ed. New York: Penguin Classics, 2002.

## TRAVEL

James, Henry. *A Little Tour in France*. Montana: Kessinger Publishing, 2004.

Johnson, Diane. *Into a Paris Quartier: Reine Margot's Chapel and Other Haunts of St. Germain*. Washington, D.C.: National Geographic Society, 2005.

Mayle, Peter. *Encore Provence: New Adventures in the South of France*. New York: Vintage, 2000.

Palmer, Hugh, and James Bentley. *The Most Beautiful Villages of the Loire*. London: Thames and Hudson, 2001.

# PHOTOGRAPHY CREDITS

All images in this book are held under copyright by Francedias and are credited to the following photographers:

Benoît A La Guillaume 97
Patrick André 29t, 32, 41, 63t, 67, 98, 100, 185b, 226b, 234
Christian Arnal 19
J.L. Barde/Scope 84, 95, 142, 147b, 155b, 183, 184-185, 197, 199
Alain Baschenis 110, 144, 146-147, 149
Eric Bénard 169, 171, 172, 173, 176, 177, 178, 180r, 180l, 180-181
Philip Bernard 156
Francis Bertout 101
Yvon Boelle 50t, 167, 175
Pierre Canivenq 148, 151
Marie-Hélène Carcanague 152
Michel Carossio 107, 140, 141, 194
A.J. Cassaigne 21, 66, 168
Jean-Yves Catherin 240t
Ludovic Cazenave 18
Jérome Chabanne 33, 89t, 89b, 90-91, 91b, 120
Thierry Charlon 10
Philippe Chenet 35, 60, 61, 62-63, 63b, 64, 70, 71, 72t, 72b, 188, 196, 205
Lionel Chocat 36, 42-43
Patrice Coppée 136, 145, 154-155
Costacurta 29b
Paul-André Coumes 46, 47, 178, 190, 191, 192t, 192b, 192-193, 200
Daniel Czap / Scope 38
Joël Damase 27, 34
Sophie Deballe 198
Catherine & Bernard Desjeux 65
Jean-Pierre Duplan 165s
Laurence Fleury 150
Étienne Follet 143
Patrick Foure 163, 164-165, 225
Philippe Fournier 218, 248, 249, 250, 251
Olivier Frimat 13, 76, 78t, 128b
B. Galeron / Scope 195
C. Goupi / Scope 204
Michel Guebardot 157, 158, 161, 162, 165d
J. Guillard/Scope 9, 69, 74, 75, 93, 113, 185t, 220
Dominique Guillaume 53
Pierre Guy / Scope 43b
Noël Hautemanière 109, 115, 116-117, 117b, 119
Noël Hautemanière / Scope 189
Roger Hemon 37, 39
Roland Huitel / Scope 86t
Jean Isenmann 40, 179
H. Joshua 235
Langrand 160
Gilles Lansard 233

C. Lecomte 77, 78b, 78-79, 131
F. Le Divenah 44, 45
Le Fotographe / Iconos 94, 242, 244t, 244b
Florence Lelong 239, 240b
Joël Le Monnier 203, 206
Fred Lherpiniere 48
David Macherel 182, 243
Marcou 201
T. Moiroux 237, 247
Quyên Ngo-Dinh-Phu 26, 31, 43t, 56, 57, 58, 59, 68, 72-73, 80, 81, 88-89, 91t, 114, 170, 174, 186, 187, 236
Stéphanie Ngo 12
Josè Nicholas 208, 215, 216, 219, 221, 226t, 226-227, 246
Yves Noto Campanella 8, 11, 14-15, 15t, 15b, 20, 124, 127, 128t, 128-129, 130, 135
Luc Olivier 30
Bruno Pambour 222, 228
Marc Paygnard 125, 126, 132, 133
Alain Pellorce 86-87, 217, 232, 238
Jean-Didier Risler 103
Régine Rosenthal 17, 22t, 22b, 24, 25, 28-29, 82, 83, 85, 86b, 99, 105, 106, 111, 112, 118, 121, 134, 137, 138, 147t, 153, 155t, 202, 210, 212, 213, 214, 230, 241
Philippe Royer 231
Erik Saillet /Iconos 244-245
Scope 38
Dan Serregio 108, 117t, 209, 211, 224
Guillaume Team 50b, 50-51
Eric Teissedre 16, 139
Théo 102, 104, 123
Michel Thersiquel 49, 52, 54, 55
Valéry Trillaud 223, 229
Jarry Tripelon 22-23, 92, 96, 122, 159, 166, 206-207

t = top
b = bottom
r = right
l = left

First published in the United States of America in 2008
by Rizzoli International Publications, Inc.
300 Park Avenue South
New York, NY 10010
www.rizzoliusa.com

Production: Colophon srl, Venice, Italy

Editorial Direction: Andrea Grandese

Editor in Chief: Rosanna Alberti

Layout: Colophon, Venice

Design Concept: Stephen Fay

English Translation: Christine Conway

2007 2008 2009 2010 2011 / 10 9 8 7 6 5 4 3 2 1

Printed in China

ISBN-13: 978-0-8478-3037-4

Library of Congress Control Number: 2007935170